Out in the South

Out in the South

EDITED BY

Carlos L. Dews and Carolyn Leste Law

TEMPLE UNIVERSITY PRESS

PHILADELPHIA

Temple University Press, Philadelphia 19122
Copyright © 2001 by Temple University
All rights reserved
Published 2001
Printed in the United States of America

Library of Congress Cataloging-in-Publication Data

Out in the South / edited by Carlos L. Dews and Carolyn Leste Law
    p.   cm.
  Includes bibliographical references.
  ISBN 1-56639-813-4 (cl. : alk. paper) — ISBN 1-56639-814-2 (pbk. : alk. paper)
  1. Gays—Southern States.   2. Gay men—Southern States.   3. Lesbians—
Southern States.   4. Homosexuality—Southern States.   I. Dews, Carlos L.,
1963–   .   II. Law, Carolyn Leste, 1961–   .
  HQ76.3.U52.S276   2001
  306.76'6'0975–dc21

                                                                    00-037706

Contents

Part III: Representing Queer Lives in Public Space

Acknowledgments

Thank you to Deborah Burlison and Linda Uebelsteadt for their patient assistance; the faculty, staff, and administrators at the University of West Florida for their support and encouragement; and Michael Ames at Temple University Press for sharing our enthusiasm for this project. Most of all, thanks to Diana Swanson, whose support never falters, and to William Lamar Polk III for arriving along with the idea for this book.

Out in the South

Carolyn Leste Law

Introduction

Reading Adrienne Rich for the first time was for me, as for many young lesbians, a watershed experience in my sense of self. As an undergraduate, I read *Diving into the Wreck* and *The Dream of a Common Language* with equal parts pain and ecstasy. But my most unnerving and ultimately gratifying epiphany came later, after graduation, after some years of growing political and personal consciousness. When I first read Rich's poignant essay of identity and self-conflict, "Split at the Root: An Essay on Jewish Identity," I remember feeling disbelief approaching shock to learn that Adrienne Rich is a southerner.[1] My reaction, like Rich's identity, was split: Was it more remarkable to learn that there were and are Jewish people in Birmingham, Alabama, or that a lesbian with deep Alabama roots (only Mississippi, in my mind, could have been more astonishing) could be so engaged, so articulate? At that moment, I was challenged to confront my own self-loathing prejudices about the South, to reconcile my own southern identity with the powerful anti-South attitudes I increasingly encountered and absorbed as I moved farther and farther north and farther and farther away from my working-class southern roots. The greatest gift that Rich's body of work ever gave to me was a challenge to mediate my southern shame and my southern pride.

I went to college in the Ozarks. I've learned not to phrase it quite that way in mixed company, though, for I've been met with laughter on more than one occasion and probably not a little unspoken contempt. And equally important, I came out in Springfield, Missouri—not as a debutante but as a lesbian. Springfield is the Queen City of the Ozarks, though few of its citizens fully appreciate the irony in that sobriquet. It is perhaps most well known as the world headquarters of the Assemblies of God Church, an evangelical, fundamentalist Christian denomination. A city of 140,000, it is also home to at least two fundamentalist Bible colleges and two conservative four-year colleges affiliated with evangelical churches. To say that fundamentalist Christianity influences most aspects of life in Springfield and indeed all of southwest Missouri and northern Arkansas is an understatement. When I was in school there, Springfield tolerated a single gay-welcoming bar (though even that was pretty precarious); there was no gay or lesbian organization of any sort on campus at Southwest Missouri State University, with a student population of over 15,000 at that time. Even into the late 1980s, the heart of the lesbian community beat in the closet of a seemingly innocuous bookstore in a respectable strip mall on the south edge of town.

Still, I thrived in Springfield in the early 1980s. A young English major, I appeared pretty near ideal: born again and white. And as I day by day inched my way out of the closet after years of anguished heterosocial conformity, having failed repeatedly since adolescence to succeed at it, I was also learning to unlearn racism, to unlearn internalized misogyny, to unlearn naive xenophobia. Those who have only a mass-media understanding of the South might think such a social education unlikely in Springfield, or anywhere in the South, where so much fear of difference is woven into the fabric of society, but in fact the South may be the very best of all places in which to study issues of social justice precisely *because* of the glaring examples of institutionalized racism, misogyny, homophobia, and xenophobia on daily display there.

Springfield's conservatism and fundamentalism, however, then and now, do not fully represent Springfield or the South in general, though many people refuse to believe it. Despite every gun rack in a pickup, every Confederate battle flag on a rusty bumper, I met men and women in the Ozarks who deplored violence, racism, and sexism and who worked tirelessly and courageously for social justice. These were my role models, what I call the Southern Resistance. Even today, they simultaneously represent the best of the South and by the necessity of their ongoing work testify to the worst of the South.

The South is a complex region full of the most remarkable paradoxes, and that complexity is ultimately the subject of this book. These essays about life in the South for gay men and lesbians confront those issues (for better and for worse) that affect every southerner's life—racism, Christian fundamentalism, classism, compulsory masculinity/femininity, right-wing politics, the bitter legacy of a civil war—with unflinching honesty and extraordinary sensitivity. This complexity arises, of course, because there is no single South. The genteel brutality of the plantation Deep South is as unlike the Third World–scale poverty of some parts of Appalachia as the isolated valleys of the Ozarks are from the Gulf Coast beaches of the "Redneck Riviera." And New Orleans is simply unlike anyplace else. Still, these diverse regions and cultures comprise a single monolithic South in the minds of very many Americans who think they know what the South is; southerners, by extension, form a single "peculiar people," a term that, according to R. Bruce Brasell, has carried both negative and positive connotations throughout history in the South. This collection, however, represents an attempt to sound out the various subregional, racial, gender, and class differences in queer experience of the South that both enrich and challenge the South. These essays attest that everything you think or believe about the South and southerners is at once absolutely right—and absolutely wrong.

My kin came to northwest Missouri from Virginia and Kentucky, bringing with them two great southern industries: tobacco and whiskey. But the ancient stubby Ozark Mountains of southwest Missouri are my spiritual landscape. The peace and comfort I feel there are really not so surprising when I recall that the Ozarks has a notorious history of attracting and harboring society's outcasts. Its thickly wooded hollers and ridges conceal all manner of marginal people. One summer in college, I worked at Silver Dollar City near Branson, Missouri, that weird born-again Las Vegas and self-aggrandizing "family values" center of the universe. In a matter of weeks, I came to know a commune of ragtag monks, a land co-op of lesbian separatists, and a trailer park cluster of anarchists who were not beyond killing a state trooper when necessary.

Driving north from Eureka Springs, Arkansas, one breathtaking fall day several years later, I passed a road sign for the Adopt-a-Highway Program of the Arkansas Highway Department that announced that the stretch of road on which I was driving was sponsored by the Knights of the Ku Klux Klan. In my imagination I saw a dozen sheeted, hooded "civic-minded" racists picking up Moon Pie wrappers and beer bottles in the ditch. This sign was just a stone's throw from comparatively liberal Eureka Springs with its visible and prosperous colony of gay and lesbian artists. The sign was also probably visible from the top of the towering Christ of the Ozarks (a gleaming white monument that must be seen to be believed) and was surely passed by hundreds of Christians en route to the Passion Play every weekend. But while this area has been popularly described as the Bible Belt of America, it is also part of another, less well-known belt, the Faerie Belt, that "runs along the 36th parallel from Virginia's Tidewater area, through North Carolina, Tennessee and Arkansas, as far west as Taos, New Mexico."[2] Along that latitude lie dozens of pagan sanctuaries, communes of Radical Faeries, and lesbian separatist land cooperatives. Without doubt, the South is a very queer region where such extremes can coexist.

The South has also been an easy repository for all that is backward and hurtful in the United States, past and present, and while the South should be accountable for its shameful past and contemporary political and social failings, I recognize as well that it is treated unfairly as often as not by those in other regions of the country. It seems not a little disingenuous of the United States to heap all the racism, bigotry, and ignorance of an entire nation upon one region. As pernicious as the attitudes and prejudices *of* the South may be, so also are the attitudes and prejudices *about* the South that reduce and often misrepresent it. The essays collected here do in fact hold the South accountable for its spectacular homophobia and other forms of bigotry and hypocrisy, but they also acknowledge that there may be some process of making peace with the region by reading the South through queer eyes.

It is a popular myth that gay people cannot live in the repressive atmosphere of the South, that all gay and lesbian southerners are driven out, indeed are suspect if they choose to stay or cannot leave. The result, in the logic of the myth, is that there cannot be gay culture in the South. Like all stereotypes, there is a kernel of truth in this one, but the essays in part 1, "Claiming Queer Space in a Hostile Place," refute that myth's conclusion. These essays about or by those who stay in the South illustrate the ways many southern gays and lesbians, often in rural areas, find to expand what Bonnie Strickland calls the "closets of opportunities" that do exist there. Some of them are fighters, like Wanda and Brenda Henson at Camp Sister Spirit in Ovett, Mississippi, in Bonnie Morris's essay "Women's Festivals on the Front Lines"; others pass for straight in their familiar communities, like Emmett in Russell County, Alabama, interviewed by Joseph Beam; and others, like the mountain people in Kate Black and Marc A. Rhorer's essay, "Out in the Mountains," struggle to make a way out of no way in the small towns and rural counties where they've always lived and feel they belong, all the while expressing the pain of also feeling that they surely don't belong.

Inevitably, one cannot critique the South without considering race. In "Race and Gay Community in Southern Town," an analysis of one representative small city, David Knapp Whittier describes the segregation that characterizes so many gay communities in the South. The politics are superficially polite, but the divisions, prejudices, and mistrust on both sides are clear. For whatever political and social interests gay men and lesbians in the South might share, race often cuts them through, making development of any real gay community difficult. But racism in the South is not exclusively black and white. Patti Duncan transcribes a conversation with members of the Asian/Pacific Islander Lesbian, Bisexual, Transgendered Network in Atlanta in an effort to "intervene in popular understandings of southern racial structure, reinserting [themselves] into the paradigm, forcing the paradigm to shift and (we hope) eventually to be transformed." That paradigm shift calls for the dismantling of what Charles I. Nero calls, in part 2, "Striking Out/Striking Back," the culture of "white tribalism" that lies at the very heart of racial injustice in the broadest sense.

Part 2 indeed strikes back at racism and hypocrisy, but it also strikes out. Those gay men and lesbians who leave the South for gay-friendlier places form a kind of diaspora of queer expatriates across the nation. These essays explore the conflicted relationship a queer southerner always has with the South no matter where he or she lives, no matter what he or she believes or works for. But like all expatriates, queer southerners in places like San Francisco, New York, Minneapolis, or Northampton often trace a coming home by going away. As Donna Smith writes, "I moved to San Francisco to become gay, and there found out that I was southern." The striking back comes in recognizing that this trajectory should not be confused with nostalgia or romanticism, both of which drape the South like a quilt, too often concealing pain and hatefulness.

James R. Keller lifts the corner of that quilt in his indictment of the "public secret," an institution of southern culture that leads to "dissimulation and fabulation." The public secret, however, is ultimately about hypocrisy, of course, as Keller illustrates in his case study of Tennessee Williams's hometown, Columbus, Mississippi, where lies are condoned so long as they support the public secret, and the military is valorized despite its "Don't ask, don't tell" policy. This theme is picked up by R. Bruce Brasell in part 3, "Representing Queer Lives in Public Space," who understands that unless the notion of the public secret is recognized and its significant power in some degree respected, the forms of activism effective in other regions of the country will surely fail in the South. Brasell's analysis of Ellen Spiro's video *Greetings from Out Here* concludes that coming out, repudiating the public secret, is a potent political strategy:

"For southern lesbians and gays, activism emerges out of their day-to-day existence, for just to live one's life openly is a kind of activism."

Part 3 represents the lives of southern gay men and lesbians in the openness of performance, in religion and the arts, essential sites of activism by existence. Like race, religion affects every southerner regardless of one's personal history with any church or religion. Edward Gray and Laura Milner develop critiques not so much of organized religion in the South as of the performative nature of religion and ritual itself. Separately, they trace the double edges of coming out and being born again, the debutante and the queen, the butch and the belle. In the arts, along with rock 'n' roll and jazz, literature has been the South's great gift to the country, but it too is double-edged. Mab Segrest assesses the canon of southern literature from a lesbian perspective while critiquing the southern legacy in methods of literary study themselves. In "'Lines I Dare': Southern Lesbian Writing," Segrest explicates the peculiar challenges facing the scholar of gay and lesbian southern fiction—not only in arguing the validity of such a focus of study but even in identifying and defining the parameters of the field itself.

In the past few years, as publishing in queer studies has increased exponentially, there has been a marked increase in work that might be called queer southern studies or southern queer studies. One recent sign of the growing interest was the first-of-its-kind conference held at Emory University in June 1997, "Queering the South: A Gathering of LBGT Arts, Activists, and Academics." Even so, book-length treatments of gay and lesbian life in the South are overwhelmingly historical, ethnographic, or documentary. This collection contributes to the growing field of southern queer studies by adding a layer of analysis to its consideration of the institutions that often define and limit the terms by which the South is understood.

A final word about vocabulary. Arguments of definition are inevitable in projects like this one. Defining the South as a region is no small feat, but it pales in comparison to the heat inspired by terms such as "gay," "lesbian," "bisexual," "transgendered," and the most hotly contested of all, "queer." Defining the borders of what we consider the South in this book or our definition of "queer" is ultimately an exercise in futility, because to limit ourselves so would be to compile a book with two essays, mine and Carlos Dews's. The reason we let go of worrying about vocabulary and definition is that we recognized early on that we did not actually intend to compile a book *about* the South or *about* gay men, lesbians, or queers, for that matter. The book is about *relationships* between and among those terms, the intersection of gay and South, queer and southern. Each contributor to this volume has considered his or her own relationship to the South and then self-identified in whatever ways seem meaningful: some were born and raised in the South; others have lived significant portions of their lives in the South. Many of them see the South with a double vision, from within and without, as insider outsiders.

We hope these autobiographical essays that also pay attention to history, sociology, politics, and culture will help open the door of the southern closet. As Jim Grimsley writes, "Our own first steps toward finding our gay and lesbian freedom have led us to understand that we must work not only for ourselves but for each other." In that work we learn that it is possible to be out in the South, to talk back to the good-book-style hatred and institutions of the South that abhor gay men and lesbians, and further, it is possible to find others—many, many others—who also love and struggle with their southern roots.

Notes

1. Adrienne Rich, "Split at the Root: An Essay on Jewish Identity," in *Blood, Bread, and Poetry: Selected Prose, 1979–1985* (New York: Norton, 1986) (reprint; originally published 1982), 100–123.

2. Barry Yeoman, "Faerie Culture," *Southern Exposure* 16, 3 (1988): 34.

Part I

Claiming Queer Space
in a Hostile Place

Joseph Beam

Emmett's Story:
Russell County, Alabama

*Together we are creating and naming a new community while extending
a hand to the one from which we've come. We are bringing into the light
the lives which we have led in the shadows.*

Joseph Beam, In the Life, 1986

Editors' Introduction

Originally published in Joseph Beam's groundbreaking 1986 collection, In the Life: A Black
Gay Anthology, *"Emmett's Story: Russell County, Alabama," helps to undermine the prevalent stereotypes of southern black gay men. Emmett's story affirms that not all southern black
gay men are drag queens (despite the most widely recognized popular images of southern black
gay men—RuPaul and the Lady Chablis of John Berendt's* Midnight in the Garden of
Good and Evil*); not all southern black gay men live in cities (or even want to live in southern cities with large gay communities—New Orleans, Atlanta, Nashville, Birmingham—
Emmett says, "I was afraid of Atlanta"); and not all southern black men are poor (Beam
writes of Emmett, "He owns his own two-bedroom home and car, and has a manufacturing
job with a future").*

*As Beam indicates in his introduction to "Emmett's Story," "Emmett" is a pseudonym.
The invisibility needed to protect his life in rural Alabama ironically prevented us from finding him to update his story since his interview with Beam. We hope that Emmett has found
the "loving, kind, and honest" lover he was searching for and still finds Russell County,
Alabama, "peaceful," and "very, very comfortable."*

Beam wrote in the Philadelphia Gay News *in 1984: "Black gay history, not recounted by
white gay media, compounds and extends our invisibility. Transmitting our stories by word
of mouth does not possess archival permanence. Survival is visibility." We hope by reprinting his interview here to add more archival permanence not only to Emmett's story but to all*

Reprinted with permission of the estate of Joseph Beam from *In the Life* (Boston: Alyson, 1986).

the stories of southern black gay men, in the cities and on the farms, in pumps and in work boots, in unemployment lines and in line at the bank.

Emmett and I met through a web of connections: friends of friends of friends. I traveled down to see him in April 1985; my first real trip to the rural South. By either urban or rural standards, Emmett's quite a catch. At twenty-seven, he owns his own two-bedroom home and car and has a manufacturing job with a future. More importantly, he's warm and down-to-earth. What follows is most of our conversation on the evening before I left. We had spent the previous four days getting to know each other, enjoying the sunshine, and comparing notes. We sipped whiskey and Coke while he spoke candidly of his past, present, and future.

[*Joseph.*]*   What kind of gay social network exists here?

[*Emmett.*]   Well, mainly there's just the gay clubs and bars really. On Auburn University's campus there's a gay club, which I really don't know much about. Most of what I've heard about them is through my cousin Nate.

[*Joseph.*]   When you say club you mean an organization?

[*Emmett.*]   Yeah, a group of guys, hanging out together, whatever. Sometimes they have meetings on campus, I understand.

[*Joseph.*]   So that's the only formal kind of thing outside of the bars, of which there aren't any?

[*Emmett.*]   Exactly. They've all closed.

[*Joseph.*]   So, how do you identify other gay men?

[*Emmett.*]   How do I identify other gay men? Mostly by the way they look at you. Sometimes the way they dress. It all depends. There are a lot of gay guys who dress very girlish; there's others that may wear their hair girlish. You know—the eyes, always something. It's not very hard to tell.

[*Joseph.*]   I don't see people doing keys and hankies and that sort of thing here, which is still in common use in Philly. Gay men aren't using signals like that?

[*Emmett.*]   I think mostly it's body language.

[*Joseph.*]   I would imagine that a lot of gay men in small communities move to bigger cities like Atlanta or New Orleans. What has kept you here in Russell County, Alabama?

[*Emmett.*]   I find Russell County to be very, very comfortable. It's sometimes hard, difficult to find a friend that you can really get into, but I feel that if you do, if you

---

*Dialogue names have been added for ease of reading and were not in the original essay from *In the Life* (Boston: Alyson, 1986).

are successful enough, that it can be very nice. Because . . . Russell County . . . is very peaceful. I think the springtime is the most loving time of all because of the smell of the greenery. It's just real comfortable.

[*Joseph.*]   You have a little girl who will be four in October. How often do you see her?

[*Emmett.*]   Oh, I see her about every other week. She stays with me mostly on weekends and when I'm off from work, on vacations and holidays. I see her quite a bit, really.

[*Joseph.*]   So are you out to her mother? Does she know you're gay?

[*Emmett.*]   Well, I think she knows but it's something we really don't get into. 'Cause, there are things that she has heard and she has come back to me about it. You know, I approach her with the attitude like: Wow, people always talking, so what, no big deal! She says, "Well I don't care; I like you the way you are because you're Sharon's father." And that's that. She knows that, and everybody else knows that. She makes me feel good when she tells me that because she lets me know—OK. I feel that she knows what's happening, but she lets me know that she doesn't care because I am the guy that made a baby by her. Two of us made a baby together, and we both love her, and we care a lot about each other. We're good friends, good friends. And I can appreciate that.

[*Joseph.*]   Have you had a lover before?

[*Emmett.*]   A lover? Yes, I've had a lover before. I've had a couple of lovers before. But most important of all there's Wayne who I find to be very sweet and kind. A person who's very easy to love and understand. And I feel that he's very honest because . . . because we've never really been together during our relationship; we were always separated. We had to correspond by mail or telephone or something of that nature. And all kinds of things have happened to both of us. Wayne who has fell in love with a female and decides to be married, then change his mind and don't want that. And then again he's not sure what he wants. He feels like he wants me, and then sometimes he feels like he should be with a female. 'Cause he feels like that's the way it should be.

[*Joseph.*]   Were the two lover-relationships before Wayne short-term or long-term?

[*Emmett.*]   Short-term, very short.

[*Joseph.*]   Months? Weeks?

[*Emmett.*]   Oh, I'd say a couple of months. There was this guy named Randy that I knew when I was in the Job Corps. And he and I—first of all—we became very good friends. When he first got to school his grandmother died. She had raised him from an infant, and he was really shocked, it just twisted him up a little. So he went home for awhile, then he returned to school. That's when we really became close. We spent a lot of time talking, talking about the situation with his grandmother, her raising him and everything, and the shock of her death. He shared those feelings with me, and so we became more than friends. We fell in love, which was very difficult to express at first. For him and for me. I kind of broke the ice. After spending so much time together and realizing what I was feeling for him and what I felt he was feeling for me I decided to write him this little cute note expressing my feelings and whatnot. I sent it to him by a friend of mine. He got the note. I was down in my room, he came down, and it was just what was needed—just what the doctor ordered. He came out and expressed his feelings about how he felt about me, him being in love with me and everything. It was really the first experience I ever had of love with a guy. Because I thought it was something that really couldn't happen to me.

[*Joseph.*]   You were eighteen.

[*Emmett.*]   Yeah, about eighteen, yes. Before that I couldn't imagine myself falling in love with another guy. I knew how I felt sexually about guys, but I never felt that I could fall in love with one. My feelings for him were really a shock for me because I was determined not to be that far out. But it was really very beautiful.

[*Joseph.*]   So what happened to Randy?

[*Emmett.*]   Well, Randy, well . . . after our relationship went on for awhile I graduated and left and went to Atlanta for awhile. We were supposed to meet there and live together and work and everything, build a future. But it didn't quite work that way because I got to Atlanta and just wasn't ready for it. I thought that I was but the city was much faster than I was at the time. And I was really afraid.

[*Joseph.*]   Afraid to settle down?

[*Emmett.*]   I was afraid of Atlanta. Because at the time my lover wasn't there. He was still in school and so I stayed in Atlanta about two weeks and during that two weeks I was hanging out, doing this, and doing that, meeting different guys. It was all going much faster than I wanted it to go. And I decided I should be back in Alabama because it was nothing like Atlanta. At the time I felt that Atlanta was a place not for you to live but to visit. I felt that Alabama was a place for living and building a home and a relationship with somebody that you really love.

[*Joseph.*]   And you think you can do that here with your people so close by?

[*Emmett.*]   Well, I feel that I can do that here with my people, but not close by. With me being so close I feel that they feel that I'm still a child, so to speak. That they always got to watch over me; tell me to do this, tell me to do that. Make sure I do this right, make sure I do that right. And still that's not what it's all about. I'm not happy with that at all, but I can deal with it for a little while.

[*Joseph.*]   Does that mean you'd move into town or would you—

[*Emmett.*]   No, I would still live in the country, but not so close to my parents. I feel like with them being so close they're just too into my affairs. If I could just be a couple of miles away that would be even better. But next door—it's just too close.

[*Joseph.*]   Was it in the Job Corps that you first started having sex with men or did it happen earlier?

[*Emmett.*]   No, that happened earlier when I was in high school. I say really around the ninth grade was when I first experienced sex with another male. At the time it was really just a game, but I grew up liking it—and enjoying it—wanting to experience it more.

But I think I felt that long before high school because I grew up not really being a guy, enjoying the things that the boys around me enjoyed like BB guns and bicycles; I wanted dolls or something like that. I really did. And really that's what I had. I grew up just wanting to do girlish things from a very young age, then as I got older, around age ten or eleven, the guys and I were getting closer and playing around all the time— just checking each other out—physically—and enjoying it.

[*Joseph.*]   What did your mama say when she was buying you a doll instead of a G.I. Joe?

[*Emmett.*]   I don't know. I think she thought it was cute. I really did.

[*Joseph.*]   Did you play jacks?

[*Emmett.*]   No, never, I don't play jacks.

[*Joseph.*]   Well, I played jacks a lot—always on the back porch. I couldn't play them on the front porch. And I was fierce at them, too!

[*Emmett.*]   I wasn't good at jacks, but I played a good mother's playhouse. [We both laugh.]

[*Joseph.*]   Are there any gay male couples who live together in this community?

[*Emmett.*]   No, there's none. There are people you suspect—but in this neighborhood—no.

[*Joseph.*]   Maybe not in the neighborhood, but say a five-mile radius?

[*Emmett.*]   People I suspect as being lovers? No, I really can't say there are any. At least, not that I know of.

[*Joseph.*]   Will you talk a little bit more about why you feel comfortable here?

[*Emmett.*]   I feel it's comfortable here because . . . there's not a very big population. You got less people to really deal with and less congestion. I sometimes think—this may sound strange—that just the smell of the air puts me in a certain mood. 'Cause sometimes the freshness can be so nice and so loving and peaceful that there's just nowhere else to be. It's just . . . hard to describe. It seems to be hard to find words to express what I really want to say. Just . . . comfortable: the atmosphere. The people is a little difficult to deal with sometimes but I feel that people are going to be a big issue wherever you might go. So, I'm willing to deal with that; there's a lot less of them to deal with here.

[*Joseph.*]   It seems like the feelings of comfort are also related to your family being here.

[*Emmett.*]   I like being near my family, especially my grandmother really. Well, she's my grandmother, but she was like a mother to me. She raised me; I've been with her most of my life, and I love her a lot. She's not very young now and I just like being with her. For some reason I feel . . . a certain security with her or something. I feel that she feels that with me and wants me around. I feel happy being near her.

[*Joseph.*]   But not this near!

[*Emmett.*]   No, not next door!

[*Joseph.*]   Why do you think you've been unsuccessful finding a lover?

[*Emmett.*]   Why? I just feel I haven't been in the right place at the right time. I feel that if there's a lover for me I can find him. I can find him here somewhere. It's just a matter of time.

[*Joseph.*]   Do you think that maybe a lot of men aren't about anything?

[*Emmett.*]   I find a lot of guys in this particular area, most of the ones who will approach you are unemployed, not very serious. The type of relationship I want is not just a one-night stand, but something that can be special and long lasting. And most of the guys I run into, at this particular time, are just hanging out for the night, so to speak. And it's getting very tiring.

[*Joseph.*]   So do you think they describe themselves as "in the life" or do they jump the fence and think of themselves as bisexuals?

[*Emmett.*]   Well, frankly, they consider themselves as heterosexuals. They just doing something, trying it out. It's just an excuse that most of them use. They do it every now and then, but they consider themselves real men: heterosexuals. They will deny to the last minute that they are bisexual or homosexual. And yet you know something ain't right; they're either gay or bisexual. You know they are and they know they are, but they're not willing to accept this; otherwise, I don't think they'd be interested. But I've found that a lot of them are, a lot of them.

[*Joseph.*]   We've talked some about your grandmother and mother. What about your father?

[*Emmett.*]   My natural father and mother were divorced when I was two. My mother remarried. My stepfather and I are not very close, not close at all. We don't have any conversation: hello, goodbye, anything. He lives over there; I live over here.

[*Joseph.*]   Does he live in the house?

[*Emmett.*]   He, my mother, and my grandmother live nextdoor. But they are in the process of getting a divorce. It's a long time coming. Very late; it should have been years ago. As I said, my stepfather and I have never been very close; there's no love lost between the two of us.

My father and I—I know him; we visit each other, but still we're not that close. We never see each other that much. I really didn't know my father until I was sixteen or seventeen. I mean I knew him. I knew of him, saw pictures of him. But I really didn't know him and know what he looked like till I was a teenager. Still, we're not very close. We see each other every now and then. It's not like he's my father and I'm his son. 'Cause he never has been a father figure to me, so I really can't claim him as such.

[*Joseph.*]   Sometimes as I go through (maybe that's not a good word) the men in my life, I keep thinking that maybe I'm really looking for a father substitute. In terms of the men I like, how much do they resemble my father or the father I wanted. Do you think that the kind of man you like now has any resemblance to your father?

[*Emmett.*]   To my father, no. To what I would like to have been my father—yes. What I see in my heart for the man for me is what I would have liked to have had for a father. 'Cause I prefer a man who is . . . will be loving, kind, and honest, and I would have preferred a father who had been the same. But I've never really thought about it that way. But—yeah . . .

Kate Black and Marc A. Rhorer

Out in the Mountains:
Exploring Lesbian and Gay Lives

This essay focuses on the lives of gays and lesbians and their experiences growing up in the Appalachian mountains. The idea for this project began when I wanted to do a research paper on lesbians and gays in Appalachia and asked Kate, then curator of the University of Kentucky Appalachian Collection, about prior research on the subject. Kate said, "There isn't anything." A few months later, while returning from the 1993 Appalachian Studies conference, we decided to present something about lesbians and gays at the 1994 conference. We knew we could find people to ask about their experiences of growing up gay in Appalachia. We wanted to give a voice to that experience, while at the same time giving ourselves voices as a lesbian and gay man at the Appalachian Studies Conference.

Until this research, gays and lesbians did not exist in the context of Appalachian scholarship. Because of the ubiquitous "hillbilly" stereotype, issues of representation are frequently explored in Appalachian studies. Even though scholars worked diligently to establish the richness and diversity of Appalachian social life and history, lesbian and gay representation in Appalachian culture had been ignored. We hope that this exploratory work will stimulate other researchers to include gays and lesbians in the conversation of Appalachian Studies.

Though neither of us is from the mountains, we both grew up in the rural South. As longtime residents of Lexington, Kentucky, we both knew other lesbians and gays in Lexington who grew up in the mountains and migrated to Kentucky cities to study, work, and live. We talked with five lesbians and four gay men, all white, from Eastern Kentucky, West Virginia, East Tennessee, and Western North Carolina, ranging in

An earlier version of "Out in the Mountains: Exploring Lesbian and Gay Lives" first appeared in *The Journal of the Appalachian Studies Association* 7 (1995). © Center for Appalachian Studies and Services, East Tennessee State University, 1995. Used with permission.

age from twenty to forty-five. Only one of them continues to live in the mountains; the other eight live in Lexington and Louisville. Pseudonyms are used for all interviewees. These interviews are now part of the oral history collection at the University of Kentucky.

Before the interviews, we agreed on areas to explore: coming-out experiences, homophobia, AIDS-phobia, and community building. We felt that these were key issues based on our autobiographies and those of our friends who grew up in the rural South. It is the process of navigating these issues that, in part, forms our identities as lesbians and gay men. We found several common themes in the rich stories of the participants: feelings of isolation, the importance of community, fears from inside and outside the closet, various forms of oppression and discrimination, and multiple, fluid identities based on place and sexuality, in a dynamic relationship with one another.

Feelings of Isolation

When we asked people to talk about the differences between being gay in the mountains and in urban areas, all expressed feelings of isolation in the mountains. While growing up, they had no one to turn to for guidance, support, and information when they began realizing they were homosexual. They felt there were no others with same-sex attractions, even to the extreme that some did not know gays or lesbians existed. When some interviewees mentioned the possibility of moving back to the mountains, they noted that the most difficult part would be coping with the isolation from other gays and lesbians. One person made contacts in Lexington before moving back home to insure some access to the gay community. A few participants had a sense that mass-communication technology (particularly cable and satellite television) has the potential to reduce feelings of isolation by providing young lesbians and gays in the mountains access to nonheterosexist images.

These feelings of isolation were expressed in a variety of ways. Karla, a lesbian put on academic probation her first year at Morehead State University in Morehead, Kentucky, said: "A lot of the problem was I discovered the gay community. I never knew one existed. It was unbelievable! Every other person was gay." As a young person in high school, Allan also thought he didn't know any gay people. Speaking of high school friends who he now knows are gay, Allan remembered: "At the time I thought they were people I got along well with, but I didn't realize why. . . . I didn't know people who were gay."

A forty-five-year-old lesbian, Phyllis, who often gives talks on homophobia at Kentucky colleges, told us a story reiterating the sense of aloneness that young mountain people struggling to come out may experience. Once when Phyllis was speaking at Morehead State University, a young man came up to her afterward and asked, "How old did you say you were?" She answered, "Forty-two." Then he said: "You're the same age as my Mama. I didn't know there were any gay or lesbian people as old as my mama!"

But being isolated and silenced by heterosexual hegemony can have serious reper-
cussions, as Ann described:. "The saddest part to me about growing up in the mountains as a gay person is that . . . you end up feeling like an outsider; you've got no one
to talk to about these strange feelings you have, and you have to end up like lots of
young people growing up gay, being isolated, and you think about killing yourself
cause you're so strange."

Some of the interviewees described resourceful ways in which they managed to give
a name to the sexual feelings they embodied. For example, Karla came out to herself
when she was thirteen. She found out the definition of "lesbian" when she "went to
the public library and looked up 'homosexuality.' . . . There was absolutely no one to
talk to."

Brent also elaborated on the characteristics of isolation, while considering the difference between his rural Powell County and its county seat: "To be gay in Clay City
[Kentucky], it's hard," but it is harder out in the county where there isn't access to
cable TV. "MTV is preaching 'Free Your Mind,' [but] your mind is not going to be free
if you don't live inside the city limits."

Finding a Community

This sense of isolation diminished when people moved from the mountains to the city,
because in the urban setting they could meet and be with other gays and lesbians.
While finding a community of other gays and lesbians was crucial, paradoxically an
increased feeling of anonymity in the city was equally important. Anonymity, which
many could not obtain at home, allowed greater freedom from the scrutiny of those
who might condemn them; most people expressed a much greater sense of comfort
about being out in the city. In contrast, at home people felt as if they were under surveillance and subjects of the gossip networks, even after moving away to the city.
However, several people mentioned a positive aspect of the tight-knit nature of rural
community: if a person came from an established family lineage in the mountains,
she or he was less likely to be harassed for being lesbian or gay.

While discussing the differences between being gay in the mountains and in Lexington, Donald mused about the nature of urban anonymity and rural visibility.
"When you move to a bigger city, your reputation doesn't necessarily have that much
weight," he said, implying that reputation has different definitions and meanings in
these two worlds. What is a boon in one place may be a hindrance in another. But
Karla saw the rural community with a more steely gaze: "Appalachian queers migrate
out of there . . . the few that do live there are usually not totally rejected by the family but rejected by the community. They'll be real kind [to your face] but still say stuff
behind your back." Thus you might be despised but not necessarily be treated as if
you are.

Ann, a woman in her forties who came out in the late 1960s and often drove to the
gay bar in Lexington from the mountain home where she still lives, described her

forays as a familial quest: "You had community [at The Bar], which gave you family, family of choice." Two decades later, twenty-year-old Greg made a similar assessment about his life in Lexington: "Living here, there's a lot more opportunities to meet those of your kind—a lover, a boyfriend, a fuck buddy. To live in Clay City, I wouldn't want to do that . . . it's just not open enough."

One interviewee sees himself as both mountain insider and outsider, a perspective from which he can examine the tension between the two. When Donald was eight, he and his mother moved back to her family's Eastern Kentucky community after years of living in Ohio. He described both his parents as coming from old mountain families. Theorizing about the relationship between being gay or lesbian and what constitutes social status in the mountains, he said, "If someone comes in from the outside—straight or gay—it doesn't make any difference. They are going to have a very difficult time fitting into the community. If, however, they are from this long lineage, they will find it much easier to be who they are, regardless if they're gay or straight."

Because finding lesbian and gay community, especially as a newcomer, depends on identifying others who are lesbian and gay, we asked the interviewees to talk about how they found other lesbians and gays, either in the mountains or in their city homes. We heard a variety of creative responses. While several people mentioned being invited to lesbian and gay parties, especially in mountain college towns, others seemed to rely on their instincts and what might be dubbed a homosexual common sense: "You go to the gym, you find gym rats." "[I]t takes one to know one." "Gaydar." But Allan, a thoughtful, garrulous twenty-eight-year-old, came up with multiple, less instinctual, ways in which his generation of lesbians and gays found each other in Boone, North Carolina, home of Appalachian State University. "[T]here was a lesbian softball league. It wasn't an official lesbian softball league, it just happened that most people on it were probably lesbian. There was a student group. A lot of people would go to a regional gay bar. Recently, I know of people in Boone who get on e-mail and try to meet people that way."

Identity and Community

We believe that identity and community are intricately linked. In fact, identities are formed and informed by communities. Conversely, communities both affect and can be an effect of identities. Many people are members of more than one community simultaneously or through a life span, just as many of us consider ourselves to have multiple identities. In short, since community and identity are not necessarily tidy concepts—both in our everyday lives and in the abstract sense—the process of identity and community formation can often be a tense one. One identity can be at odds with another one. In the worlds we live in, for example, urban gays or lesbians may judge us to be too "country," too rural, or just outright hicks. At home, that is, the place where we grew up, we may still be considered persona non grata as a lesbian and gay man.

We were curious about how people reconciled these tensions. For example, we wondered if people identified themselves as both gay and Appalachian. While everyone readily identified themselves as gay or lesbian, we found that many of the interviewees seemed to avoid directly addressing their Appalachian identities. In addition, some had not resolved their sense of conflict over being from the mountains.

Brent was among those who remained conflicted about the place where he grew up. He referred to his "trapped" life in the mountains, equating living in the mountains with cultural isolation: "If I was trapped in Clay City, I would be myself, just like I was when I was trapped there. Information and exposure to different cultures and different people is what really changes minds. That's what causes accents, when people are trapped up in the mountains." Brent obviously saw being from the mountains as a kind of "mark of the beast" and something of which to feel ashamed. The youngest of the interviewees, twenty-year-old Greg, told us proudly, "People are surprised when they find out where I'm from. [My friends] say, 'I can't believe you turned out the way you did.'" In other words, Greg "passes" and feels pleased about his transformation.

Ann, the one interviewee who has continuously lived in Eastern Kentucky, readily identified herself as Appalachian. Without embarrassment or remorse she declared, "It's home, this is where the roots are." Another lesbian, Karla, described matter-of-factly what being Appalachian means to her: "It's the family, the heritage." One man who used to live in Boone, North Carolina, toyed with the idea of moving back there while questioning whether such a move was possible for him. In Lexington, Allan is part of a vibrant gay and lesbian community in which he has made a place for himself, most notably in gay politics. Yet in Boone, he feels a certain freedom not found in Lexington, which he expressed pensively: "I feel sometimes people [in Boone] know me more as a person than as a gay person."

Facing Fears

Because all the people we talked to expressed an overwhelmingly greater sense of freedom and ability to be out in the city, we wanted to know how the dimensions of the closet change with a move to the city. People talked about what was scary or fearful about being out at home versus being out in the city. Though fear of being out was experienced in the city, everyone generally felt that the situation was more hostile in the mountains for gays and lesbians. Men experienced much more physical aggression at home and seemed to have a limited definition of the term "fear," equating it with the threat of physical violence. Males also endured much verbal taunting in junior high and high school. Both men and women told us stories of physical violence and verbal taunting directed toward gay males in the mountains.

Interestingly but not surprisingly, women tended to include psychological as well as physical violence in their descriptions of fearful situations. Women seemed to sustain more social ostracism (that is, from family, friends, and church), were forced into psychiatric care for a "cure," or both. None of the men reported being sent to a therapist. Men were tormented because those around them suspected they were gay, while women were more likely to face threatening conditions if they were caught actually being sexual with a woman. However, one woman contradicted this representation when she told us a story of her local police cruising places where teenagers parked. She said when she was caught making out with her girlfriend, the police would generally laugh and tell them to go home, but when her gay male friends were caught, they were likely to be brutalized.

When asked about what had produced fear when he lived in the mountains, Allan said: "I've been scared that people would find out. I've been scared that if people knew I was gay, I would lose my job, people would say something to me, that I wouldn't have any recourse, wouldn't have any place to go." He went on to say how he was scared to kiss his lover goodbye when he dropped him off for work. Also, Allan was afraid that "they'd hear my partner and I and they would come and bust down the doors and get us," a fear grounded in the North Carolina sodomy law.

Donald, who talked about physical violence in the mountains, told us that he'd "heard stories of incredible physical violence against [gay] people." One of the more horrific incidents Donald remembered took place in Breathitt County, Kentucky, where a man was dismembered and killed by local people because he was thought to be gay. Kelly, a young lesbian, said that one of her gay male friends was stabbed twenty-seven times while shopping in a country store in West Virginia, solely because he was homosexual. In another hostile incident, Kelly left her truck overnight at a body shop and "while it was there someone painted on the tailgate [near the pink triangle and rainbow decals] 'die fag' and slashed the two back tires." Because of the reference to "fag," she thought that the perpetrator probably assumed the truck was owned by a man. Several men noted they were persistently taunted with words like "fag" and "sissy" throughout their adolescent schooling.

Lesbians, in particular, said that the social ostracism they endured as young people was often orchestrated by adults. "When I was in the eighth grade," Kelly told us, "because I came out to a couple of my friends, that proceeded to get me ostracized from overnight parties and church." One of the women we talked with had a relationship during high school that was discovered by her girlfriend's parents. The parents, driving a long distance in the middle of the night, arrived at the motel room where the two young women were staying for a softball tournament and pulled their daughter out of the room at 4:00 A.M.

One of the interviewees, Ann, attended Berea College, located on the edge of the Kentucky mountains and known for its student industries of crafts production and hotel keeping. While a student there, Ann had a relationship with one of her teachers. After Berea College officials exposed her to her parents, Ann was caught by her mother at the lover's house at 1:00 A.M. "It turned out to be pretty devastating for both of us. She lost her job over it. I became this crisis point in my family. They decided I needed psychiatric help." With her typical wit and the advantage of age,

Ann concluded, "Here was this woman corrupting some poor little Appalachian girl who obviously didn't know what she was doing." At this point Kate, the interviewer, and Ann began to giggle, and Kate said, "Yeah, you're supposed to be making brooms." Ann came back with, "Yeah, or spoon bread at the Tavern!"

Levels of Discrimination

Gays and lesbians face discrimination both in the mountains and in the city. We defined "discrimination" as the public or civil face of homophobia because the people we talked with defined it that way. Not surprisingly, those who work with children or young adults appear very susceptible to discrimination. We heard the story of two teachers in the mountains who were fired because they were rumored to be homosexual. Karla, who is out in most parts of her life, says she would never come out at her job working with schoolchildren in Eastern Kentucky because she "would be fired in a heartbeat."

Many people expressed fear of being out at their jobs in the city, even when they did not work with children, because they were afraid of being fired or passed over for raises or promotions. Two people told stories about gay bars that involved discrimination or the threat of it. These incidents gain even more importance because bars as public meeting places are historically central to the gay and lesbian community. Ann remembered police surveillance behind The Bar, a gay nightclub in Lexington, Kentucky, to observe those who went in and out. One man spoke about a bar owner in Huntington, West Virginia, who was gay, who did not want to be associated with anything "political," in this case having an AIDS literature table in his bar. The interviewee explained that the bar owner felt too vulnerable to actions of the local authorities and, therefore, did not want to do anything to call attention to his bar or his clientele.

In most rural and small-town communities, churches and public schools are often the most important and influential social institutions. A man told us of how a lesbian high school teacher in North Carolina lost her job just because one of her students perceived that she was a lesbian and proceeded to openly accuse her. Allan explained how people in the community "prayed for her" publicly at church. The teacher was fired "on the pretext that she cussed in class, but it was well known that it was because she was a lesbian," Allan concluded.

Kelly related how she experienced discrimination at her Lexington workplace. "I can't prove anything from this, but I would swear I'm being discriminated against at my job." Kelly elaborated: "After I'd been working there for three months, one of the people who was in middle management took me into his office and told me that I shouldn't be working there because of my sexual orientation and that there was no reason for me to come back. . . . Apparently he forgot to tell anyone else this and the next time my shift rolled around I got a call asking me where I was. So I went in, didn't say anything about it, and I've been working there ever since."

Several of the people we talked with told stories of discrimination at public meeting places. In Boone, North Carolina, in the late 1980s, a group of gays who were not students wanted to start an off-campus gay organization and meeting place. Bomb and death threats were made. Allan, who lived in Boone at the time, said the police provided protection and "were pretty good about dealing with it [but that] people would have to come in around the police when these meetings first went on." Recalling earlier times, Ann described how she frequently went to the gay bar in Lexington, Kentucky, during the early 1970s: "It was frightening, going to The Bar. It was rough, tough. Police cars parked out back. People said, 'Don't drive your car, they're taking down license plate numbers,' so there was all that harassment. So coming to the bar was not only an act of celebration, but an act of defiance."

AIDS-phobia

We also asked people to talk about AIDS. We included AIDS-phobia in the discussions about various forms of homophobia, since the two have been viciously linked ever since the early days of the epidemic when AIDS was called GRID—Gay-Related Immune Deficiency. Surprisingly, one of the gay men we interviewed did not know anyone who is HIV positive or has AIDS. Everyone acknowledged that AIDS-phobia exists, but they did not seem to think it was more rampant in one place or the other, except for one man who said he'd experienced more AIDS-phobia in Lexington—by both the straight and gay community—than in the mountains. He correlated AIDS-phobia with a higher HIV incidence in Lexington. Two people said that because they stick closely to the lesbian and gay community or are outspoken advocates for the lesbian/gay community and for people with AIDS, they are not as likely to hear AIDS-phobic remarks and discussions.

When we asked Karla if she heard AIDS-phobic statements at home, she said, "More than anything else. More than homophobia, more than racist things. . . . It's not really [expressed] as trashing people with AIDS, it is just terror that they're gonna get it." A few people said they had experienced people correlating AIDS directly with homosexuality. Greg told us that when he came out to his grandmother, she responded irrationally by exclaiming, "You're gonna get AIDS!" He noted that she is an intelligent, politically aware woman, yet she immediately connected being gay with being HIV positive.

Kelly said that when she comes out to people, they often respond with "Aren't you afraid of AIDS?" She also told us a story of AIDS-phobi, not explicitly tied to homophobia. In her workplace, an urban YMCA, all employees are required to take an AIDS awareness class. This Y's policy is to notify the supervisor if an HIV-positive person is in a class or program. This information is then passed up the ladder to the executive director. Kelly pointed out to her co-workers at a postclass discussion that no one needed to know this information since one of the tenets of the AIDS awareness course was to treat anyone who is injured as infected to prevent infecting anyone else. In short, universal precautions should be universal. Kelly "was knocked down by everyone else in the room, saying that it didn't matter, they [YMCA employees] deserve to know because they work with these children and adults and if they were infected they [YMCA employees] were going to treat them differently."

Internalizing Homophobia

Like racism, homophobia not only is perpetrated by those who dominate but also can be internalized by those who are dominated. Because organized religion played an important part in most of the interviewees' lives—socially, morally, and spiritually— we found that many had deep inner struggles over their homosexuality rooted in religious notions of sin and guilt. This powerful underpinning of internalized homophobia was sometimes acted out in religious proselytizing. One of our interviewees told us that before she came out in high school, she used the Bible to try to convince a lesbian couple she knew that their sexuality was a sin.

Two of the lesbians we talked with, however, resisted the oppression and repression of the church by questioning and railing against it. Kelly described her church experience this way: "The church was the only social outlet in the town. So I wasn't going to church so much for religious/spiritual reasons as I was for social reasons. In fact, I learned quite early to keep my mouth shut when discussing the Bible and other issues because I asked too many questions that the answer was always 'Pray about it, and you'll see the truth.'" For Karla, the conflict was not reconciled for many years. She told us that she "really struggled with religion and going to hell. I really did not want to be gay. I've had a hard time accepting it. Probably [over] the last five years, it has gotten easy." Finally, another woman, at a young age, was able to transform her questioning into a belief in social justice.

For most of the interviewees, the extreme isolation from other lesbians and gays contributed to their internalized homophobia. Many spoke movingly of the need to help lesbian and gay young people in the mountains know they are not abnormal or alone. Many suggested lesbian and gay visibility as a partial solution to this problem. One of the youngest interviewees, Brent, connected the isolation with organized religion, seeing it as a potent force for his own suffering and confusion. Brent, who went to mass every day when he was thirteen, prayed, "Why do I have to be different? Why can't I be like everyone else?" He poignantly concluded:

> I would hate for another generation of gay people to have to grow up and feel alienated, to feel like they are outcasts. I consider myself, in a way, one of the lucky people who have finally been able to draw themselves into another community and find other people like themselves, so that they don't end up being drug addicts or jumping off a bridge or hanging themselves, just because they have no role models, have no other friends that they can come out to. They need someone to show them that they're okay, that they're not bad, that they're not going to hell.

Some Last Thoughts

Over the course of these interviews, fresh questions for subsequent interviews and new conceptual categories began to emerge. For example, class differences and perspectives surfaced from the interviews even though we did not probe our interviewees with questions about class. One of the interviewees, Karla, for instance, conflated class and gender roles when she described her lesbian community at a state University as being divided into the *A*, *B*, and *C* crowds. The *A* crowd consisted of "the pretty ones who were well dressed and acted like they were better than other people. Then there was just the average people in the *B*. In the *C*, of course, was the real butch people."

While we neither explicitly nor implicitly asked people to talk about their whiteness or notions of race, a few interviewees freely offered the information that their families were more racist than homophobic.

Neither did we ask questions directly about gender identities, yet several people brought up the categories of "butch" and "fem" for lesbians and "butch" and "queen" for gay men. For example, Allan theorized: "People [he means gay men] in rural areas of Kentucky and North Carolina tend to be queenier. It is like they try to mesh with the stereotype of gay people more than people in larger cities, who feel free to emulate other things." This statement possibly provides a window into class and gender differences, roles—both chosen and prescribed—internalized homophobia (the interviewee's), varying notions about power and resistance, and, perhaps, rural and urban dissonance. In addition, several people talked about the contentious role religion played in their lives. In short, this exploratory project begs for more exploration.

Nine interviews hardly constitute a scientifically valid sampling. But they reveal much difference among these nine people who grew up lesbian and gay in the Appalachian mountains. Their identities are multiple, sometimes contradictory, and always complex. Rural and small-town people—in Appalachia and in the South—are far more complicated than the media and, often, scholarship portray them. These nine people were, in fact, grappling with creating a synthesis of multiple identities—class, race, gender, place, religion, and, of course, sexuality. Even in this preliminary research, the evidence cautions all of us against categorizing lesbians and gays as a homogenous group, and for that matter, Appalachians, also.

The common threads among the interviewees were the pain that synthesizing can evoke (though the pain seemed to be experienced and coped with variously) and their desire—desire for same-sex relations, sex, love, community. Together, the pain and desire seemed to produce this incredible resistance—albeit manifested by varying strategies and tactics—to the ever lurking and ever pressing homophobia and heterosexism.

Patti Duncan

Claiming Space in the South: A Conversation Among Members of Asian/Pacific Islander Lesbian, Bisexual, Transgendered Network of Atlanta

Transcribed, edited, and introduced by Patti Duncan, with Trishala Deb, Sunita Bhatt, Janet Guerrero, Ami Mattison, Kelly Patillo, and Paula Xian

Introduction

When we considered taping a conversation for this anthology, we decided that we wanted to speak of our differences, our common understandings of certain aspects of race and culture, and our place within the polarized racial structure of the American South. This conversation performs at least two simultaneous functions. First, we attempt a critique of common stereotypes surrounding Asian and Pacific Islander Americans—that we are the "model minority," that we are all the same (that is, male, heterosexual, middle class, of East Asian descent, and so on, a description that of course represents only a tiny fraction of the experienced reality for Asian and Pacific Islanders), and that all of us in this country live only in the Northeast or on the West Coast. In fact, we live in the South too. Second, we intervene in popular understandings of southern racial structure, reinserting ourselves into the paradigm, forcing the paradigm to shift and (we hope) eventually to be transformed. As nonblack people of color living in the South, we have been forced to identify ourselves and our cultural space as unique, distinct from those of other people of color in the South and of other Asian and Pacific Islanders Americans in various other regions. Finally, as Asian and

Pacific Islander queer women living in the South, we continue to struggle against myriad controlling images that attempt to tell us who we are, where we fit in, and what we are capable of. It has been in the context of such struggle that we have created a name and a space for ourselves, at once painful, difficult, and empowering.

The conversation that follows involves only seven members[1] of our group and in no way can reflect the entire group at large. Also, due to busy schedules, one member left early, and two members joined the conversation after it had begun. The unevenness of the transcription does reflect a reality for our group—coming together despite differences, obstacles, and scheduling conflicts, and often getting what we need from one another in fragments gathered when and where we are able to do so.

On Being Asian and Pacific Islander in the South

Patti.   Let's start by talking about who we are and what it means to be queer and API (Asian and Pacific Islander) in the South, in terms of how each of us identify, who identifies as southern and who doesn't—that sort of thing. To explain how I identify, I call myself Korean American, mixed race, queer, a dyke, biracial, and a dyke of color. I identify in many different ways. Whether or not I identify as a southerner though, has been this really kind of strange thing because I don't think I do.

I was born in the South, in North Carolina, and actually lived in the South for the first couple years of my life. But then, because my dad was in the military and we moved around, I didn't come back to the South until I was twenty-two, coming to graduate school. And what I remember is that my first reaction to being in the South was really bizarre. I had gotten so used to being part of communities of color, especially Asian American—East Asian American—communities, that coming here and feeling really, really isolated and invisible, and the idea that "people of color" in the South often equals only African American people, was really off-putting to me. And all of the new stereotypes I kept confronting. I don't think I'd ever been in a place before where it was so hard to find another API person.

And really, that shouldn't be true here—there are a lot of APIs in Atlanta, but that's how it felt, and something about that really suggested to me our invisibility here in the South. So I think part of why I wanted to do a project like this had to with really thinking about these issues, and really feeling like hardly anybody is talking about APIs in the South, let alone queer APIs in the South. And when other API queer organizations hear about us, their first reaction is usually one of pity, like "Oh you poor things, what are you doing down in Atlanta?"

Janet.   Really?

Everyone.   Yeah!

Patti.   And the assumption is always that "you must have no community down there."

Janet.   Like, "You must be constantly persecuted there"?

Patti.   Yeah, and in some ways I would say maybe that's true, but in other ways I think about how we have a group here that is truly amazing, maybe because we've had to struggle through more obstacles, or face more issues of difference and exclusion. But here we are in the South with this API queer group doing things, pushing boundaries, in a way that I don't think I'm hearing about in New York or San Francisco or LA. So sometimes it kind of amazes me.

Janet.   For me, maybe one of the reasons why it's different here than in those other cities you named is because queer APIs in those cities have gotten a little complacent, and they're able to move within their own API communities, like I always felt very comfortable within my own Pacific Islander community [in California]. I wasn't out— I was going to say I wasn't "very" out, but in fact I wasn't out within the Pacific Islander community. Even though I never officially came out, most people knew that I was a gay woman. And I could move in and out of the two different communities which I never felt overlapped in any way, you know, being gay or being Pacific Islander. And I was always caught between those two, so I sometimes think that also, at least in my culture, they—my family—knew I was gay, and it didn't matter, well, to my mother it mattered a lot, but to everybody else it was not necessarily fine, but they could deal with it, 'cause I wasn't sucking face in front of them or anything like that; so it wasn't that big of a deal, you know, for me.

And I never had the need to go seek out other Pacific Islanders or other APIs. You know what I mean? We didn't have a very active API group in San Diego—a queer group. I guess every now and then I'd see an ad for them getting together, but I never went to any of it and I know other API men and women who never went either. We had our own set of friends. Our lives seemed to be fulfilled as far as our cultures were concerned through our families and just through the magnitude of other APIs there.

Ami.   I think ultimately it is about need, and what people need, socially and culturally and communally. Patti was saying it seemed like you couldn't find other APIs here, but it seems like there's a much larger Asian American or Asian community than there is a Pacific Islander community. I know that within our group we do talk about APIs—Asian and Pacific Islanders—and that's because we have Asians and Pacific Islanders in the group. In a lot of other groups, they include Pacific Islanders as part of the community but in fact there aren't many (if any) Pacific Islanders in the group, or they're not active or they're marginalized within the group. I don't think that's true in our group. But it still seems really important to not just conflate API—that's a huge conflation on the one hand, but it's been a necessary kind of coalition, one that has made more sense here and maybe not necessarily in other places.

I know for me that not growing up in a community of Pacific Islanders or mostly Pacific Islanders, not even having a Pacific Islander family, it did become much more important for me not to simply find other Pacific Islanders, per se, but to find other women of color who could identity with my experience of displacement, the experience of on the one hand feeling connected to but also feeling disconnected from one's culture. I wanted to meet other people who understood having to straddle different kinds of cultures at the same time, and it was important to meet people who were more like me in that way, as opposed to identical to me. Though it was kind of funny that I met Janet because, you know—that I would meet another Chamorro dyke in Atlanta, Georgia, is just crazy! It's crazy but really great at the same time, something I totally wasn't expecting ever, to come across or to meet, certainly not to become good friends with like we have, so that's a really great thing, but I never expected that as much as I was seeking out a space where some of the kinds of experiences that I had felt would be similar to other women and that I would somehow learn to articulate my own experience by listening to other women's experiences.

Trish. Growing up . . . in the Northeast, I think my kind of unspoken sense of identity was more of an immigrant than as an ethnicity or some kind of constructed racial term or whatever. I think some of that was because of where my family lived. A lot of times there wasn't a large Indian community. So what was clearest to me was that we were immigrants and that we were different, and there didn't seem to be large communities of other families like ours wherever we were. And that was especially true of North Carolina—we moved to a small town in North Carolina when I was sixteen, and I just was really clear that I could never, ever, ever fit in there. And it wasn't because I was Indian but because I was an immigrant. I felt much more marginalized as an immigrant than as a person of color.

And I think it was not until college when I became politicized that I understood what that also meant was to be nonwhite in a paradigm of white supremacy, which I think is still very articulated in the South, whereas it exists in the North, but it's not quite as articulated. I don't know. I guess that's something I was just realizing talking to you all, that kind of the irony for me is that our API group is the first API group that I've really felt at home in, and that I've tried to find other API or South Asian groups in cities that I've been in and I've never fit in, for other reasons—because I was queer, because I'm a feminist, or because I don't reflect their politics.

Sunita. I grew up in the Northeast as well, but completely surrounded by the Indian community. That's the community I grew up in, so even when I came out to myself I couldn't come out to the community because everyone knew my parents and that was just, well, it wasn't accepted to be queer and if people knew you were, the gossip would go so far and wide that you'd completely be shunned. And so in a way for me, coming to the South and meeting this group was something that I really enjoyed because it meant, like Trish said, it was where I first felt at home, where I could really be myself.

And also the other thing I notice that is different from growing up in the North and being active in the South is that I think a lot of the groups in the North are able to be complacent because they're so used to having privilege, they're so used to being accepted as people of color communities, because the North has such a political correctness attitude in the sense that they feel as if they need to be politically correct even if they may be suddenly racist; outwardly they are politically correct, and outwardly they do pretend to accept people of color communities, so you don't really feel the racism. Whereas coming to the South was a huge culture shock and a huge eye opener because growing up in the North I didn't really experience the racism at all since I grew up in the Indian community and was pretty much sheltered in that respect.

Coming here, the first thing I noticed was being the only person of color in a restaurant where all the waiters were people of color and all the patrons were white. And being in this group made me feel at home also in the sense that this is probably the first group I've been in that's been API where South Asians are actually integrated. It's not a group that has an East Asian focus, whereas all the groups up North—they may say they're API, but like Ami said, it ends up being mostly an East Asian focus. And the South Asian groups are pretty much split from the overall Asian groups. You have the Asian groups and the South Asian groups, and they don't really mix as well as I think we do down here.

Patti.   I feel like this group is really special for similar reasons. Though I'm of an East Asian background, being mixed race and feeling like that has never allowed me to fit into any group of people of color very easily. This group has never even questioned it—I've never felt that that was an issue, that someone was going to ask me "What are you doing in this group?" In fact, the kind of shit that I've encountered has been from people outside of this group. Especially—well, maybe not especially but maybe it just hurts the most—from the white queer community. Here. I mean in terms of questioning my race, in terms of questioning my identity. Always that feeling like when I moved down here, I was constantly feeling like I had to come out both racially and sexually, and it's interesting to me that it was never you guys—or this group— who made me feel like I don't have a right or I'm not entitled to claim my identity and my space as a member of this group. It was often white queers saying things like, "Why would you be part of a group like that?" "You're white enough," or "You can pass." Or just kind of questioning my desire to be part of this group, and even questioning the creation of a group like this. There's a critical attitude, that we're isolating ourselves, we're being exclusionary, there's something wrong with us creating a group for us.

Janet.   It's meant a lot to me to be among women of color. And I do feel strongly that we need to keep Pacific Islander distinct, that we need to recognize that Pacific Islanders have a completely different culture. But I've never felt like anyone was treating me differently because I'm Pacific Islander. And I have to tell you I'm really glad I've met South Asians, because I didn't know any in San Diego. There it was like I was hanging out with Pacific Islanders or I was hanging out with white dykes. And I honestly have never been exposed to Indian culture. So I enjoy the diversity of the group.

Ami.   Yeah I do too, and I've learned so much from my friends. And I feel like that's a really important way to have cultural experiences. Because otherwise it seems really appropriative. On the other hand, it's really important to me to be as open and as broad a person, I feel like that's what makes me a bigger person, is that I know more about other people's experiences that might be very different from mine.

Distinct Forms of Racism

Trish.   Lately I feel like I've been experiencing a different kind of racism. I think that as a progressive organizing community emerges in the South and especially in Atlanta, there's a growing network of supposedly progressive queer organizing venues in Atlanta. I'm starting to feel this whole other aspect of tokenization, particularly from the white queer sector or the white feminist sector. People learn that not only am I a feminist, or queer, or an activist, all of a sudden I'm this hot commodity because I'm like all of the things they need for their political correctness potion wrapped up in one. And I feel like as the queer community kind of emerges from its black/white dichotomy, all of a sudden our presence is sought out here in places, even if our voices and the diversity of our experiences are not.

And I feel that there are times when I've been asked to be in spaces and the people in those spaces realize I'm not going to say what they want me to say, which is like how glad I am to be part of a diverse community in this country, or some bullshit like that, and I start talking about racism too, and that's not what they want to hear from me. Or I talk about how historically the white feminist movement has alienated not only women of color but immigrants specifically or queer women of color specifically, or queer Asian women specifically, or whatever, you know, they don't want to be hearing that either. I just think that's really interesting, that as our access to spaces becomes broader, my range of experiences around racism also becomes broader.

Patti.   And a more insidious form of racism sometimes too. There's a different twist to it when it comes from people who you want to trust, whom you align yourself with or identify with in some way. Like the kind of shit from other feminists when I really strongly identify as a feminist. To have the kinds of things you were saying, Trish, repeated over and over and over again, and people wanting you to fit into this particular space and when you question it, they don't hear you.

Trish.   Yeah, then you're a traitor.

Ami.   Yeah!

Trish.   Then you're good for nothing.

Patti.   And I feel like history is getting rewritten by these people all the time in really dangerous ways. For instance, did anybody read that *Southern Voice* article a few weeks ago by a white woman feminist about the history of the women's movement? Okay, she begins by explaining how she's been hearing about the "race" issue over and over again—"We need to be more inclusive and more diverse racially, blah, blah, blah," is how she put it. But this was simply lip-service. Because then she goes on to argue that it was the feminists early on in this country (Susan B. Anthony, Carrie Chapman, et cetera) who really knew that the issue of race must be addressed along with gender issues. And that's a total lie! For her to credit those particular women—that's just historically inaccurate! And here's *Southern Voice* printing it. It was like a huge slap in the face to all the African American feminists and other women of color at the time who really were arguing for some understanding about the interrelationships among social categories like race, gender, and class, and for inclusiveness, and they basically got betrayed by these women—and that's still happening.

Ami.   Yeah, and these women who were doing early activist work within black communities were pressing not only for freedom for African Americans, but also freedom for women and freedom around class—women needing to be independent. It is a real slap in the face when somebody can take something that was ultimately talked about by Sojourner Truth and turn it into something that Susan B. Anthony came up with.

Trish.   Or ignore the fact that Margaret Sanger was a white supremacist who advocated birth control as a form of eugenics.

Patti.   Or that some of the early white feminist suffragists betrayed Frederick Douglass and other African American activists, saying that they would rather get the vote for themselves first than "allow" black men to vote—like, what an insult to them to have "colored men" voting before they could vote, was how they put it, to have black men voting when they couldn't.

Ami.   Instead of refusing to even make that kind of choice, and questioning power.

Patti.   And of course no mention of Ida B. Wells and the antilynching campaign— a movement that in many ways was distinctly southern, and required the participation of southern women to transform what was happening. So all through history we have examples of people of color and their allies being the ones to really talk about how freedom and equality have to be fought on all fronts at once. But everywhere I turn lately here, I'm seeing these messages being rewritten through this discourse, as though it came from somewhere else and we have no association with it or it has nothing to do with people of color.

Ami.   As though it came from white supremacists.

Trish.   And I feel like the other way that's happening lately is that there's no class analysis present in the national mainstream, predominantly white, queer movement, so when you pick up [southern queer newspaper] again and again, the message is, like, "Buy your way through America," like, "Buy your way into this middle-class or upper-class dream." And it's becoming increasingly clear to me that my life in the next fifty years is going to be as molded by economic factors as it is by safety on the basis of who I love or my color or the fact that I'm a woman. I think my survival is going to be challenged as much by economics as by those other things. And I'm becoming more and more fearful of how things are going to start splintering off if we don't start having some discussions soon. Like how we're going to lose any parity to fight back.

Ami.   It's really telling, the ignorance that is so rampant in the white queer community, not just in the South, but in the South it's articulated in very particular ways, I think. Like going to a community forum that was supposed to be about racism in the queer community and sitting through that, which was just painful, and what was going on was that people were talking about how black community and white community were too segregated from one another, and they were doing this without really listening to people who kept standing up and saying, "You know, the queer community isn't just black and white, there are a lot of other people of color." In fact in the scheme of things, there was a really good showing of nonblack people of color, as well as African American people and white queers as well—it was a very diverse group.

And some issues around class were raised, about like if we do something practical like throw big parties, that sort of thing, we have to worry about door fees and bar fees that some of us obviously can't afford. Well, you know, right after I stand up and say, "We really need to rethink this whole black and white thing and how we're looking at the racial structure of the South and understanding it," a white prominent leader in our community, businessman, capitalist, stands up and says, "I think we should have a party and we should have a sliding scale so people of color don't have to pay as much as white people." Well, you know all of the middle-class people of color are like, "Excuse me, I can pay my own way to a party." But of course there were other people of color there who were really like, "Yeah, I want in free."

But the problem—it was really telling that in some ways even though the racial diversity and the economic diversity has shifted over the last fifty years, there's still an equation of poverty with people of color. And that's no longer an accurate paradigm. It was accurate in the South at one time, but it's no longer true. I really think that that's a real telling ignorance about the community. And if people can't look at the racial and class reality now, then you know that it's going to be difficult into the [twenty-first] century.

Patti.   And I think that those things work alongside stereotypes of all southerners as poor.

Ami.   And it's also that all southerners are white too. The stereotype itself makes the southerners out to be usually male, some kind of Bubba redneck type, or maybe an aristocrat—plantation owner—or a southern belle, which obviously is a white woman.

Patti.   And think of that working in conjunction with stereotypes of Asian Americans—and Pacific Island[ers] on some level but maybe mostly the stereotype focuses on Asian Americans—as being the "model minority" with lots of money. So there's this idea then if all southerners are poor "Bubbas" and all Asian Americans or APIs are these rich—

Janet.   And send their kids to Harvard, play the violin, and all that—

Patti.   Then it's like, Where do we fit into this system?

Sunita.   And even then, the thing that I've really noticed here, especially in the South, is that our group is the one that really thinks about class issues, thinks about race issues, whereas the South Asian group which is predominantly men [Trikone]—they may be men of color, they may be South Asian—they are the model minority. And I think in a lot of ways, granted, our two groups [APLBTN and Trikone] may be integrated on some level, but I know on the class level we're definitely not integrated because they don't understand a lot of the issues we face, as women, and especially as women of color who are not rich, who are not wealthy, who are working really hard to make ends meet. They don't understand that. And I think on some level they even discount it, discredit it, and even make fun of us for that.

Social Geographies of Race, Class, Gender, and Sexuality

Janet.   Can I ask a question? Are there places that you just won't go here in the South or in Atlanta, or that you avoid or try to keep the lowest profile that you possibly can?

Ami.   I avoid Buckhead.

Everyone.   Yeah!

Ami.   I avoid any of the areas that are predominantly white and predominantly rich or upper middle class. And I'll go there with friends, I'll meet people out, I'll do that kind of thing. But I wouldn't just volunteer to go. I really don't like going over to Midtown, the Piedmont Park area, where there are a lot of rich white gay boys. I really avoid that area, except for PRIDE. I used to go over to My Sister's Room [local lesbian bar/lounge] before it was shut down, and we'll go to the movie theater over there, but you know, I don't really go over there. And I have to say, on some level I think Patti and I hang out in areas that are predominantly people of color, not necessarily queers. And here in Decatur, it's not really that big of an issue because there are so many queers, it's like you get in your car and you see queers everywhere.

Kelly.   There's a different kind of feeling over here. It's not as pretentious. It doesn't feel like there is as much money over here.

Ami.   It is predominantly dykes. There's not as much money. And you don't feel like you're underdressed everywhere you go.

Janet.   Do you do that because it's a class thing, or because it's a color thing?

Ami.   Well I think it's both. It's a combination of feeling like I want to go somewhere where I can see people who seem real to me, and when I say real, I mean people who aren't so concerned about the money stuff, who aren't going out just to be seen, that kind of thing.

Janet.   I thought I was one of the only people who was avoiding different places, and I was feeling that maybe part of me is being, well, maybe racist in a way, because I'm from the West. And I come here and I don't really quite know how I'm going to fit in, but there are places in San Diego like Buckhead that I don't want to go. There are places here on both levels—and I don't know if it's because I'm queer or a woman of color—that I try to avoid.

Patti.   It seems so much more extreme here than in other places, the extreme segregation. Like for example, Einstein's, I will not go there. All the clientele is white.

Kelly.   I don't think I think about doing that, not going to certain areas. I don't think I think about it, it just happens. And I don't really stop and think about it until I try and make plans with somebody who I really don't see that often. And they say, why we don't go to such and such place in Buckhead or Midtown, and I'm always like, I just hate driving that far.

Sunita.   I don't like driving on Peachtree.

Kelly.   And you know how you were asking is it a class thing or is it a race thing, I think it's both, but I think for me personally—and maybe this has to do with the fact that I can pass for white—but for me it's a class thing first. And that I guess in Buckhead it's heterophobia too. I really have this heterophobic response when I'm in that part of town. And that's probably one of the few areas where that really comes out in me, because on the weekend it's so predominantly, flagrantly heterosexual. [Everybody laughs.]

Ami.   Well I know that I don't spend much time outside of the perimeter either.[2] Because my parents live in Montgomery, Alabama, and I have good friends in Tuscaloosa, Alabama. So I go to those places, and we'll stop at a fast food place or something, and we go into the restaurant, and everybody looks at us. And at first Patti would ask, "Why do people stare at us here?" And at first I was like, "Well, that's just the way white southerners are," and it wasn't even just white southerners, it was actually like black southerners too, like everybody there looks at you. She asks, "Is it because we're dykes?" And I say, "Well, they may not know we're dykes but we're just foreign. We don't belong." We don't look like we belong there. Even if we do belong. So they stare at us and stuff.

Kelly.   What's funny was that I was raised in the South and my parents taught me that it was rude to stare at people. I don't know if it's just southerners either, if it's an American phenomenon, or what. We have this story, when my parents were still married, because my grandmother lives in Alabama as well, and we would go over there and visit, and most of the time we would eat at my grandmother's house, but there was this one time that we went out to this barbecue place, and I swear my mom got so many stares. We were joking, we had to just laugh about it because you know, what else are you going to do, you know, get angry? My father was talking about how she was staring back at these kids who wouldn't stop looking at her. And we would make jokes about how when we walked in, the music stopped because everybody was so busy staring at my mom, who is very obviously Asian and has the long black hair. I mean we could hardly eat, because it was just so there.

Janet.   I have to say that when I get outside the perimeter, like when we go to the beach or camping, whatever, we try not to stop anywhere.

Kelly.   I don't feel safe stopping at some places.

Janet.   I don't either. I always send out Pat [my partner] because, you know, she's white—she doesn't really fit the stereotype. And I'll stay in the car a lot of times, if we stop. Or we won't go into places.

Ami.   It's funny because when I moved to Atlanta—well, in college—I came out in college in Tuscaloosa, and then I moved to Atlanta and in Atlanta I felt much freer to shave my head, to pierce my lip, you know, to start dressing like a man or whatever, so basically just being my freaky self, and at first when I started going home, sometimes I would make a concession to my mom by, you know, wearing a dress and being bald, that sort of thing. But when I first started doing that, I'd get like more and more angry, like the closer I'd get to home, and I'd be like, "Just let somebody say something to me," you know, because I'm southern and I grew up here, and I feel really strongly that the South is my home, the South is my culture, and I have as much right to claim it as anyone else, and I refuse to let people's stereotypes or people's attitudes somehow take away my home. And I've had to carve my space myself, you know, with my bare hands, so I get really defiant and I go in and almost just beg people to do something, and they don't, you know, every time. They're just like, "How ya doin'?"

Janet.   If I do go in, I'm treated fine, you know, but it's the staring, it's that uncomfortable staring that really kind of gets me. And I kind of didn't know if it was me, you know, just in my way those stereotypes of southerners were just exaggerated and I just didn't feel safe, or if it was really other people too; they don't stop.

Patti.   And those stereotypes about southerners being mostly white, being rednecks—that kind of thing, I think there is an assumption that the South is more racist, more homophobic, more sexist, and therefore more dangerous for us than the rest of the country. Of course we know these things aren't necessarily true, the kinds of racism and homophobia and sexism here maybe are just different. But I remember before moving down here feeling like, Oh my god, I'm moving to the Deep South, and how am I going to be treated as a woman and a dyke of color?

Kelly.   Well I think there's also the element of—since it's like, we are queer, we are women, we are women of color—it's like, if you don't fall neatly into one of those categories and appear that way, like you might walk in and they could be staring at you because you're not white or black. But they could also be staring at you because you're Asian but you're not the stereotypical Asian girl—you have more of a boyish look about you, and so they don't know what to do.

Patti. It's like, Is it a boy or a girl? Is it black or white? Is it this or that? It's like you have to fit neatly into one of these categories.

Kelly. So they know how to talk to you, I guess. I mean, if you stop and think about it, you almost just have to feel sorry for people because they can't adapt. I mean, it would appear that they just don't have enough diversity in their lives, I guess, to really be comfortable dealing with this new whatever it is.

Janet. Throwing a fastball at them! [Laughter]

The South: "Home of Fried Chicken and Inbreeding"?

Patti. We talked a lot about what it's like to be here, or how the queer mostly white community is here in Atlanta, what that's like for us. I think some things that would be really interesting for us to talk about would be how each of us identify in relation to the idea of being in the South, or being southerners.

And something else that I've been wanting to talk about is an issue I brought up earlier, having to do with other people in other parts of the country who are organizing around being API or queer or both, saying that they feel sorry for us. Or saying that we don't have anything here, and how wrongheaded that is, how in fact we have so much going on here on the one hand, yet on the other hand we've had to build it all from scratch, and why maybe that makes it a really different experience for us. A few years ago, for example, Ami, Svati, and I were at a conference—Asian Americans in the South—and the three of us did a workshop on being queer and API. Later, in California, a UCLA newspaper happened to print a story about us because a woman at that university had attended the conference and had written about it (a friend of mine sent me the piece).

And she wrote about how she attended this conference for APIs in Atlanta, "in the deep south, home of fried chicken and inbreeding," and she was sort of trying to say that these were the stereotypes, for better or worse, but it didn't quite work. Instead, her attitude came off as, like, "Here I am in this horrible, horrible place, where there's nothing going on, and it makes me really appreciate L.A., because we have a real community there, as opposed to these poor people in the South." But part of her point was she thought that Ami, Svati, and I did a really good job and were very articulate, and how amazing it was to actually hear articulate people speaking at this conference—she tried to pay us a compliment, but it came off sounding like she was surprised that there were actually three articulate people in the South. And it was crazy, because we didn't know how to take it at first except to be really offended.

But it certainly made me think more and more about how we as a group, as a community, as a racial group, or as a sexual group, are perceived in other parts of the country. And in other parts of the world, but especially thinking of this country and its perceptions of the South.

Ami.   Well, to go back to the whole idea or question of how we relate to southern culture or some kind of southern identity, I do identify as a southerner, primarily because the South is the region that I'm most familiar with, the culture that I'm most familiar with, and also just the people—the way people interact, that kind of thing. Though it's very diverse from community to community in the South, I still sort of feel like it's legitimate to claim that identity.

And I think that it's always been important for me to claim that particular identity, because growing up as a nonblack person of color in the South has meant that my racial identity was always inevitably questioned by everybody else. And so there was always this idea, and I always have people ask, "Where are you from?" and you know I'm from Alabama, so it's kind of like they just assumed that I wasn't southern somehow. So not really having some other kinds of identity, to not have a racial identity that I could really understand, or to be really certain about growing up, made it difficult on the one hand for me to claim a southern identity, because so clearly I wasn't southern if everybody could question that. But as an adult it's been really important for me to claim that.

When I was a kid, I think that I was kind of embarrassed to be southern, because it's a stigmatized identity outside of the South. I mean southerners are seen as stupid, racist, white people for the most part, right? That's the stereotype. And I really didn't want to be a part of the white supremacist history of the South—I didn't want to be identified with that, I didn't want to be identified with the ignorance that is associated with the South, which is very often just a stereotype or falsehood, but nonetheless there. And also just the sort of lack of sophistication that is associated with the South.

Janet.   The South has its own culture that nobody ever recognizes as a valid culture.

Ami.   Yeah, and if it is, then it's the stereotype, like fried chicken and inbreeding.

Janet.   Yeah, exactly.

Patti.   Which is interesting, when you think of the stereotypes of inbreeding, like there's this idea or myth that southerners have this really perverse, fucked up sexuality. And here we are queer, claiming that, or claiming that we're sexually different and in the South. And that raises all kinds of issues for me, here we are being told that the South already has this really deviant sexuality, and then here we are as queer women and as Asian Americans and Pacific Islanders being told that our sexuality must be perverse or different, that we're hypersexual, we're stereotyped, you know, as somehow sexually wrong. So here we are claiming that sexuality—what does that do?

Ami.   Well, and other southerners, particularly those tied to fundamentalist religions, are very much letting the gay and lesbian communities know that we're perverts, we're sinners, we're unnatural.

Paula.   I spent four years of my adolescence growing up in a small southern town, in northeast Georgia. And that was a really quite a unique experience, a town of maybe 3,000 people. And from day one when I moved there—in that place, the telephone book was so small it was really more like a pamphlet, and if you were looking for my name, I was the only *X* in the whole book—that was the first time ever in any place that I'd ever experienced any kind of racism. And the thing was, it wasn't even from the white majority people there. It was from the black people who lived there.

It was very difficult trying to deal with that, and also being queer but not really knowing it, but having it expressed in things I do. People always assumed that I was queer or different or something, and I was always made fun of because of that also. And that added on to make me even more stigmatized. It kind of brought up some kind of resentment for being in the South, and growing up here, but really I learned to look at it in a different way, you know. Not all southerners are like that, because I did have friends who, regardless of the way I acted, the way I looked, were still my friends. And so it took me a little while to get over it, but I am over it now.

Janet.   Do you identify as southern?

Paula.   I identify as growing up here. But I don't know about the word "southern." "Southern," to me, really does bring up all those pictures of living out on the farm, and milking cows and having chickens and everything like that. To me, it's always been "You're from the south and you grew up here, and you know what it's like," and its not about being southern. It's about claiming who you are no matter where you are. And being in the South just happens to be where I am.

Kelly.   That's funny, because that sounds kind of like how I was relating to what Ami was saying. When I was younger, I was like, "Well, I may be from here, but I'm not a southerner, you know." And as I got older, though, for some reason I started to latch onto identifying more as a southerner. And I think that probably some of it came out of reacting to other people's responses to me when they found out that I lived in Georgia, so kind of like, at least initially, more of a defensive reaction, like, "Yeah, well I am from the South. Yeah, well I am southern, and do you have a problem with that?"

But something I feel should be noted since we're in Decatur, we're right outside of Atlanta, one thing that some Georgians, at least—and I'm sure it's like this in some of the other southern states that have major cities—that there are people that consider themselves southern and then they look to Atlanta and they say, "That's not the South." You know, like, "They're a bunch of freaks up there." It's much more rural areas, you know. Maybe this is a bad attitude, but I almost feel like maybe they should have a bigger claim on it, I don't know why. I appreciate living in a city and what comes with living in a city. And if I wasn't living in this southern city, I would be living in some other city, whether it was in the North or the West or wherever.

Ami.   So many queers from rural and suburban areas around the South, they move to Atlanta because it's the closest big city. I know that's what I did. My first girlfriend and I had just enough money to come to Atlanta and pay a deposit on an apartment here. And she was a southerner as well.

Kelly.   And as queers, especially, I would imagine that there are things that they'd be seeking that they might have an easier time finding in a bigger city, in Atlanta.

On Relations with Other Queers of Color

Patti.   Paula, I thought you brought up a really interesting point about the racism you faced in a small town coming primarily from African Americans, because I think that there's often this assumption that we're facing racism only from white people. And that's not the case at all. Here we are in Atlanta, or in the South, and so often we're rendered invisible not only by white people. Or we're hit with those questions not only from white people.

Paula.   It was very different. I was twelve years old, and I had never experienced any kind of racism at all. And I moved to this small northeastern Georgia town, Toccoa. At one point there were a bunch of black guys and us walking on the bus, and they just started calling me all kinds of names like "chink" and other names. It was something that I really had a hard time dealing with because I saw blacks as being a minority themselves, and then having my first racist experience like that, from black people, that really confused me a lot. I didn't know what was going on, why they were doing that. And it really didn't make any sense to me, why I was getting that, especially from blacks.

And then I found out that really it was the whole town, not just those guys, it was really the whole area. Having lived in that atmosphere, and in the city, in Atlanta, it's like two separate worlds. They had their own culture there, they did their own things there. And the blacks and whites there, they grow up differently, they're raised differently as opposed to the people here. It was really a unique experience, I think. I really don't know how to think about that. It was really something that I worked out over a period of time, you know. And for the whole four years that I lived there, I never did make one black friend.

Kelly.   Do you think that that experience with those guys calling you names, maybe you kind of put yourself in less of a position to make black friends, like a fear or an attitude or something on your part?

Paula.   Yeah, well, actually I did. Initially, yes. I really did carry a resentment toward black people in general for a while, until I saw that not all of them were like that. But the majority of black people who did live there were like that, I thought. So, yes, that did make a stumbling block right there, for me to make any black friends. And so I never did while I was there.

Patti.   Well, I know that when our group got together with a black queer organization here in Atlanta about two years ago to have a conversation, it was really interesting because I think a lot of us and a lot of members of that group came to it really, really excited. We felt a sort of alliance, we felt like here we all are, queer and women of color—dykes of color—and we wanted to connect. And we thought—especially some of us and some of the women there who were already friends—we felt like this was something really important for us to do, to come together and talk about our similarities and differences. And maybe it was a structural problem on some level, but something that was really disturbing, what happened was a large number of women in that group, African American and black women, began asking us questions like, "When did you arrive in our country?" and "So how did you guys learn to speak English so well?"

Janet.   No way!

Paula.   Yeah, I can totally understand that.

Sunita.   And implied was "When are you all going back?"

Patti.   Yeah, so it felt like, "Where are you from? When are you going back? Why are you here?" Underlying all those questions was an attitude or suggestion that we didn't belong here, that we don't belong here.

Ami.   Questions that were really sort of ignorant and insensitive to our issues as Asian Pacific Islanders. Just assuming that we all were immigrants—

Janet.   And recent immigrants.

Ami.   Because those are the kinds of questions that might make more sense if immigrants are talking to other immigrants. Like "where are you from" and that kind of thing. But it didn't make any sense in our context, and so it came off as offensive.

Sunita.   And it was almost as if instead of conversation we were on display.

Ami.   Yeah, that was it. Well, I know for me, growing up in the South I was the only Pacific Islander that I knew of in Montgomery, and part of me thinks I probably was the only Pacific Islander, you know, I mean I don't know for sure. And in actuality, Montgomery has become a place for fairly new immigrants, so it actually has become a more racially diverse area. And my brothers, both of whom are Native American, they were the only Native Americans growing up [there]. And so, other than some of my mother's friends—my mother had some Asian American friends—but other than them, we were the only nonblack people of color that we knew of, and so we were sort of having to deal with, not precisely racism, but simply a kind of ignorance around race and racial diversity from everybody, from blacks and whites.

And I know that it was very difficult for me in high school, college, and on after college when I moved to Atlanta, to be involved in communities of color. I remember that I actually helped to start a group, to try to keep a group going, that was a women of color group that was constantly forming and disbanding and reorganizing, and there were a lot of reasons for that. But I know for that group—it was predominantly black women though there were other women who were Latina, Chicana, and myself. But because it was predominantly African American, many of the women just assumed that women of color meant African American. And so the other [non-black] women didn't really stay, and I was the only one who kept thinking that "oh, any minute now this is going to be a space for me too." But it just wasn't, ultimately. Because there were too many differences and there were too many resentments, I mean a lot of the black women felt a resentment towards me because they really couldn't connect to my experiences of racism as being racism, as being experiences of racism. They couldn't connect to how my identity was a racial identity that had been marginalized and oppressed, not in identical ways as African American women are oppressed, but certainly in ways that are similar.

So that was a really hard thing for me to come to terms with. Really, on the one hand, I could deal with my own light-skin privilege, and I could deal with the fact that I wasn't oppressed in the same ways that black women are oppressed—I felt like there was really a kind of an unwillingness to even grant me any kind of oppressive experiences around race. Which was really oppressive! It's so oppressive to have people try to deny your experiences as oppressive when you know that they have been. And they tell you, "Oh no, you haven't experienced racism," like you don't even know, because if you're not me or just like me, then you don't even know what racism is. And like I was four years old and in church of all places, the first time somebody called me a "nigger," whereas I have a friend who is African American and the first time she ever had to experience racism—because she moved within a black community and she was very sheltered from that—so she was like twelve or thirteen the first time anybody ever did something like that to her. And I was four. I mean, there's no way to compare, but it's not as simple as some people want it to be.

Kelly.   It's strange how people will latch onto that too, like, "This is my oppression and it is so big, and there is no way that anybody can relate to it." And it's not like a relative kind of thing, it's just different, period. You know, like we all experience things on different levels and in different ways, and just because you've done it one way doesn't mean that I haven't done it in some other way. And it's really hurtful, I think, to have to hear that.

Your saying that made me think of just recently how I was in my U.S. history class and some girl was talking about U.S. politics, and she was saying something about gay rights and she was talking about the black Civil Rights movement and she made some sort of comparison in some way. And there was this woman in the front row that I saw—an African American woman—and she looked at her friend like, "How can she even?" Like, "How can she even compare gays to blacks?" And I was like, "Why do you have to be so offended by that, though? Like yes, it's different, it's a different thing, but why does it have to be such a—why do you have to be so defensive about it?!"

Ami.   Why not some sort of critical thought about how if it's not the same, then how is it different?

Kelly.   Yeah! I mean maybe there are more differences than there are similarities, but that doesn't mean that it can just be discounted. It was just homophobic, and it was just really frustrating to me.

Patti.   It is really frustrating. People are so quick to jump on that, to say, well, you can't compare this to that, or APIs aren't victims of racism.

Sunita.   Or that APIs are benefiting from the struggles of African Americans, which is in the theory that's going around today.

Patti.   The model-minority myth. And that always makes me think that we really need to think about what racism means. This idea that racism can only be "this"—like this one type of experience—leaves out a whole range of experiences. Like what does it mean to have your accent made fun of if you are an immigrant? Or what does it mean to be constantly asked where are you from, and when are you going back? Or how did you learn to speak English? I mean maybe that's just as harmful as being called a "chink" or a "nigger" or something else. Maybe it's a different kind of discrimination but just as harmful to always be treated like you don't belong here. You shouldn't be here. Or like your food smells bad. Your language sounds funny. I can't pronounce your name. Your culture is wrong.

Ami.   And ultimately there is a difference between racism and colorism. I think that if people continue to focus on just one part of the picture, we leave out a whole range of experiences of oppression. Part of the problem is that people really do think of race as being about skin color and physical features.

Janet.   And it's so many other aspects too.

Ami.   Yeah, and ultimately if it's just about biology, like people so often want to believe, well, what does that leave out? Why do we have that whole notion of color blindness? It's just about how we see people, or how we look at people, what people look like, when that's ultimately not all there is to race, and that's not necessarily the only way in which racism happens.

What makes that situation from your class, Kelly, so disturbing, is that on the one hand, it does seem that when those comparisons are made, that sometimes it seems like some straight African Americans get really offended by that because they do perceive that on some level, the gay rights movement is all about white people, white queers, and then there are white queers who are totally appropriating the black civil rights language, strategies, et cetera, and making all these comparisons that don't even apply and are just racist and are appropriative. Like for instance, white activists calling up the rhetoric of Martin Luther King, you know, there's a real problem with that, that's not cool either. And it feels like those of us who are more conscious of this, particularly queers of color, end up getting caught in those debates. It's almost like you can't speak anywhere in those debates, you know. Because one more time it's this dichotomy, it's like gays versus blacks in those situations, or gay people versus people of color. What happens when you're a person of color and gay?

On Relations with Straight Asian Pacific Islanders

Patti.   So how about the communities of color here in Atlanta or anywhere else in terms of us, that are of our own ethnic backgrounds, our own racial communities, what's it like for us to be a part of those communities (or to not be a part of them)? For example, for me, going to Buford Highway and being around other Asian Americans, East Asian Americans, Korean Americans there who are straight, who don't necessarily want to know that I'm queer or hear anything about it, it's really, really painful, you know. There's a loss there that is really hard to name or identify. I'm not even just talking about my mother or my family, I'm talking about people who I don't even know, but who I know reject me if they see me walk in with my lover, or they give us a dirty look, or they stare. Or they speak to me only in English. I mean I speak English, but often that's a signifier that you're not one of them. What's that like for you all?

Paula.   I, for one, did come from a large community of Asians here in this area. I mean I grew up all around them, and that's mostly what I did, growing up. I was never encouraged to go out and make white friends or black friends or Hispanic friends. I was always told, "Stay with your own kind," "Only date people who speak the same language as you, that look like you." It went so far and so deep that even if I dated someone else who was Asian but didn't speak my language [Hmong], that was wrong. That's how bad it was.

   And then after coming out and telling everyone that I'm this way, that I'm queer, you know, it was like I almost had to let go of that whole community. I was more or less ostracized, and people, when they saw me, they didn't say anything, they just looked at me. Some gave me dirty looks, some just looked at me like I was on display, like "Hey, look at that person—she's a he," always whispering. And so I felt shunned around my own people. It was hard at first, having experienced that kind of rejection from people who you've known all your life, and people who are supposed to encourage you and support you because you're Asian, and you grow up around all this racism and everything. But then there's also reverse racism of "We're better than them so we don't need to be around them." And then coming out as queer and having your own people reject you, it's like, where do I go now? What is there left for me now?

Kelly.   It's like, "We wanted you to stick with your own type before, but now that you're queer . . ."

Paula.   Yeah, now it's like, "Go find your own people."

Patti.   You've told me bits and pieces, Paula, like that when you came out, it was almost like you were outed to everybody in your community all at once.

Paula.   Oh yeah, and I knew that would happen, but it spread really fast and really wide, and it didn't spread only here in Georgia, it also went to other communities in other parts of the U.S. So it's like I'm known nationally, really . . . which is kinda nice! [laughter] But on the other hand, it's something that's a personal issue of mine, but now it's become common knowledge not only to people here but to people everywhere else—I mean, I had people in North Carolina calling my father, asking him questions and telling him, "Well, this is how you solve the problem."

And really it bothers me in a way that first of all you're saying that what I have is a problem, when I don't see it that way. And secondly, you're telling them how to solve my problem, when you're rejecting me throughout the whole period, throughout the whole time, it's like you don't want nothing to do with me, but you want to tell me how to live my life. So it really doesn't make any sense to me why they want to do that, I mean, yes I'm different, but we also have a lot of commonalities that we share, and just because of that one fact that I'm different means that all the things that I'm going through are totally different from what you're going through. That's been something that I've had to deal with, and basically they don't want to hear it. They don't want to listen, so I'm not around there to tell them.

And recently I just went and attended my brother's wedding reception, and my mother, she kept telling me, "If you want to come, you have to do this, you have to do this, and you have to do this." Like, no, I'm just going to come as is, and so we had a big argument, and then I showed up. And the first thing that happened when I walked through that door was everyone looked at me, it took them maybe a minute to register who I was, and then they just kept looking. Some started laughing, some just didn't know what to do, it was like everything stopped and all eyes were focused on me. And I was really on display. I mean I walked around, and people who didn't know me didn't treat me any different, until they found out who I was.

So having experienced that kind of prejudice from your own people because you're queer, it really makes me ask questions like where do I stand as an API person? And I still face life every day, I still experience racism every now and then. But I'm also queer, and so that adds on to it too. Like I'm seeing someone right now, and her father has a problem with her seeing me, but then also because I'm Asian, that's another problem. So really there's a lot there to deal with. But how do we deal with it?

I mean what can we do about it? Where do we find a place where we feel safe enough to really be ourselves and come out and talk about issues like this, other than small groups like this one? I mean we really have to make a name for ourselves out in the general open community.

Kelly.   It kind of puts you in a position of having a really fragmented family and social life, like this little piece of me gets fulfilled here, you know, thinking about how you hang out with us, and then you've got your family and other friends, and then I know that you go to the transgendered group sometimes.

Paula. Sometimes.

Kelly. Just like, well, what do I need most today? What do I need most this week? Which part of me needs something? And it's like this, I guess, for everybody in a lot of ways, but some of us have more trouble with it than others, it's like those one or two best friends that you make that you have so many things in common with. I mean I've felt really at home in this group, but didn't realize that there was something that was missing until I hooked up with Nikki, who's half white and half Japanese. And it's funny because maybe in terms of personality, I have more in common with some of the other members of the group. But just that week, right there, sometimes exactly what I needed, like, Let's just go out to dinner—I mean, we'd have completely different styles of communicating at times and stuff, but just to know that that one link was there was at times really, really important. So I'm thinking that we just feel the need to address different parts of ourselves at different times with different sorts of conditions.

Paula. There's also a problem there with spreading yourself too thin.

Kelly. Uh huh. Oh yeah, I'm not saying it's easy by any means.

Paula. It's like you're giving and getting here and here and here and here but never enough to where you feel complete.

Ami. Right. I think everybody wants somebody, even just one person, to accept them precisely for everything that they are, wholly—I mean, people don't want to have to hide themselves or put it away, not even have to hide it, but be able to talk about it, you know, be able to show off every part of it. And it doesn't seem like too much to ask out of life. But then for some of us, to be a whole person, to be treated as a whole person, to be respected as a whole person, some of us certainly have a harder time of that than others because ultimately that is what oppression is about. It is about fragmenting us, dividing ourselves, not only dividing us from one another but dividing each of us, you know.

Kelly. I guess that has to do with two different kinds of spaces that can be desirable, like wanting to be a whole person and be accepted by anybody, regardless of what their makeup is or whatever, which is always a great thing. But then there's also the realm of shared experience, which is also really important.

Ami. Well, I was thinking about this when we were at Charis [local feminist bookstore], when our group led a discussion. We were talking about how diverse our group is, and yet at the same time we felt like we had things in common. And what I found was that the one thing that we had in common seemed to be something—not really identity, but some particular take on identity politics. Which was kind of interesting to me that it wasn't really identity that we had in common, but identity politics. And that was kind of illuminating for me, that it was not identity but the idea of identity.

Patti.   Which is so interesting and so important, because personally I don't think I could have survived these last few years in Atlanta without this group, without these people—you people, as well as other members. Because there's this feeling that you're supposed to be able to get what you need—different parts of you—from all of these places, but there was no place. You know, the queer community that didn't have a space for us, that would go so far as to either ignore us, make us completely invisible, stereotype us, or misname us—we actually were called by the wrong name more than once. Remember when a photo of our group was printed in a magazine under the wrong name—[they called us Trikone]—this idea that it doesn't matter, as APIs or as people of color we're all the same, we're interchangeable.

Ami.   And that's frustrating because we come together consciously knowing that we're all very different and we're all coming from different backgrounds and different cultures, but then we get lumped into the same thing, like we're all "Oriental," "those Asians." Like we're all just "Asian."

Patti.   And the idea, of course, is always East Asian, immigrant, middle class, you know, it's a very specific generalization, and it's never clear—it's never South Asian, it's never Pacific Islander, it's never mixed race, it's never any of the complex identities that we have.

Ami.   It's never poor, I know that! [laughter]

Patti.   But here we come together with all these differences, and yet I feel at home. And I could go out and find people who are mixed race and Korean American who are straight, who might either treat me badly and hate me, or—

Ami.   Somebody did, actually, right?

Patti.   Which one?

Ami.   That woman who was Korean American and entering your [academic] program.

Patti.   Oh, right. She was like, "You're Korean???!!" She was Korean American and straight. When I came out to her, she kept asking, "How can you be Korean and lesbian??! What do you mean you're Korean??" And when I tried to talk to her about her homophobia, she said, "Well, it must be because you were raised here, and you're half white." She had the nerve to say that to me!

Kelly.   There are no queer people in Korea! [laughter]

Patti.   Right. My mother said that, that there are no queers in Korea—actually I think she used the word "homosexuals." She said that the reason I must be "like this" is because I'm mixed race, and because she let me grow up here in this country. She kept saying, "It was my mistake, I should never have married that white man, I shouldn't have let you grow up in this country, if we were in Korea this would never have happened."

Everybody.   Like she should have never married your father! Then you never would have been born!

Patti.   Yeah, it's absurd! But the idea is somehow that you can't be both this and this. So I'm supposed to believe that I can't be both Korean and queer. And then if I add on to it and tell you that I'm a feminist, or that I come from a working-class background, it just gets more and more convoluted. Like okay, I can be Korean if I'm male, middle class, I went to Harvard, I play the violin, I'm gonna be a doctor, et cetera.

Claiming Southern, Queer, and API Identities

Ami.   I want to return to something, what I was talking about earlier about claiming a southern identity, and how that did take time, for me to claim a southern identity. Because when Paula was talking, it occurred to me that it was when I came out as a lesbian and felt very much disconnected from my family—I felt exiled—and growing up, family was very important to me and to all the members of my family. Because we were lower middle class, working class, and my mother and father had come from poor communities, there was a real belief that your family is really the only thing that you have, you know, that you possess, so you have to maintain those connections because if you're in trouble, your family is the only people that are going to be there, that sort of stuff, which on the one hand is maybe a good ideology, but it's also a very oppressive one—you need freedom from your family.

But I think it was because both my mother and father grew up in the South, and their parents and probably their parents. I think that's when it became much more important to me to claim a southern identity, because it had a lot to do with wanting to claim my family, and wanting them to stop trying to disown me or deny that I was lesbian. They weren't really trying to disown me, but they were trying to disown my lesbianism. And so having them come for my and Patti's commitment ceremony was just this huge breakthrough, and just to have them come and actually for the first time see my world and my friends, and begin to get a clue about who I am, was just an amazing thing that I never thought would happen.

But I think what is really interesting, sad too, is that because when I was growing up I've always known that I was Pacific Islander, but it was always kind of downplayed in a sense that it was a difference that on the one hand made a difference only because it was "special" and "exotic" and "unique," that sort of thing. But otherwise, we were supposed to be white, like my parents. Our race, ultimately, "didn't matter," wasn't supposed to matter at all, which made for a really bad racial experience growing up.

But I think that my mother, for instance, though she hasn't said anything to me, I know that she was uncomfortable at times about the fact that Patti is Korean American. Like we haven't had an explicit conversation about it, but because she, first— she kept forgetting that Patti is Korean American was like the first thing. You know she just kept forgetting, kept erasing it. And every time she was told that Patti is

Korean American, my mother would start talking about Chinese medicine or something like that, like a movie she saw, you know, "Ancient Chinese medicine, they know everything—they know much more than us." And then she had all these stereotypes about Asian women being able to sew really well. She said, "You know, all Asians are really good at sewing and stuff like that." I said, "Mama, that' s not true." And she just said, "Yes it is." She just changed the subject—she had to be right, and then she changed the subject.

I don't know what she was thinking, because her mother, who was white, was an excellent seamstress—that's what she did for a living, and here's my mother saying that all Asians can sew and "it's cultural." I was like, "Okay, Mom, whatever." And I really think that we would have had more trouble around the interracial thing if Patti had been a man, if I were marrying a man, but because we're lesbian, it was already freaky in her mind that we were even trying to do this, so the interracial thing was maybe like the least of it.

Patti.   On this subject of family, Sunita, I know you're close to your parents but you've had some issues with them, and I can't help but ask you what's going on with your family.

Sunita.   Yeah, part of the reason I won't come out to them is because of the fact that we've been so close and I am an only child, and they've always been there for me in all the other instances when I've needed them. And again, it's that fragmented identity bit too, it's like when I'm with them, when I'm in the Indian community I'm a straight Indian woman, that's the identity I've tried to portray in the past because I'm scared—because I'm scared that if I lose this community, what will I have to resort to? Especially given the racism in the greater queer community. It's almost like you're trapped inside of the community that's supposed to support you—and will support you as long as you're not yourself, in a sense. I mean that's what it is for me in the greater Indian community, and then with my parents, if I did come out to them, they'd still love me, they'd still accept me, but they'd feel as if they'd done something wrong, they'd blame themselves, and I don't want them to blame themselves, I almost feel an obligation to protect them.

Patti.   So it's really more about protecting them than being afraid that they'll disown you.

Sunita.   Yeah, I know that will never happen, I know they won't disown me. But they'll blame themselves, and then they'll try to change me, they'll try to convince me that what I'm doing is wrong, it's just a phase. I mean they're already in denial as it is because they don't want to admit it to themselves.

Ami.   And they kind of know.

Sunita.   Yeah, but they kind of know.

Ami.   Yeah, because your mom harasses you all the time—she knows! She accuses you of going to these lesbian and gay things.

Sunita.   And even the fact that she tends to associate "progressive" and "liberal" with gay. That's her association, you know, because that's not what good Indian girls talk about. Good Indian girls go to college, get their career, get good husbands, and have their children–it's like, what is this activist issue thing? They don't understand that because it's not part of their world. And if I am an activist, if I am progressive, then that must hint that I'm also associating with people who are gay, and does that mean I'm gay too? They're already beginning to make these kinds of associations, but they don't want to hear me vocalize it because that would make it true, and that's not what they want.

Kelly.   Do you think that if they're in denial about your being gay that they still recognize you as being progressive or liberal? And an activist? Do you think that knowing, recognizing those things, do you think already with those things in hand, they're blaming themselves for anything, or is that more okay?

Sunita.   I don't know if they're blaming themselves or if they're blaming the college I went to. Several times my dad has said, "If I didn't send you to Wellesley, things would be different." It's like Wellesley ruined you, Wellesley made you a rebel, it's Wellesley's fault.

Janet.   My mother told me that I was overeducated and that that's why I'm gay. It's not that I went to Wellesley, it's the fact that I went to school! [laughter]

Sunita.   For my parents, it's not about overeducation, it's the fact that I went to a women's college. Because I was supposed to get educated, I was supposed to go ahead, have a career, be a doctor, which I'm sort of doing but not because of them. But in terms of school, for them I should have gone to Harvard, or I should have gone to M.I.T., I should have gone to a coed school where I could have found a nice Indian boy.

Patti.   Who you could be engaged to by now.

Sunita.   Right!

Patti.   I think my parents are somewhere between yours, Sunita and Janet. Because on the one hand, I'm already too educated, and that's really awful for them because they're not educated, and they're intimidated by that and they associate it with everything that is foreign or strange to them—like, for example, my sexual identity. But also that I went to Vassar kind of makes it all the worse—not that they really know what that means but they saw pictures so they know that it was—

Sunita.   One of those freaky liberal colleges.

Patti.   Yeah, and that it used to be a women's college. And that forces them to ask what's wrong with me—why would I do that? Why would I go somewhere where there weren't as many men as women?

Paula.   My mother even found a reason to blame it on the military. She says, "If you hadn't gone into the Marines, you wouldn't be like this now." How do you get that? It's like explain that to me, Mom. Like someone drugged me or something? [laughter]

Kelly. Wow, so being around all those men turned you into a woman.

Paula. Yeah, it really doesn't make sense!

Patti. I'm wondering, Paula, how you feel in this group, being the first member who is open and out about being a transgendered, transsexual queer woman. I know that there are other people in the group who identify in some ways related to being transgendered, but in other ways I think of you as the first person who has really pushed that issue and made us have some good conversations. And I just want to ask since we're talking about this, I've often wondered if that difference makes it hard for you to feel like you're at home.

Paula. Well, honestly, truthfully, it does. I mean, I've known some of you for over a year now, but still I haven't found that comfort level, you know, where I can be completely open and out and say everything I want to say. Because I don't know where your comfort levels with that issue are, and also there's the fact that not only am I a transsexual, but I'm a transsexual lesbian.

Now that raises issues there too, and so it's really kept me on my toes, especially in the greater community, not knowing how everyone would react to that, and not knowing how people would respond to what I say. Whether they would acknowledge that my issues of lesbianism are real, you know, which to me I really don't understand myself. It's something that I've had to come to terms with. I mean it was really hard to keep coming here and feel like I was invading a personal private space, where you come here to feel acknowledged and to get support, I mean I almost felt like I was intruding because I wasn't born female. And even though I really appreciate all the welcoming efforts that everyone's put into to try make me feel comfortable here, it's where I've had to deal with my own issues of not invading your space. And trying to find a space where I can be comfortable, and everyone else can be comfortable with me.

It's one thing being a transsexual, being a transsexual woman in an API queer women's organization, but being a transsexual lesbian woman, you know, in this organization, is like, Okay how do we deal with this? How do we handle this? Do we make this person—do we acknowledge all this person is going through as the same things as what we're going through.

Janet. No, it's not the same.

Paula. It's not exactly the same. In certain ways, yeah.

Ami. I think what I hear you saying is that if you're born female, and you have sexual relationships with other females, then there is a claim to lesbian identity, to naming yourself as lesbian, in a way that it sounds like it hasn't been some direct or natural connection for you, and I can see how you might even feel that some of us who also identify as lesbian wouldn't necessarily see you as lesbian in the same way.

Paula.   Yeah, exactly. Because this far, for basically twenty years, I lived as what people would perceive as a straight male, though I never perceived myself that way. And then when I crossed over, then everyone assumed that I was a heterosexual female. And having to explain to them that No, I'm not that way, I don't like men, I still like women. It's like people don't understand that, and what people don't understand they tend to really be afraid of, or they stigmatize, or they push away and don't even acknowledge. And so it's really been something very hard to say, I mean even now, I mean right now I'm involved in a relationship with a girl. And she totally sees it as a lesbian relationship, and I do too, but not everyone else does.

Ami.   Did she identify as lesbian, before your relationship?

Paula.   No, before the relationship she identified as bisexual, and then when we got involved, she identified as lesbian. It's even really hard to call myself a lesbian because I wasn't born female, you know, because I became female. It's like no one word really describes me, who I am, you know, so trying to fit in to any kind of group is really hard for me. And I don't know if I can find that place. I mean, granted, I love seeing you guys, I love coming here, I wouldn't stop, but finding that one space where I'm comfortable enough to completely let everything out, I don't know if I can find that.

Ami.   I totally think you can. I think, you know, it takes time, it takes someone you know, it takes more experience. But I just believe that you can because I identify with where you're coming from because I feel like on some level I was saying the same thing you're saying ten years ago—and you are like ten years younger than me—and not for the same reasons, not for the same kinds of personal issues, but very similar ones, and I really think you can.

Patti.   Ami, you've told me that ten years ago you walked around feeling like you were the "only one"—the only one.

Ami.   And I still walk around sometimes feeling that way, but at least now I know that I'm not. I know now that it's more of a feeling.

Kelly.   I hope that that lessens with time, because I think that part of the answer for that, within our group, is that it has to do with time and it has to do with communication. And I think that there are issues that may or may not have been addressed within our group because it was really easy to fall back on either that we're API or we're dykes, okay, that's it. Because I recently had issues about—and I think this might affect you too—I had had issues about starting to come out to myself and my friends as bisexual, but still not being real comfortable with that terminology. Because I don't really know what that means for me yet. Like in the past, it was that I slept with men and I slept with women but I only had relationships with women. Now I think it's conceivable that I could have relationships, emotional relationships, with men as well, which is kind of freaking me out. So I'm kind of trying this on, I don't really like using that word but it's the best one I can come up with to describe myself and where I am now, but I'm still not being quite comfortable with it, and then also feeling like within this group, I hadn't really felt like I had seen somebody who had openly addressed bisexuality within the realm of our group.

Sunita.   Yeah, it's a topic that we've been meaning to discuss for a really long time.

Kelly.   Yeah, and it kind of comes and it goes, because people see different kinds of people and they identify one way or another, but like what we were talking about—what would it be like to bring a boy to a social event or something like that? Like what a concept, you know?

Ami.   I guess we kind of talked about that, but I guess on some level we never really followed up on that. I guess that was something that might have been really useful for everybody.

Paula.   It's like, How do the lesbians deal with the transsexual lesbians? It's like, Do I fit in?

Kelly.   Well, honestly, I think that something that might have helped me out from hearing that, from whatever you may have told me and you use the word "lesbian" or you made references to being in relationships with women, is that you see so many transgendered born-male people who are with men—and I hate to admit it, but honestly I think that might have kept me from just hearing that, hearing you saying that to me, because maybe I would imagine going into a transgendered space and hanging out with a bunch of women who like guys. Is that how it is for the most part?

Paula.   That is it. Most transsexuals who identify as transsexuals have heterosexual orientations. But then, you know, it's just like in the greater population, there's statistics, that 10 percent of the population has homosexual orientations, so 10 percent of the transgendered population has homosexual orientations. The 10 percent of the 10 percent! [laughter]

Patti.   The marginalized within the marginalized.

Paula.   Yeah, if you want to oppress me, oppress me for this and this and this and this. [Everyone laughs.] Do it all, don't just do one.

Patti.   I think that we should all talk about these issues more and maybe talk more openly. I think it feels great to be talking about some of these things that we've been wanting to talk about for over a year now. For years, some of us, and perhaps we can continue some of these conversations and really try to build these relationships and to trust that we'll probably make mistakes in the process, cross boundaries and step on toes, but that's okay.

Sunita.   As long as we keep up honest communication. I almost feel as if sometimes that has been the problem, that we haven't been able to speak honestly, because everyone is so afraid of what the other person will say or do.

Kelly.   Something about the Asian thing with the girl thing.[Everybody laughs.]

Everybody.   It is! It's a girl thing!

Kelly.   Like, "I don't want to offend anybody."

Patti.   Everybody saying, "I'm sorry, but can I say something?" [laughter]

Ami.   We're not maybe talking as honestly as we should, but I think too it is about not wanting to risk being offensive, because I think people—it comes with this sense like, "Well I don't want to lose the friends that I have" [laughter], and I think that for us that's a very real thing; we've all had experiences of rejection and loss from the very people who we believed and were told would be the people to be there for us, and so it makes a lot of sense that we would want to be careful about not losing our good thing, or even our so-so good thing—like not perfect thing but it is good, we don't want to lose it.

I was thinking we've been meaning to have a conversation about bisexuality, and we never really sat down and talked about it—it's more of a piecemeal kind of thing, we never had somebody bring a male partner or male friend to the socials. So never being tested around those kinds of things. But that was one reason why we made the decision to do socials versus meetings. Because I know I personally was one of the people saying I would really appreciate a woman-only space and an API woman-only space, I just feel really adamant about being able to create that but also wanting people to feel like their partners or their friends could be included and accepted.

Kelly.   Which interestingly enough comes back to what I was saying about the whole person thing and about wanting to be with people who could share your experience, but at the same time, needing the people who just accept you as whole. Bringing your partner, your lover, or your friend, or whomever to an APLBTN function is bringing another part of you in so people can see that or embrace that or whatever they're going to do, but at the same time you go off here and deal with the fragment or whatever, shared experience.

After concluding our taped discussion, we realized that for each of us, this organization provides affirmation of our identities as queer and Asian/Pacific Islander in the South, as well as a space in which to consider the meanings of our many differences. We raised themes that have continued to be in the forefront of this group's conversations. Since the time of this taping, several members have moved away to other cities or countries, while many new women have joined the group, bringing new dimensions to our collective experience as Asian/Pacific Islander and queer in Atlanta. We hope this conversation provides insight into our lives and identities, fragmented as they may be, and that it will be considered in the context of the richness and diversity of Asian and Pacific Islander histories, social and economic circumstances, and collective struggles in the United States.

Notes

1. Some personal names used in this discussion are pseudonyms.

2. The "perimeter" is a major expressway that encircles Atlanta and represents to many local people a division between the (predominantly white) suburbs and the (more multiracial) "inner city."

Bonnie J. Morris

Women's Festivals
On the Front Lines

I am not a southerner, but I lived through five of my most important adolescent years in Durham, North Carolina, and earned my high school diploma at the legendary Carolina Friends School. There I fell in love with my best friend at age sixteen and met my first real lesbians when I daringly attended the 1978 Southeastern Gay and Lesbian Conference at UNC–Chapel Hill. Now I return to the South every spring to emcee the Gulf Coast Womyn's Festival in Ovett, Mississippi.

My "day job" as a women's studies professor and historian allows me long weekends and long summers for field trips into lesbian turf. For a decade or longer, my real work has been at women's music festivals, those much misunderstood events bringing artists and activists together under the stars. Make no mistake, festivals are radical institutions, inviting all women to examine how homophobia, sexism, and racism limit our lives. But what occurs when a once-a-year women's music festival spills over into the surrounding community, creating a year-round lesbian presence? How does such interaction change and challenge communities where festivals put down roots?

In the case of the Gulf Coast Womyn's Festival, the town more or less declared war on lesbians. The story of Wanda and Brenda Henson's fight for a feminist retreat in their home state eloquently demonstrates the inconsistency of equal protection for lesbians around these United States.

The Mississippi Spirit

By now, most festiegoers and indeed many Americans in general are familiar with the saga of Camp Sister Spirit. Wanda and Brenda Henson's battle with the citizens

Another version of this essay appeared in Bonnie J. Morris's *Eden Built by Eves* (Boston: Alyson, 1999). Used with permission of the author.

of Ovett, Mississippi, has been spotlighted by media coverage from the *Oprah Win-frey Show, 20/20,* the *Jerry Springer Show, Larry King Live,* and newspapers across the country. The Hensons, whose original goal was simply to provide quality commu-nity outreach and educational resources to women in rural Mississippi, have become controversial folk heroines in the southern land they insist they will not leave.

Mississippi is the poorest state in the nation. It graduates the fewest students and pays the lowest wages. It is a right-to-work state where women, black and white, struggle to find promising job opportunities. Haunted by the bloody civil rights years of voter registration drives and lynchings, Mississippi's black and white residents remain divided, though united in a profound Christianity that has also made con-troversial headlines of late (certain public schools include daily Christian prayer and Bible reading, despite the presumed separation of church and state).

Despite these challenges, Mississippi also draws on a rich oral tradition of women's words and stories; the language of women speaking and singing is woven into the lush coastal landscape and deltas. This, too, is a culture and a place where women look to one another with love and commitment. Here, song traditions draw from Native Amer-ican languages, Cajun cadences, slave lullabies, blues, gospel hymns, fishing and river-boat legends. In response to those who mock the idea of a lesbian festival taking root in Mississippi, Wanda Henson's quick reply is that these are her people; this is her envi-ronment—and why should a woman-loving identity make refugees of individuals, require all activists to relocate to urban gay communities like San Francisco?

The arrogant assumption that progressive Mississippi women have the resources to move out of state is another point. Not only is the idea of uprooting every lesbian feminist a slap in the face to folk with kinship ties and emotional history in their own land, it is impossible for those women who lack the discretionary funds to leave town. Women without the cash flow to attend the more distant festivals might well benefit from an affordable, local festival at home, tailored to their own concerns. With this in mind, Wanda and Brenda Henson founded the Gulf Coast Womyn's Festival in 1989. What no one could foresee was that this small statement of grassroots feminism, based in the belief that every region deserves its festival, would become a national symbol of the fight against intolerance.

Wanda and Brenda first met in January of 1985 at an abortion clinic–defense during the anniversary of *Roe v. Wade.* Brenda hailed from a Unitarian family in Ohio, whereas Wanda grew up in Mississippi's strict Holiness subculture and preached as a young woman. The two women nonetheless had much in common. Both had married at six-teen. Both had two children from those marriages. And both had left behind husbands who battered them, electing to start life over in service to women in need.

As a committed lesbian couple, legally sharing the surname of Brenda's mother, the Hensons found a model for community change in the first festival they attended—Robin Tyler's Southern Women's Music and Comedy Festival in Georgia. Reminisc-ing about that life-changing first festival, Wanda later told the readers of *HOT WIRE: The Journal of Women's Music and Culture,* "I went into Robin's festival a desperate, tired woman, full of pure hopelessness … and for the first time began seeing people that were expressing things like what I thought." She added, "When I hear sisters say to me that the feminist movement is dying, I feel like, 'You can't die, we haven't had our chance yet.' I get real desperate over that, because I know where I was, and I see it in my sisters every day. There's so much hopelessness, lack of education, and poverty here among women."

Rather like the radical feminist writer Sonia Johnson, who transferred the vision-ary fervor of her Mormon upbringing to festival activism and rhetoric, Wanda caught inspiration from Robin Tyler's festival and began working and fundraising to open a women's bookstore in Mississippi. Southern Wild Sisters Unlimited opened in November 1987, and a host of other Henson projects followed. Brenda would even-tually joke, "Instead of a community starting a bookstore, our bookstore started a community." The Hensons' goals were twofold: to host cultural events that were clean-and-sober alternatives to the bar scene and to work politically on child custody, incest, and other issues. (Wanda had lost custody of her children for being a lesbian, thankfully regaining that custody later on.)

With the support of festival veterans Therese Edell and Sue Fink, who trained the Hensons in everything from sound production to emcee work, the first Gulf Coast Festival met in 1989 at a Girl Scout camp and attracted over 250 festiegoers. Brenda boasted proudly, "Wanda put the whole thing together in ninety days with thirty-three volunteers—her spirit is catching." With almost no precedent for its Gulf Coast cul-tural focus, the festival quickly gained a reputation for emphasizing regional favorites such as red beans and rice, boiled shrimp, and a Mardi Gras night with a parade of women throwing Moon Pies and beads into the audience.

In support of southern women who, like Wanda, felt overwhelmed by the con-trasting messages of Pentecostal and feminist spirituality, the Hensons also began hosting a separate event, Spiritfest, in 1991. By the Gulf Coast Festival's third year, Wanda and Brenda were still renting from Scout or church camps and anxious about land privacy, yet their commitment and friendly outreach continued to attract top-quality performers. And because the festival met on Easter weekend, the only spring holiday for the state's workers, the Hensons instituted a Passover seder as well, edu-cating Mississippi women about Jewish culture and inviting all festiegoers to partake in this appropriate ritual of liberation.

The festival came up against its first real ideological backlash when the Methodist camp used in 1991 refused to rent space for 1992, citing concerns about the Jewish seder ritual. A verbal contract notwithstanding, the camp board denied use of its facility well after the Hensons had begun advertising the 1992 festival. As a result, in 1992 the Gulf Coast Womyn's Festival had to switch to a Boy Scout camp, where male caretakers were very much present and male violence at the outside gate created a series of confrontations.

Angry, weary, and desperate to continue her search for safe land, Wanda Henson greeted the 1992 festival audience with a moving lesson on anti-Semitism and orga-nizing.

Good evening, and welcome to the Fourth Annual Gulf Coast Womyn's Festival.

This is the second time that we've had to change camp plans. And I come here tonight as an angry southern woman! I am sick and tired of the oppression we live under, and what I've been through this year nobody should have to have endured. It was bad enough when the Girl Scouts—the people who taught me integrity, the place where I got my first hickie when I was nine years old!—it was bad enough when they told me that I couldn't have their land back. I'm here tonight to tell you they lied to me. And I'm angry.

I'm angry at the Methodist Church camp that we were at last year, because they are liars too. Two days after festival last year, our money was embezzled by the camp director. They asked us to keep it all a secret. A grand jury was held—I was not invited to the proceedings. But the judge ordered a reimbursement of money to this festival because they had severely overcharged us. I'm having to sue them, and I want my money back! I wouldn't set foot on that land if the judge gave it to me. I want land that is sacred woman land, and I want land that comes from our hearts, and I want land *soon.* Real soon. If we don't get this land back, this Boy Scout camp, next year we'll be at a university, and what that means is that every year we have lost more and more and more.

To backtrack: in January I went pleading to the Methodist camp board. I wanted their land again. We gave a long, long ordeal, about an hour and a half with them, and all they could do was sit and ask me a multitude of questions about the Passover seder. They didn't understand why there would be a seder at our festival and wanted to know all about it. And sisters, I didn't see anti-Semitism when it was staring me in the face. But we are all here today because of it. So if you never thought your lives would be affected by it, as non-Jewish sisters, then you're wrong, because here we are. And each year it will be because of oppression, because they will find a hook to land us with, and I'm sick of it.

I hate to have to start the festival off like this again. But I'm telling you, I'm angry, and I'm tired of it. I wrote some little thoughts down about organizing, so I'd like to share with you what goes on in my head all year long.

Sisters, we must organize ourselves with a new mindset; then we can build a new meaning for ourselves and transform, bring life to, the existence we now live. One thing that has kept us apart as southern women, forever, is our individualism, and it is not serving us well at all. We must learn collective action with responsibility. Then our society and our reality will change. The power for meaningful change is within our hearts and we can do it by our own hands; no one can do our work for us. We must begin by building trust with each other. And that is what the Gulf Coast Womyn's Festival is all about.

Consciousness-raising groups in the Deep South are a must; we must get them. And we must take the responsibility, each one of us here tonight. It is

necessary. We need to face the reality of our issues together; we can no longer
sit back and wait for change to happen. Our denial has rendered us powerless
and without voice. Our anger is consuming us.

Who will build these spaces? What sisters am I talking to tonight? And who
is gonna risk being in that space? I know hundreds of sisters here on the coast
who are afraid to be in this space because they don't know what this festival
is about. Think about it: the greater risk for us is to choose not to be here. We
must come together to understand what our strengths are; then we must share
our differences so we can accept each other and each others' truths. My sisters'
truths will then become a part of my truths.

That's what the Gulf Coast Womyn's Festival is all about: it's about bringing
all of our groups together. And feminism is what this festival is about, for we
must become feminists. Feminism is the politics of this space; and I sometimes
like to think it's the politics of my morality. Already we have evidence to show
what can happen when women embrace feminism in the Deep south. Look at
this festival: this is our fourth year! We are here because women embraced
feminism! Because we wanted to live in freedom, like our sisters do outside
of our existence here.

We are here because we love women, because our lives are valuable, because
we can no longer leave our lives to chance. We are here because we know it is
up to us to create safe space—a space that is free of oppression, for the
empowerment of ourselves.

Sisters, the winds of change are blowing across the Gulf Coast, and tonight
I hope you feel the winds of change . . .

By the following year, the festival was forced to meet in one corner of a Louisiana
state park, where an early evening noise ordinance and patrolling park rangers placed
obvious limitations on festival freedom. Yet even under circumstances that would
have seemed intolerable to, say, veterans of the Michigan festival, Gulf Coast festiegoers made clear their appreciation for any organized lesbian event. For example, the
state park location made it easy for festiegoers to drive into town for snacks and sup-
plies at any time—a convenience most festivals lack—but few southern women
attending left the land, preferring to invent a parked-in feeling like that of the Michigan festival.

I overheard the following conversation: a woman invited her lover to drive into
town for munchies. The invited partner rooted herself more firmly into a splintered
picnic bench, gestured to the many lesbians conversing around her, and replied with
almost transcendental serenity, "Now, honey, why would I leave *heaven* to go to the
grocery store?" Only Wanda could have expressed more tellingly the important role
a local festival plays. In a word, heaven.

At that same 1993 festival, the producers indeed took their moments at the microphone. Wanda and Brenda Henson, who had closed their women's bookstore and
gone back to school for graduate training in education, were now far more experienced

speakers and had successfully raised the seed money for a land purchase, winning a $14,000 grant from the Minneapolis-based Lesbian Natural Resources Foundation.

A cheerful Wanda Henson, drawing on her background as a preacher, wowed the festival audience with a revival-style update on Gulf Coast organizing: 1993 would be the last year of a "homeless" festival.

This past year all of my friends have begun to say, "Wanda Henson, just hush; we ain't in the mood for no more projects. You just about to kill us!" Well, Gulf Coast women have been busy, busy, for five years now. Busy doing all the stuff you might not know about: we have a food bank that we make available to old women, primarily, up to the tune of 40,000 pounds last year and 60,000 pounds this year. We also have a second-hand shop that sisters run themselves, making the money to get the food, and we got a Federal Emergency Management Assistance grant for this, and the Catholic church funded us a thousand dollars this year.

So, you see, I tell you my work is in Mississippi, but it's just about the same here in Louisiana: working in this part of the country, we're working with very poor people. For instance, one-third of all Mississippi women cannot really read or write. And it means that you work in jobs that are horrible—*if* you can get work. And so the poor have very few choices in my state. We started our work at the basic level; it's been really tough, but it's growing, and we're happy. We are now ready for the challenge of the land.

We keep talking about this land, this land, this land, and many sisters keep saying, "Well, when are you getting this land? When are you getting the land?" You? It's not a you. It is O-U-R. It has to be a community effort. Right now, the community has raised around $10,000. There is also $13,950 that has been raised as a grant from Lesbian Natural Resources, sisters up in Minneapolis. We've done fundraisers in all the different communities: Tallahassee, Memphis, Jackson, Mobile, New Orleans—a couple (three of them) in New Orleans. And there's been individuals who have stood up in meetings and said, "*This is important*, take out your checkbooks and write your checks!"

It dawned on us that we don't know exactly what women *can do* for community money. This is because of classism, and I'm eat up with it. I'm eat up with internalized classism! We have not had the chance for what feminism could be in the Deep South!

Now, sisters that have had privilege, able to get out of this area and go other places, have a lot of wonderful feminist spirit. But for sisters that can't leave, there's just literally hundreds of suicides happening all around. You know what happens when you don't have hope? This work is saving lives, sisters, and we are desperate for this land space.

This year the patriarchy has pushed us out of Mississippi, and it's gonna push us out of Louisiana. What I have learned from my history is that the civil rights movement wouldn't have got off the ground like it did if Ella Baker[1] had not gotten with the folks and organized, and she said that the black farmers owned their land and couldn't be moved off it. They could stand in defiance and defend their land. And I'm screaming now because that's what poor women do when they're upset and they need something; thanks for being here!

It does me a world of good to do this because when I'm at home doing this, everybody's worried about me. They don't like it when I cry, and they say, "Don't get upset." But if we don't get upset, what happens to feminists? What happens to you when you have the passion of love in your heart for your sisters? What happens is internalized stress, and there's a lot of cancer in our communities. So it is with passion that I work.

What's gonna happen when we get our civil rights, but sisters are sitting in a closet? I know what happens when the laws change and the people don't. That's why it's hard for sisters of color to trust coming to this space, to come to Mississippi in the first place! Because of the racism that's in this community. And if you can say that you're working on this shit, then sisters can organize across the lines that are separating us.

But you're gonna come home to apathy. You're gonna come home to sisters who look at you like you're a strange woman because you dare to come to a festival, because you went to a seder and learned, as a Christian, about liberation and freedom. They're gonna look at you, and they're not gonna understand. And then you're gonna be oppressed by your own people; your own people is gonna look at you and make fun of everything you say. That is my experience! But what I know is, I can't wait thirty or forty years until there comes a trickle-down in the patriarchy here.

And one by one we will change. And if we don't change, I challenge you to get the black women's anthologies and read what Pat Parker had to say.[2] She said, "Where will you be when they come? And they will come!" I can't remember poetry, I made a F on it in the eleventh grade, dropped out of school over poetry. Actually, I was pregnant. Thought I was heterosexual! But I use that poem to piss people off. I was at the March on Washington in 1987 when her booming voice came over the microphone. There were 650,000 people there, but everyone stood still and we heard what Pat Parker had to say. Pat's not with us anymore, but her words live on. Read that poem! Use it to piss off everybody you know! And then, once they get angry and start talking, then maybe you can move them off their apathy and into a space that is for freedom!

If you look around this room, there are some empowered sisters here. We have our first group of lesbian feminist–identified sisters from the State of Louisiana on the national women's music scene, Sisterbeat. From Mississippi, our first lesbian-identified women's musician on the national scene, Pam Hall. And sisters from Florida beginning in the women's music scene now. This is the first wave of feminism coming through here. We can't ride on the third one that some folks tell me about.

But if you think there ain't no way that you can do something, I want to tell you I felt that way, too, eight years ago, before I went to *my* first festival: the Southern Women's Music and Comedy Festival, Robin Tyler's festival. After I left there, I went up to her and told her, "Sister, you have changed my life *forever!* Forever!" And I just cried and cried in her arms. I didn't know how to organize, but we did a craft show, made a little money, started from there.

I was in the Pentecostal Church with thirty sisters; you can laugh, but that's the culture I come from, in case you hadn't noticed. I used to preach in children's church. A sister at a festival told me I'd never be effective with my speaking style, and it silenced me—up until last year. I've longed to get up on stage and say the things that are on my heart, but it is my speaking style that I was afraid of—that sisters would not understand. But it's the language that I have! When I was in the Holiness church, we met every Saturday morning and we made peanut brittle until we had blisters on our hands. This was serious business, because we wanted a church. And I dare say the South would not be where it is today if we didn't have those damn churches. I got five churches within two blocks of my house, and there are two hundred within an eight-mile stretch on the lower coast of Mississippi, and not one of them gave one dollar when I sent out a plea for money for people living with AIDS. Not one; bunch of hypocrites! And if I'm stepping on your toes because you claim Christianity, well, I'm just telling you about the people that I've had to deal with.

Anyhow, we made peanut brittle, we had blisters on our hands, every Saturday. And come Monday, when the women at the sawmill got out and the women at the paper mill got out, we stood there. We stood out there in our long dresses and our hair poked up like this and looking the way Holiness sisters look, and we asked, "Can you buy some peanut brittle?" And every time they'd buy it, we'd say, "Bless you, sister!" "Thank you, sister!" "You're doing the Lord's work!" And we raised $65,000 in two years, selling peanut brittle.

So when we needed food for our food bank, I decided to make little bracelets and send them to feminist bookstores. I made $1,500 in a year! I don't have a jewelry pattern, I just got me some leather and string and a couple little beads, put it all together and said: *This is a bracelet, help support us, we're working for change in Mississippi.* And the sisters heard me! And so now we've been making food available where there was none, where sisters had to choose between medicine or food the last week of the month. That's the level of poverty I'm talking about, see? Toni Armstrong Jr. from *HOT WIRE* magazine said to me, "Hang on, Wanda; one day the sisters will not remember not having the land." That day will come. It will!

So, I want to leave you with a challenge. What will you do? What can you do? I don't know you. I don't know what your circumstances are. Every one of you gonna leave out of here with a different interpretation of what I mean.

Being foremothers—of the groundwater of the Deep South feminist movement—we have a challenge. I want to invite you, I want your input, just come on and we'll process. Or maybe we'll just visit with each other; figure out what to do. I invite lesbians, bisexual women, straight women, celibate women, any woman who is here, who has found it important to be here. Just come on, even if you think you might not know how. Just come on.

Wanda skillfully reminded her audiences that for a southerner, one's place and having a place is everything, yet her mission appealed to supporters from all regions. The stage was set for a land purchase, and in summer 1993 Sisterspirit Incorporated paid $60,000 for a 120-acre former pig farm in Ovett, Mississippi. The goals for the land went beyond having secure festival space: the Hensons were dedicated to creating indigenous lesbian culture, building a feminist educational retreat, and maintaining their community work running a food bank and a literacy program. They also sought an economically self-sufficient "landyke" community, using this term to reach interested women through the country lesbian magazine *Maize*.

The new land, quickly named Camp Sister Spirit, was situated in a dry county and effectively continued the Gulf Coast Festival's policy of clean and sober space. The land site was the most affordable option for the Hensons. Yet it quickly placed the women under scrutiny—not only from their overwhelmingly born-again neighbors but from northern festival activists critical of the site. Writing about the ensuing months of controversy, feminist author Phyllis Chesler noted:

> Questions abound. Why should the feminist government-in-exile choose Jones County, the historical heart of the Klan, as its first outpost on earth? Why build a future where you're not wanted? (Tell that to the Israelis and the Palestinians.) "Why not in Mississippi, the poorest state in the nation, and the most oppressed?" Wanda asks. "It's where I was born, where I'm from." Anyway where exactly are radical lesbian feminists wanted? And where is land as cheap (120 acres for $60,000) as in Ovett, Mississippi?

Trouble first began in November 1993, after a Camp Sister Spirit newsletter, *The Grapevine,* was removed from the Henson's mailbox and made available to local Christian activists. On November 8, a dog resembling the camp's three-month-old puppy was found shot through the stomach and draped over the mailbox, with a sanitary napkin attached to the side of the mailbox, reading "Die Bitch"—a clearly symbolic statement of hostility to women's interests and an incident that has consistently been denied and misreported by local law officials. What followed were bomb threats, obscene letters and phone calls, roofing tacks placed on the driveway (as well as spikes commonly used during war to disable tires), and incidents in which camp volunteers were shot at or driven off the road. Despite keeping meticulous records of these threats, the Hensons—and caretakers Cheri Michael and Pam Firth—were up against the biases of local law enforcement officials, who clearly opposed their presence. On January 3, 1994, Jones County sheriff Maurice Hooks himself passed the collection plate for an "Ovett Community Defense Fund" at one of the many anti-Camp meetings.

As the outside press quickly zoomed in on what looked like new civil rights egg on the face of Mississippi, state and local leaders quickly rallied to protest the "gay agenda" in their midst. A Mississippians for Family Values group formed, led by James Hendry, for the sole purpose of driving the Hensons from their land, enlisting the support of Beverly LaHaye's Concerned Women for America organization. U.S. Representative Mike Parker [D-Ovett] expressed his opposition. Paul Walley, attorney for the Perry County Board of Supervisors, quickly began investigating state sodomy and building-code laws that might force the Hensons out. Eventually, the local threat grew so intimidating that by February of 1994 Attorney General Janet Reno asked for mediation from the Justice Department and sent a letter of support to the National Gay and Lesbian Task Force.

In spite of Reno's few gestures, however, the spotlight of the U.S. Justice Department did not create change in the situation, and a war of words—in both print and television media—escalated. Ironically, although in many respects the Gulf Coast Festival was one of the newer women's festival gatherings in the United States, its producers were the first to become household names across the country—names with faces, as the Hensons described their plight on the *Oprah Winfrey Show* in December 1993, on *20/20* in January 1994, and on the *Jerry Springer Show* and *Larry King Live,* as well as in *Time* and *Newsweek* articles, in February and early spring. Astonished festiegoers turned on their televisions to see, for the first time, festival founders as media spokeswomen. If the Hensons offered a grassroots rather than glamorous media image, they also brought home—in a new era of "lesbian chic"—the message that tolerance and visibility were privileges enjoyed by only a few gay and lesbian communities nationwide.

Transformed into educators whose testimony moved millions of viewers, the Hensons were forced to take to the road and support their cause through speaking engagements and fundraisers. Throughout calendar year 1994, while festivals and Gay and Lesbian Pride Events flourished in other American states, the Hensons traveled to college campuses and conferences nationwide while Pam and Cheri (and Wanda's adult son, Arthur) kept the camp secure and built its first structures.

News clippings from the eight-month period between November 1993 and July 1994 show the degree of hatred:

December 7, 1993: If they approach any of the women of the community, they ought to run. (Ricky Cole, *Hattiesburg American*)

December 17–23, 1993: The focus of their existence is something I consider an abomination to nature. (Paul Walley, *Philadelphia Gay News*)

January 1994: When I heard that rednecks were attacking Camp Sister Spirit, I was disappointed because I think they should be attacked by all kinds of necks: black necks, white necks. (Reverend Ken Fairly, *Clarion-Ledger,* Jackson, Mississippi)

February 1994: It's a known fact that all your violent crimes comes from homosexuals. (Deputy Sheriff Myron Holifield, *Mississippi Press*)

March 25, 1994: I'm going to go out and buy a gun for me and my wife. We are going to keep loaded shotguns in our cars. (James Hendry, *Hattiesburg American*)

Frightened by the publicity of gunshots and other threats from the Ovett community, most performers and festiegoers stayed away from the spring 1994 Gulf Coast gathering; a loyal group of some fifty-three women instead held a quiet celebration of tenacity and commitment, and Sonya Rutstein of the band Disappear Fear was the sole guest artist. Brenda Henson recalls: "Ten minutes before that first-night stage concert, upon learning that only one performer had shown up, sisters in the audience rallied together and we had a 'Make Your Own Festival Stage.' Women came forward with music, poetry, Goddess dancing, and Picard the pot-bellied pig assisted his mom Allison (an attorney!) in doing tricks."

In the following year, however, Camp Sister Spirit took a turn for the better. Dozens of college-age feminists who had learned of the Hensons' struggle came to Camp Sister Spirit as volunteers, assisting in the construction of several buildings, as well as a security fence. As local residents gradually grew more accustomed to the retreat center, threatening incidents lessened; instead, the women living on the land received thousands of supportive letters from all over the world (the Associated Press had picked up their story). Donations helped ready the land for the 1995 festival. I served as emcee and performer at that festival, and the usual Passover seder took place without incident.

It is both startling and disappointing to note that a vocal minority of lesbian critics have denounced Camp Sister Spirit. Two women wrote to the January–February 1995 issue of Lesbian Connection, "We have finally had enough of the glorification of the very dangerous situation in Mississippi. The Hensons' own personal and financial choices and miscalculations in no way warrant the Lesbian community's unquestioned allegiance or the elevation of the Hensons to the status of cultural heroines." More disturbing still are those women in the festival community who have stated that the Hensons are martyrs seeking publicity or are bad for other lesbian businesses or should simply get out. Despite Phyllis Chesler's fall 1994 article in *On the Issues,* which concluded with the important point that no region is safe for women, some educated feminists continue to insist that the Hensons have deliberately placed Mississippi women at risk.

Mississippi women know better. Pam Hall, a dynamic festival performer from Jackson, Mississippi, and one of the very few women of color to perform at the Gulf Coast Festival for several years, has often pointed out that women in her home state need alternatives to the alcoholism and violence of the bar scene; other women with barely the gas money to drive through Camp Sister Spirit's gates have made moving statements in the camp journal after a first visit: "I thought I was the only one." "I am the only lesbian in my town." "I thought I was a sinner." "I was so scared, I turned back three times, but now I am free."

"If we're gonna take a movement from the head to the heart, it's got to be through music," Wanda told me at a Halloween bonfire on the land in 1994. "We're here to teach nonoppressive lifeways. There's been enough social change that Congress could be compelled to enact social justice legislation protecting us all . . . but by fleeing to gay ghettoes, removing ourselves from our own homelands, we make it easier for the government and the right wing. They say we're too hostile; I say, middle-class people are too silent."

Welcoming the festival audience to the reconverted barn stage on Easter/Passover weekend of 1995, Wanda Henson stood at the microphone a changed woman; a two-way transmitter on her belt, her voice steady, the producer who was once too shy to speak sang to us.

Well, there's been many women before us that have decided that if they could not have their freedom they would rather be dead. But when you get on that line, sisters, it's a real hard line to walk. And the silence of your friends is hard to take. But I'm not here to bring you down.

I'm here to explain to you what has kept us going. What has kept us going for the past year and a half has been the new sisters that have come, the feminists that I didn't even know about. I did not know about the young feminist movement that is in this nation. It's not in the lesbian press, it's not in the gay press, I'm not seeing it in the mainstream press—Mississippi's got a lot of censorship! But the sisters have come to this land, and I'll give you a sense of what we've been up to.

Not only have we protected this land and made safety for each other, but this *barn*, in the beginning of March, still had pig sties in it. I don't know if you've ever tried to bang some of these oak boards apart, but it takes a lot of strength. And two of the three caretakers on this land live with disabilities: me and Brenda. The first person who moved in on this land was Cheri Michael. The media moved in on a sound byte that sounded funny to them, "The Hensons," but Cheri was the first dyke to be here full time. Brenda and I were here four days a week; we were going to school. I think everybody knows that we've been forced to drop out of school; we're very disappointed—we're just eight courses away from dissertation, and for women who didn't get a chance early in life to go to school, that's a real big disappointment to us. But the movement work that we're doing now is more important and there's not enough hours in the day to do what we have to do.

Getting ready for this event was incredible. We've been trying to get ourselves out of a sixteen-foot travel trailer that Brenda and I and our son Arthur lived in for a year. We got here in March, and that's when the sisters came down from the universities. They've now left the land and gone back home to organize. We are charging them with "You have to organize in your own community," and I'm telling every one of you that, here, now. Because if you want this event to grow, or our work to continue, you have to do the organizing. We can't go into your community and have access to your friends. Unless you invite us to come there and speak, and even then we're only there for hours. Movement is the one by one, the people deciding to act.

And these sisters, at different universities where we spoke this last year, decided to come and be on the land here for their spring break. And *my, my,*

I couldn't believe it! The women from Smith College learned how to use power tools—and everybody here learned about gay and lesbian rights that we do not have, and we also talked about the human rights that have been violated against Camp Sister Spirit—seventeen out of the thirty!

We don't have civil rights. This is one thing we have learned, and we're having a hard time trying to file a lawsuit, getting the right attorneys, and figuring out what our strategy's gonna be against this Mississippi for Family Values group. But we also want to press forward for civil rights, and the way to do it is to grow, and for people to come to this land and to make a stand and for us not to be pushed off of this land. We have to be here. And we can only be here as long as we are financially empowered to be here.

Wanda, Brenda, Cheri, Kathy and Pam—our fifth caretaker, now in California doing personal healing, because it's been tremendously hard for us, I can't even begin to tell you—anyway, folks want to know about us. "God, they really looking good," "They got nice new clothes," is the kind of shit I've heard. Well, we got a hundred-dollar stipend the last three months of the year, and we're getting $300 a month for January, February, and March. In April there's no money. And we have worked our asses off; our personal needs have gone by the wayside for a long time now. I want y'all to go back into your communities and do what you can to organize and raise money.

Because it is *important* that we are here. Women come up to us on the street, look up at us and say, "Please, you're doing it for women. You're doing it for all of us; honey, it's nothing about you being different. It's about you being a woman!" Begging us, begging us. Folks that don't live here, you might not know the oppression that southern dykes have lived under for a long time. But we have longed to be free, like the communities I see around the country. It's why we don't mind getting up at six o'clock in the morning, why Cheri don't mind being up here wiring this barn until midnight every night. She worked ten days leading up to festival, just getting this done. We had to have concrete, had to have a ramp; it's not completely wheelchair accessible, but I hope it has served everybody's needs for this event. Cheri can do anything!

We also put the pad into the front gate. Y'all may have noticed there's a big hunk of concrete there. Because Miss Robin Tyler of the West Coast Music and Comedy Festival made available $10,012 by passing the hat, and we have a fancy, fancy gate that's going in there, sixteen foot high! And if *they* chase my wife again, she will have her radio with her and she will be able to open that gate from half a mile away and come in for safety, because there's always safety here. They chased her home June the first; I've never been so angry in my life. But now we have the means to get in here real quick if we need to.

We've got a mile and a half of fence up, and it's working, because this hunting season they've only been on the property three times. And we know the difference between intimidation and just regular what they do around here.

So . . . the boys ain't messed with us this year. Our security team is doing a mighty fine job.

It's so empowering to be in this kind of space. If you don't have it, if you only get it for two or three days, and then gotta go back to the patriarchy, this is so important. If it wasn't as important to us as it is, I would have been gone a long time ago! But seven years ago, I walked onto a stage, and I could barely talk into a damned mike, and I begged, "I want to be a producer. This is what we're trying to do." I made circles with my arms; I couldn't explain women's spirituality. But I wanted something to happen. And I knew if we made this space available, women would make it happen. And one of these days those cars are gonna be lined up to Hattiesburg. Nobody's gonna stop the flow of justice.

Wanda concluded her speech by singing "Which Side Are You On?"[3] And since that triumphant moment, the festival has continued yearly, without incident. Artists and audience are asked to sign a liability release form, but no harm has come to those of us committed to attending this festival. The buildings and performances grow every year. Performer Sandy Rapp recently recorded "The Ballad of Camp Sister Spirit"; several books on the festival are in the works. Judith Sloan, a longtime Gulf Coast Festival comedian, performed off-Broadway in "A Tattle Tale," her one-woman show based on the political justice work of Brenda Henson's daughter, Andi Gibbs.

THE BALLAD OF CAMP SISTER SPIRIT
© Sandy Rapp 1996

I went down to Ovett, Mississippi.
I flew all day then drove an ol' two-lane.
Red tin roofs and junk yards lined the dusty way,
And an ancient mill town spoke of better days.
The armadillos fled along the roadside
And a buzzard had a rattler in its claws.
'Til violet tree trunks told us we were not in Kansas now,
And the barbed wire told us nor were we in Oz.
A purple gate arose to let us enter,
But only when security was cleared.
Later down the drive a dance of ribbons came alive;
Camp Sister Spirit magically appeared.
And Brenda sat amidst the flags and flyers,
And Wanda waved hello from on the run.
And I had met the Hensons who had made a dream come true;
They had built the sister camp and we had come.

CHORUS: But did you hear Mississippi's still a burnin'
           Up in flames, the sacred spaces all around.
           And though you know Sister Spirit ain't a turnin',
           They been shootin' at the old camp ground.

Buchanan wrote a scathing little column
Implying they were shooting at themselves
To boost attendance at the campground;
He's unaware that shellfire keeps attendance down.
Meanwhile a truck ran Brenda off the highway
And a black/white couple caught some special fire.
An automatic discharged 87 rounds one day;
And the Caretaker got shot at from a car.

REPEAT CHORUS

Well, the Hensons won a lawsuit filed against 'em,
For turning Mississippi on its ass.
And the judge is spelling womyn with a "y" now,
And the farmworkers salute them when they pass.
And a hundred people come each month to campground
For a pantry that the campfolk have on hand.
And I am told that there are those who've learned to love out loud
This living lesbiana in their land.

FINAL CHORUS: So when you hear Mississippi's still a burnin'
                Up in flames, the sacred spaces all around
                Remember every Sister Spirit from the journey,
                And the rainbow flyin' high and shinin' through
                For that is Mississippi too.

Notes

1. The granddaughter of slaves, Ella Baker was a civil rights activist in the 1940s and 1950s, president of the New York branch of the National Association for the Advancement of Colored People and then national director of branches. Baker helped provide support to southern blacks during the Alabama bus boycott and later became coordinator of the Southern Christian Leadership Conference, as well as a proponent of the Student Nonviolent Coordinating Committee.

2. Pat Parker was a black lesbian feminist poet whose premature death from cancer in the early 1990s devastated many in the U.S. lesbian community. Pat Parker's 1978 poem "Where Will You Be?" first appeared in her book *Movement in Black* (Diana Press) and later in *Lesbian Poetry*, edited by Elly Bulkin and Joan Larkin; it has also been recorded as a song by Nedra Johnson on Johnson's debut album, *Testify*.

3. The 1947 working peoples' anthem "Which Side Are You On?" was written by Florence Reece, the wife of a coal miner and union organizer. The song defies the idea of remaining neutral in a crisis. Reece sings this song on the Rounder Records album "They'll Never Keep Us Down: Women's Coal Mining Songs."

Works Cited

Chesler, Phyllis. 1994. "Sister, Fear Has No Place Here." *On The Issues*, fall, 29.

Goodstein, Laurie. 1994. "Mississippi Mother to Sue over School Prayer." *Washington Post*, 20 December, A8.

Henson, Wanda. 1993. "The Personal Is Political in the Deep South," interview by Toni Armstrong Jr. *Hot Wire*, January, 41–42.

David Knapp Whittier

Race and Gay Community
in Southern Town

A drive to Southern Town involves passing by miles of pecan and cotton groves.[1] The town is 170 miles away from the nearest major urban concentration of at least a million people and is 50 miles away from the closest interstate highway. It is a city of almost 80,000 people and the county seat of a county of about 96,000 persons. Southern Town is at least 85 miles away from other towns of its own size or larger, each of which, like Southern Town, has at least one gay bar. (No place in the southeastern United States is more than a two-hour drive from a gay bar.)

Southern Town has an agricultural, manufacturing, and service economy base. The western part of town is a newer suburban sprawl of retail chain stores and franchises, large boulevards, and housing. About four miles west of downtown is the Southern Town Mall. The mall is now the town's commercial and social hub. The downtown looks like it is dying. Now, the mall is the center of face-to-face contact among the residents in Southern Town. Only the poor are seen walking about the town's streets in the hot humid weather. Most people get about in pickup trucks that announce them as hardworking country folks. Now and then a Lexus announces something else again.

Just a little south of the mall, is a country-club residential development where the wealthier natives and corporate interlopers now tend to settle. Many of these homes are ostentatious and very large, undoubtedly belonging to the newly moneyed few of the 1980s "me" decade. A few such homes are new pseudo–ante bellum mansions. But the New South is not lacking in such ironies.

Gay men grow up and variously leave, return, and remain in places like Southern Town. No one fully knows how many do which and why. For example, the migration of younger people to urban areas may leave closeted older and young gays in rural areas. These factors may act to inhibit the growth of the gay community and culture in these areas (Harry and DeVall 1978).

East and closer to downtown, the town looks more like a classic, sleepy, southern town. There are huge live oaks dripping Spanish moss, and the homes are clearly older than those in the western part of town. Southern Town and its county are 44 percent and 49 percent white, respectively. The farther east you go in the city and the county, the blacker and poorer are the residents. As Rosemary, the white seventy-six-year-old mother of a gay man, put it, "Southern Town is a color-divided town."

According to David Paramore, forty-two and white: "Southern Town is actually four towns . . . and it's divided by the Broad River and Cotton Avenue. And Northwest runs everything. I mean that's the money, the politics, and everything else. Northwest runs the overall town. The southwest part of it is pretty much black. And poor black. It's your poor blacks . . . it's the Watts area. The roughest neighborhood in town. The biggest crime district. . . . Then you've got your white factory-worker type people who are in the Northeast. And the southeast section of town is where you find the more affluent blacks. You have your black powers, but . . . only within the black community and even they don't have the influence that the white power structure does over the black community."

Over twice as many African Americans as whites live in the eastern part of Southern Town, while the western part is pretty evenly split racially. A historically African American state college sits east of a river that flows north-south. The downtown sits on the west bank. Railroad tracks also flank the river, serving as another symbol of the division between black and white. A predominantly white state junior college is well west. The percentage of persons twenty-five years or older with a bachelor's degree living in eastern Southern Town is 7.4 percent, compared with 21.1 percent in western Southern Town. Percentages of persons whose incomes in 1989 were below poverty level (for all ages) are 34.6 percent in east Southern Town and 24.7 percent in west Southern Town. A 1994 *New York Times* article about Selma, Alabama, describes a town much like Southern Town—poor schools impoverished by white flight, and an older white minority that retains most of the wealth and power in the town through land ownership (Applebome 1994).

The geography of Southern Town is not the only indicator of its racial division. I am white, and I felt the glare of the eyes of African American men and women when I entered the predominantly African American gay bar. I had already noticed the glare of white eyes focused on an African American person who entered the predominantly white gay bar. These were not the stares of welcome and desire that accompany the entrance of a new man (of the correct race) to either bar.

Keith Foxworth (white, twenty-nine) at one of our first meetings told me in a casual description of Southern Town that besides the bar, people have parties at their houses, cookouts, pool parties, water-skiing expeditions, et cetera. He said, "Queens get together and have barbecues and talk, and that is what a gay community is supposed to be." When I asked Keith if people mix by race and gender at these events, he told me that they do not have integrated parties or integrated swimming because "Afro Sheen is a poisonous grease that floats up to the surface of the water and makes you sick." He then said to his friend, who was sitting next to him, "That sounds racist. Well, I guess it is."

As soon as I arrived, white gay men made racist statements in my presence. I guessed they assumed that I shared their sentiments. I came just about as quickly to the belief that such racist speech is socially acceptable among many whites in town, and I learned clearly again that racist culture perpetuates itself very much by condoning, indeed even celebrating, racist talk. Various sorts of discord characterize the lives of homoerotically interested men in Southern Town. Race is one of the most pervasive divisions. There are two separate gay communities in Southern Town. These two communities, and the men's sexual connections with each other, are constructed by racism, a social practice with which I was to deal every day in Southern Town and something that I was sure would have significant ramifications for my investigation.

Not that racial division is new to me. I have seen it in Montgomery, Alabama, where I was born and lived until I was ten. I have seen it in Atlanta, Georgia, where I have also lived. And I have also seen racism "up north" in large eastern cities where I have lived later as an adult. But the racism struck me early on in Southern Town. This town must be like Montgomery, I thought. They are close cousins. Many think of Southern Town as a failure of the civil rights movement—a place where "the whites never gave an inch, even to Dr. King."

Gay Bars

Southern Town contains two gay bars—one whose patrons are predominantly white and one that draws mostly African American patrons. The locations of the two gay bars follow the same east-west pattern of racial geographic segregation that exists in the town.

The Predominantly African American Gay Bar

Candy's, the mostly African American gay bar, is located east of the city center, the river, and the railroad tracks in one of the poorest and primarily African American sections of Southern Town. The immediate neighborhood looks like a former mill town area, characterized by a hulking factory surrounded by shotgun-type shanty houses. Other, straight African American bars and nightclubs share Candy's thoroughfare. One would almost want to call these bars redneck honky-tonks were it not that they attract African American clientele. Candy's is a ramshackle former single-story ranch-type home. Inside, they have knocked out the walls between rooms to create a square bar at the entrance. Many such modifications are apparent. Casement windows look out from the room that contains the bar onto a dance floor and show room. Moving from the barroom into the disco and show room feels like stepping into the backyard of what once was someone's house.

Candy's opened as a gay bar around Christmas of 1992 and was only two years old when I frequented it. The bar is open only on Friday and Saturday nights. Friday is its busiest night because blue laws in Southern Town require establishments to stop serving liquor at midnight Saturdays and to have their doors locked by 2:00 A.M. on Sundays for the remainder of the day. On Friday nights, Candy's has a crowd of about a hundred to two hundred people (from around 11:00 P.M. until 3:00 or 4:00 A.M.) African American men and women make up the crowd in fairly even proportions. Usually there are a couple of white men and women in the bar as well. The cruising among the men appears quite intense on a Friday night, perhaps because of the relatively large numbers.

Candy's sells beer, wine, and setups (for hard liquor that you can bring into the bar for a fee). There is customarily a four-dollar cover charge at the door that helps to pay for the drag (and infrequently strip) entertainment the bar offers in two separate shows on Friday nights. Candy's features guest entertainers from out of town almost every other Friday night. Every Friday night there are usually three or more local drag-queen entertainers in addition to a couple of local male leads (men who lip-synch to vocal recordings by men, usually love ballads). Occasionally a lesbian will lip-synch as a man. I never saw a white entertainer perform at Candy's except on the occasion of a drag pageant in which the queen had paid to compete.

The complaint I heard most frequently about Candy's from its patrons was that the crowd is cold and impersonal. There are discernible cliques, and "slinging Grand Queen attitude" is an occasional feature of the entertainers' demeanor. One night the emcee announced a private party to follow after the bar closed that was open only to those who had invitations. Just as the DJ at the white bar is prone to "read" (roughly translated as poke fun at) the entertainers and customers as he emcees the show, so does the emcee at Candy's. At Candy's the attitude spills over easily into the larger crowd, who might stand on the tables, catcall, and tip the entertainers in a fashion as showy as the entertainers' own. Tipping a performer is an occasion for making a statement.

One night a very hefty drag queen came on the stage and dropped her robe, revealing not a stitch of clothing underneath. The crowd went wild. The music stopped, and it took the management at least ten minutes to regain its composure and restart the music and the show.

Disco dancing takes place between the show sets. The style of music played is distinctly urban and African American: a few house tunes usually pave the way for the apparently more popular rap genre standards as the dancing gets going. The drag scene among the African Americans at Candy's seems to echo that of the "house" organization that can be found in the Voguing-House-Ball scene in the New York City area. I have learned in my work in New York City that the Voguing-House-Ball scene is very extensive in the African American gay community up and down the eastern U.S. coast. These houses of gay African American drag performers are another example of how gay networks spiral outward from a local area.

Pictures of Nelson Mandela and Malcolm X adorn the walls. One evening during the first drag number, a young African American man running the floodlight for the show focused the light on the picture of Malcolm X rather than spotlighting the drag queen. Candy, the owner (who is African American, fifty-something, and a straight woman), often serves as DJ and emcee. In this latter capacity she occasionally gives a lecture on African American pride.

Candy's does not advertise in the local mass media or in the regional gay media. I met some white homoerotically interested men in town who did not often go to the white gay bar and had not heard of Candy's. Most of the national gay guidebooks do not list the African American gay bars in the region (out of ignorance and lack of attention and of effort). On a trip to a larger city in another state (which I call Capital City here) about two hours' drive from Southern Town, I encountered a gay man I had met many years earlier in Atlanta. This man is editing a weekly regional gay guide and asked me for contact information for the gay bars in Southern Town. His gay guide now lists the "white" bar but not the "black" bar.

Because of the large crowd on Friday nights, which periodically spills out onto the streets, the tenor of Candy's must be noticeable to the people who live in the immediate neighborhood. The chief way to find out about Candy's is by word of mouth. Perhaps if you are new in town, you could call the police department or a cab company and they could probably tell you. This is a common way newcomers find out the exact location of gay bars in small towns. I learned about Candy's by asking about the Southern Town gay scene on one of my first trips to what I afterward thought of as "the white gay bar." (People there admonished me not to go to Candy's. They told me I would "be killed.")

Harry and DeVall (1978, 139) claimed twenty years ago that "since black gays are a minority of a minority, it is understandable that only the largest urban areas would be able to support a black gay bar." An African American gay bar is a recent addition to Southern Town, and rather, though not completely, exceptional for the region. Capital City, about two hours by car from Southern Town, contains a mixed (straight and gay) bar that is primarily gay and African American on Sunday evenings. This was the closest African American gay bar to Southern Town before Candy's opened. Atlanta, which is more than three hours from Southern Town, did not have a predominantly African American bar that advertised in the gay press until the early 1980s. Obviously, then, an African American gay bar in Southern Town begs for explanation—a point of this essay. Since Candy's only advertisements are word-of-mouth, I wonder how it fits into a gay cultural trajectory. At issue is the extent to which the gay cultural model permeates the African American community, or rather, the interface between African American and gay culture in Southern Town.

Because an African American gay bar is so rare, Candy's draws customers from a radius of a hundred miles. For example, Lamar (African American, twenty-two) makes an hour-plus drive to Candy's from his hometown with some African American lesbian friends almost every Friday night. When Candy's opened, quite a few African American drag queens relocated to Southern Town to work there and be part of the scene. Areanna Valle, the housemother of the House of Valle, moved from Capital City to headline at Candy's. (This sort of movement illustrates the extent to which drag queens, their entourages, and other gay bar customers link distant gay scenes in the smaller towns and rural areas of the region, thereby effectively enlarging the gay scene beyond the local area. Homoerotically active traveling salesmen and other aficionados of male-male public sex scenes are another major source of such linkages.)

The black bar's genesis relates to a change in ownership of the "other bar" (as several African American men euphemistically refer to the white gay bar, Reflections). When Reflections changed management a couple of years ago, African Americans were reportedly no longer as welcome. For example, Alan Purdue (white, twenty-nine), an employee of the white bar, told me that the new management began the Saturday night cover charge there to discourage African American customers who the management felt were sneaking in liquor instead of buying drinks in the bar. Several African American men complained to me that there had never been an African American employee at Reflections. My understanding of the opening of Candy's comes from the manager of Candy's, who told me that some African American drag queens, fed up with their treatment at Reflections, approached her, as the owner of a defunct straight African American bar, about reopening as a gay bar. She subsequently did this under her old and actual name, Candy's. At the very least, conditions were ripe.

The Predominantly White Gay Bar

Reflections is open Monday through Saturday and has a full liquor license, so one may not bring in bottles. Friday nights are also Reflections's busiest nights, with approximately thirty to sixty patrons. The crowd is usually gender mixed, with about one female to every two males. Otis, who is African American and in his late thirties, was usually there on the weekends. (Otis told me that he never visits "that part of town" when I asked him if he ever goes to Candy's. It was apparent to me that Otis prefers white men.) Very occasionally there might be another African American man or woman at Reflections. One Saturday night there was a drag pageant at the bar, and many African Americans competed. That was the "blackest" night I ever saw at Reflections. When the pageant ended, the African American men and women filed out, and the white regulars began to arrive.

Perhaps because the customers are so familiar to each other, for whites Reflections is a friendly place. Men would readily come up and talk to me (which is different from my experience in most gay bars in big cities). On weeknights, Reflections has the feeling to me of a neighborhood tavern. The regulars make a point of talking to newcomers. The style of music is also "whiter" than that offered at Candy's. It is top-forty popular dance and disco, and occasionally Techno-Industrial. Weeknights, when the small groups of regulars gather at the bar, the television usually blares the Country Music Channel. The scene is usually one of drinking and talking (gossiping, which they refer to as "calling out") rather than cruising. Reflections is not a very fast scene in comparison to those I have seen in gay bars in large cities, but it is a scene nevertheless.

As at Candy's, Friday is the big night, and there is a slightly greater air of possibility. Almost everyone is waiting for someone new to come into the bar. Friday night, the patrons pay the customary four-dollar cover charge to venture in to socialize,

drink, play pool, and watch the drag show at midnight. Fridays, Reflections also usually features a guest drag-queen entertainer (usually white) from another city in the
region. Occasionally there is a larger than usual turnout. Perhaps it is a fluke, or perhaps a special entertainer will be booked to bring out a crowd. A male-to-female
transsexual from Capital City, who Rita (the bar owner, who is a white fifty-something lesbian) told me "has a real puss" (and displays it on stage), is a favorite of the
white lesbians whenever she headlines. On both Friday and Saturday, there were
three (then two) regular cast members doing drag as well: Chrissy St. John (a.k.a. Steve
Block, white, thirty-one) and her then current proteges—Nina Holland (a.k.a. James
Speir, white, twenty-three) and Cheryl Jonel (a.k.a. Ben Luke, white, twenty-two, who
quit doing drag after a time).

Men develop extrasexual relationships at Reflections. It is the central site of the gay
white world in Southern Town. The telephone behind the bar is available for incom-
ing and outgoing personal calls. Historically, national gay guidebooks listed the telephone as a number where callers could obtain help and information about gay life in
the town. With the new management, the phone continued to function as an informal help and referral line. (The usual help and referral requested and given consists
of directions to the bar itself.) It is not rare to see a customer help at the door, fill in
behind the bar, or run the floodlight for the drag show.

Many men who attend Reflections are protective of it. Some men who hang out in
front of the bar during operating hours, talking with each another and perhaps interested in still other men who are cruising around in their cars, say they are helping to
protect the cars parked out in front, and the bar itself, from would-be troublemakers.
Observing the patrons hanging around out front of the bar was instructive about the
connections between them and other features of life in the town. The space can be
viewed as a transition zone between gay and straight life in the locale. Observing the
zone also informed me about racism in Southern Town. I often witnessed bar patrons
assuming that African Americans walking by or in the bar were "up to no good,"
while they did not make the same assumptions concerning white passersby. Similarly,
customers often complained that the bar is in a "bad" area (meaning that the neighbors were predominantly African American).

Reflections sits in a zone of transition between the downtown and more commer-
cially vibrant areas. It is just blocks west of the somewhat vacated downtown and east
of the newer development of suburban-style tract homes and strip shopping centers,
the migration of which signals the westward march of the white residents of the town
and county (in which whites are a numerical minority). Its immediate surrounding
area is one of sparse commercial establishments and lower-income black residents.
The management and many of its patrons would like to move Reflections.

Many feel—as they do about the downtown area—that the bar is in a "dangerous"
area. But where to move the bar is a problem. The rent in another area would probably be too high. Reflections fits into a geographical niche. Rita does not advertise,
and there is no sign out front. If one had not heard of the bar by word of mouth or
read about it in gay guidebooks (which are next to impossible to find in Southern

Town), one probably would miss it. During the day, it looks like the other buildings that surround it—automobile body repair shops and used-car lots. At night, because the bar is not very busy, the club is not much more noticeable. Most Southern Town folk do not venture into the area at night. A longtime resident and heterosexual bank vice president was not aware of the existence of the bar, although his office was just blocks away in the downtown area. The bar's existence probably depends on its low rent, muffled (zone of transition) visibility, and the ignorance of the larger community. The Reflections location is the longest continuing location for a strictly gay bar in the local area.

History of Gay Bars in Southern Town

A mixed (black-white, men-women, gay-straight) and a popular bar, the Follies, existed on the southwestern edge of town in a strip shopping center in the early and mid-1980s. The Follies advertised in the regional gay media and locally in the straight media as a "Show Place." The Follies existed simultaneously with the other gay bars that were the earlier incarnations at the current Reflections location (known as Pat's, then Images). Many informants who had been either children or adolescents during the heyday of the Follies told me that it was a legend among their peers as the butt of many jokes, yet most had not been aware of the Pat's, then Images, then Reflections venue. Perhaps the notoriety the Follies achieved relates to its show-place advertisements. Two men threw teargas into the Follies in 1983. (Once while I was at Reflections, someone lobbed a rock through the window.)

The longstanding Reflections location first became a gay bar in the early 1980s, when Pat (the woman owner) converted what had been a one-room beer and biker bar with a mural of "rats fucking on the wall and a wooden picnic table." The story of the bar's conversion is that Pat announced drunkenly at a private gay party one night that she was going to turn her bar into a gay bar. The next night some gay men and lesbians went there and, over a short time with the support of the owner, discouraged the bikers from attending. Stevie Johnson recalls this as "the night the gays took over." The name remained the same: Pat's.

A little while later, a married man whose wife reportedly knew about his sexual interest in men purchased the bar. He continued to run it as a gay bar. After him another gay man purchased it so that his male lover could manage it and have something to occupy his time. Next, another gay man who was an employee of this owner's other business took over management from the lover, renaming the bar Images. This man, David Paramore (white, forty-two), had enough money to expand from serving beer and wine to obtaining a full liquor license.

When the Follies closed, Images was there to take advantage of it. Images became very popular with the lesbians and gay men in the region during the last four years of the 1980s. African Americans and whites, women and men, frequented Images. Men reported that HIV/AIDS affected bar attendance in the region beginning around this time. Crack cocaine became a problem in Southern Town in the later part of the 1980s and among many men hanging out at Images during the early 1990s. Substance abuse was a factor in the bar's decline.(Of course, drinking was always a central feature in the social organization of the bar.) Both employee and customer involvement with crack cocaine led to pilfering, bad checks, curtailment of liquor stocks and utilities, et cetera. The Images management also told me of the difficulties of holding a client base from such a large catchment area. Something new always had to be done to draw in the people from more than an hour's drive away. People in the region became disgruntled with the declining situation at Images and switched to other regional gay bars that made the ongoing required changes and did not have the extensive problems Images was having with crack. The bar under the Images management eventually was closed. The stigma of AIDS was at least partially responsible for the demise of Images, as men quit going out as AIDS arrived on the scene and the fear set in.

Rita leased and reopened the Images location as Reflections early in 1992. When she reopened, it was a relief to some of both the African American and the white people with homoerotic interest, because it gave them a public place where they could be gay without much fear of harassment. Some told me as much. With the opening of Candy's in late 1992, the African American gay exodus from Reflections was complete, for the most part. Now the regional pull at the Reflections location seems forever lost. Some former white patrons who live in the area will not frequent Reflections and call it a "crack den." The small number of whites who patronize Reflections are disillusioned by the meager attendance by other whites, even as they express happiness about the African American exodus.

Many Reflections regulars complain about the current management in terms of high prices and lack of imagination in fostering entertainment value. I did not see how the management was making much money and wondered how, given the market in the area, more than one gay bar could exist for very long in Southern Town. In the summer of 1994, Reflections changed ownership again. The man who took it over gave the bar his first name. He put a sign out front, painted gay symbols on the inside walls, and placed condoms, AIDS information, and regional gay guidebooks around the bar.

If either Candy's or Reflections were to close, no doubt the club left open would become more racially mixed. Interracial couples tended to prefer Candy's. A few white men with cross-race sexual interests frequent Candy's, just as Otis (who is African American) frequents Reflections out of his interest in white men. There are some other points of connection between the two clubs. Drag contests are an occasion for crossing the racial boundaries between the bars: occasionally the organizers tried to involve contestants of all colors. (AIDS benefits held from time to time seemed more segregated.) Nina Holland (James Speir) began going to Candy's on occasion after she first competed in a pageant there. For many of Reflections's regulars, I was the first white man they knew who went to Candy's. Some of them occasionally followed suit, especially when Reflections would close earlier on a Friday night and they were not yet ready to stop partying. One night (early Saturday morning), as

Nina/James and Cheryl/Ben clomped around drunk in high heels, dresses, wigs, and makeup at Candy's, Cheryl/Ben explained her presence there with, "It's the only place you can get you something."

Homoerotically Interested Men in Straight Bars in Southern Town

Historically, there were other bars at which homoerotically interested men and women gathered that were not strictly gay bars. A tolerated vice (gambling, prostitution, liquor) district existed in the downtown area before and during World War II. Then, homoerotically interested and active men and women gathered clandestinely among the other patrons of a particular cocktail lounge located in a downtown hotel.

In the 1950s and 1960s, there was a downtown block that contained two prostitution and drug bars at which homoerotically interested men reportedly congregated among the demimonde. Presently there is such a scene in a cluster of bars just south of the downtown area in an African American section of town, where street prostitution and drug sales are apparent. Drag-queen prostitutes work their trade in this area, and reportedly, it is a place where people can purchase liquor and drugs and pick up men, especially after hours.

In the hiatus between the razing of the block downtown and the conversion of Pat's from a biker to a gay bar, there were predominantly white straight bars that white homoerotically interested men reportedly frequented in search of other men for sexual liaisons. According to Jerome Gordon (African American, thirty-six), the homoerotically interested African American men practiced this pattern in the straight African American bars before the advent of Candy's and concurrent with the operation of the earlier racially mixed gay bar. Men reported that they could meet another man in these bars for sex (and in some, I observed men at least trying). As Tim put it to me, "After 2:00 A.M., everyone in Southern Town is gay."

They went to straight bars between the closing of Images and its reopening as Reflections. Many gay men started hanging out at a straight bar that is most notorious among them for "trade" (ostensibly straight men who would have sex with other men). Glen, Stevie Johnson, James Speir, and Bo Hunt said that the gays started going, even dancing together there, and that this created a lot of friction at the bar. Glen said that during this time, the management tried to ferret out the gays by refusing entrance to known or "obvious gays."

One bar in Southern Town usually stays open later than the rest, and, says Rick Jones (white, twenty-six), "It's the last chance pick-up joint. And so everybody who's horny and wants to get picked up goes to the Stone Pony because there is no place else to go." People assume men in a straight bar are straight, just as people assume men in a gay bar are gay. Chrissy, the head white female impersonator in town, maintains that she cannot "make out" in a straight bar because these are "men environments." Perhaps Chrissy looks too much like a femme or a gay in such a public environment for a man to approach her. Chrissy reports very rarely having picked up a drunk straight man in a straight bar even when she was in full drag. In any event, only on occasions where a man is viewed as engaging in normative gender interaction—that is, chumming with another straight male friend or picking up a woman—will men likely garner a homosexual liaison in a straight bar. The homosexually interested man in this scene will need to follow these rules even to anticipate a sexual contact with another man. To the extent that a straight bar is a homosexual scene, it is dependent on the heterosexual assumption. Not all straight bars are so unaccommodating. In some, the management tolerates the homoerotically interested. In a neighboring town, there is a working-class bar where mostly local lesbians and gay men hang out. They are tolerated where their dollars may be needed or the management is "friendly" and occasionally homoerotically interested itself.

There are not enough gay institutions in Southern Town to provide for all the needs of its putative gay residents. The best way to find out about other gays and make connections with them in a smaller town is to be a gregarious participant in the local gay information loops.

While some see the gay community as composed only of the "out gays" (those that go to the gay bars or in most situations hold that they are gay), others in Southern Town have what I view as a rather simplistic definition of gay community. They tend to view gay community as simply the aggregate of homoerotically interested men in the area, no matter with whom they affiliate or with what population they identify themselves. That is, this view defines gay community as all homoerotically interested men (and perhaps women) bundled together, whether these individuals think of themselves as gay or not.

What is absent from this description of the gay community as simply the aggregate of people with a putative homosexual trait is an understanding of the extent to which shared interests connect these people to one another. Social life is composed of connection (and lack thereof) resulting from variously compelling (and *meaningful*) social processes and structures or domains of social life, such as gender, race, age, class, and sexuality. The possible and complex intersections of these social practices by which people may ascertain shared attributes, positions, and like-mindedness is what I mean by "community." In Southern Town, I found a variety of social supports operating among the homoerotically interested men that for the most part these men did not seem to notice or acknowledge.

Local Thinking

Chrissy (white, thirty-one), a regular at Reflections, expressed the problem of local gay organization in her endearing (although drunken) way on two subsequent weeknights in the bar. One night she proclaimed: "I love Southern Town. Southern Town has treated me good. And I am the oldest [drag queen] that is still around. We may not have a big gay community here, but we have a tight-knit one. We don't let outsiders come in here. Atlanta is just too fast. I came from a smaller town and thought that Southern Town was big."

In this instance, Chrissy sings the praises of the connections the homoerotically interested have established in Southern Town (while effectively ignoring the crevasse between whites and African American gays in Southern Town). Chrissy was talking about her friendship network, but on a subsequent night, she said that Southern Town gays could not come together as a community. Glen said it is because Southern Town is in the Bible Belt. I asked Chrissy whether, if someone threw a bomb (God forbid) in the bar and it killed some folks, it would unite people, and she said, "No, it would not."

The Importance of Being Gay

A sense of honor among the subordinated is an important shift in the formation of community. Herdt (1992, 63) writes that being gay represents "ultimate claims to social acceptance in contemporary society." In one of our taped conversations, Chrissy St. John focused on the annual Gay Pride Day in Atlanta in her definition of gay community, a focus that displays her understanding of the central role of pride in the formation of community.

Chrissy.   The gay community here is so split up. It really is. . . . The gay people here never come together. In Atlanta, I believe they have a big gay community up there.

David.   What do you mean by "gay community"? What is it?

Chrissy.   I believe the gays should stick together. I mean like . . . look at Gay Pride. They come out. They stick together.

Cultural pride or honor in homoerotic interest and community is the central element that allows some observers to reason that "the Gay Pride Day Parade more than anything symbolizes" the change from homosexual to gay cultural models in the social organization of homoerotic sexual behaviors in the contemporary United States (Herdt and Boxer 1993, 5). Although it is not often remarked on in the literature on gay identity, cultural change and identity change are related. Socialization into the gay community "requires restructuring of personhood and social surround, not just changes in cognitive category or self identity" (Herdt 1992, 32).

Formal Institutions

The formal institutions, of course, are the two bars and an organization that some gay men, women, and friends originally founded to raise money to help provide for the housing, nutrition, and transportation needs of people with HIV-related diseases. The organization that serves HIV clients in Southern Town began in 1985 when the manager of one gay bar put it together with a clique of men who were associated with the other gay bar, Images (including the owner and manager, who called themselves the League of Uptown White Women). They decided to include with their biannual camp-and-glamour drag pageants the Fall Ball and Spring Fling, two fund-raisers for the organization, thereby connecting the managements of the two bars for this purpose. AIDS has been a context for connection between homoerotically interested men in Southern Town.

Through the course of its formalization (incorporation), the organization, primarily through the changing makeup of its board of directors, became increasingly composed of health professionals and of nonhomoerotically interested incumbents of HIV at-risk populations. The organization became more bureaucratic as its meetings were moved out of the bar and to the regional state HIV clinic, which was located in town in 1991. During this transformation, allegiances to the organization also changed as many of the homoerotically interested men in town dropped their formal membership. Most of the men I talked with felt an obligation to perpetuate the original bar-oriented fundraiser but expressed estrangement from the organization itself.

Informal Institutions

The more and less formal homoerotic scenes in Southern Town are primarily social rather than political venues, but that does not mean they are not without consequences.[2] There are several informal institutions in the area that, at minimum, facilitate meeting other men. For instance, there are the car-cruising scenes, one at the Water Works park and another along the alleys and streets outside Reflections. These scenes and the interactions in them may also serve homoerotically interested men as a source of social support. The racial divide is mostly perpetuated in these scenes, as I observed and interacted with only one African American man who regularly cruised outside the white bar in his automobile. He has a sexual interest in white men exclusively. I never observed an African American man cruising the Water Works park, nor was I able to find a public cruising venue frequented by African American men— I believe this was because I was not accepted as enough of an insider to be privy to this potentially untoward information and because, as I was told by a few African American men, private house parties were the main form of developing new sexual interactions among them in the area.

Social Support

The literature on public sex venues commonly claims that such sites are predicated only on the nonverbal single-minded pursuit of sex (Delph 1978). The homosexual scenes in Southern Town do not seem nonverbal. It is true that nonverbal communication facilitates sexual contacts at these scenes. Nonverbal communication can show who is "on the game" through observations and displays. But at least as often as liaisons develop nonverbally, they come to fruition through verbal interaction.

Homoerotically interested men identify and "chat up" other men in the department store men's room (tearoom), and sometimes they arrange to go elsewhere. Regular participants in the scenes can become well established because the scenes are not that diverse in terms of the turnover of participants. (I noticed the same men repeatedly and heard often that "everybody has already slept with everybody else.") Many of the men at both Southern Town sites develop supportive social and economic and nonsexual relationships. One friendship network, the "trash" group (as it is labeled, for "alley trash" by one of its members, and for "white trash" by outsiders) centers on these scenes. Not the least significant of the functions of the socializing that goes on at these scenes is the support one might obtain for what people popularly described as a furtive and secretive life.

Johnny Finley (white, forty, married) reported to me that he thought he would go insane the other week were it not for the men at the park he could talk to. He recognizes as the "married gays" a group of the men on his "dick circuit" who share a common situation. He identifies himself as a member of that group. Johnny's dick circuits consist of cruising in his truck for homoerotically interested men at the Water Works park, outside Reflections, and around certain local motels, as well as along the main street in Southern Town whenever he can get away from work and his wife (as time out from his official social networks). The circuit could more accurately be termed a "range," as Johnny, like other men in the locale, occasionally drives up to two hours one way to visit similar venues, including gay bars and pornographic bookstores. Johnny had not in the past few years ventured into what had become Reflections bar in Southern Town. He has never been in or cruised outside the black bar. Johnny goes to the Water Works park as much to socialize with men like himself as to have sex there. He goes there simply to talk with others.

Homoerotically interested men in Southern Town exchange information in ongoing relationships with regulars about the local world as a way of establishing contact with new men. I traced the appearance of several men at the Water Works park to information they received from men they met at men's rooms in the Southern Town Mall. The verbal feature is true of other homosexual and gay scenes in town, where interactions and friendship groups develop and where all sorts of information is exchanged.

Friends and Domestic Help

Chrissy maintains a household that is a social scene for Southern Town gays and to which household members and habitues contribute. They pay rent and utilities, bring in food, liquor, furnishings, et cetera. I would in no way doubt that these helping relationships suggest the kind of solidarity and mediation of the values of the dominant community (such as kinship) that Carol Stack (1974, 124) found in "the black urban family, embedded in cooperative domestic exchange, [that] proves to be an organized, tenacious, active, lifelong network." Chrissy St. John's (white, thirty-one) own characterization of her relationship with her close friend Floyd Gilbert describes the rules of friendships that operate in the network: "We have done a lot for each other. I mean, if I've got it, he's got it. If he's got it, I've got it. So, there's nothing to worry there." Many kinds of helping relationships develop at Chrissy's, just as they do at other gay and homoerotic scenes in town (such as the bar and the Water Works park). Gil met Jason at Chrissy's and helped Jason get a job at the store where Gil is a manager. Bo Hunt, half jokingly, half seriously, refers to Chrissy's house as "The Commune." Historically, Chrissy's doors have remained open to just about everyone who wants to venture in, especially if they can contribute something (liquor, potential for sex, food, entertainment, etc.) to the maintenance of the household and party atmosphere.

There is a history of just such house scenes in Southern Town. Many men told me of Chrissy's predecessor, a drag queen named Felicia who died of complications from an HIV infection in the early 1990s. From my limited access, I conclude that the homoerotically interested African American men in Southern Town followed the house and private party tradition more completely than did the whites while I was there. I heard about quite a few parties, and I pilfered invitations to such events at Candy's occasionally. (Only two men ever invited me.) One invitation I swiped off a table at Candy's was to a party at Areanna Valle's. Areanna is the mother (head member) of the House of Valle. I was aware of a House of Valle member who came from another town to perform at Candy's and who with her entourage stayed the weekend at Areanna's. It was quite probable that Areanna's home operated among the homoerotically interested African American men in much the same kind of exclusively gay party scene and domestic network that Chrissy's place does among the whites. I have also been told of similar household scenes in other small cities and towns in the region. Such scenes are particularly important in towns where there is no gay bar. One man living in a rural area in Southern State built a cinder-block building on his property (complete with a stage, dance floor, disco lights, and full bar) in which he could have gay parties and his lover could perform drag.

Other helping relationships and party scenes exist among homoerotically interested white men in Southern Town, but they are not as prominent as those at Chrissy's and perhaps Areanna's. Besides these rather open house parties and scenes, I was aware of the existence of smaller closed parties among the homoerotically interested white men in town. Additionally, the clique of men who work for Greg Freeland's antique company also share domestic routines and socialize almost exclusively among themselves. These men regularly gave large open house parties in the past but seem to have stopped that, perhaps due in part to their growing older. Ronald Akers (white, thirty-eight) describes that earlier scene: "Well, Greg Freeland's and that house used to be—before the bars even opened, that used to be the place where everybody congregated. And that was just like the wild house. You know, like Animal Party. [Laughs.] I never got involved in a lot of that. They had orgies and everything else all the time up there. . . . I was always kind of disgusted by all that."

Few new men have emerged to fill the void. Chrissy often complained about the unwillingness of others to give large house parties and occasionally invited me to do so. To Chrissy's own chagrin sometimes, many homoerotically interested men, women, and friends refer to the household in which she lives simply as Chrissy's. There was some trouble at Chrissy's with the police because of noise and an investi- gation into some teenagers who went missing in town. Chrissy complained to me that she was singled out as the head of the household by the police. She said that every- one acts as if she was the only person living there, by referring to the household by her name. Because of the notoriety Chrissy's household received about this time, Chrissy began a not very rigorous campaign to tone down its activities. In the win- ter months of 1994, there were four official roommates sharing a two-bedroom duplex apartment, while at least three others slept there almost every night. On the week- ends, it was not rare for from one to five additional others to sleep over or pass out there.

Interactional Community

The Southern Town gay community is a word-of-mouth assortment of relatively sta- ble homoerotic settings and networks appropriated on a situational basis as gay or as homosexual cruising scenes. These are what I call gay and homosexual cultural strategies that men pursue in getting along and getting laid in Southern Town. As we have seen, the social world for homoerotically interested men in Southern Town is not formalized much in terms of public legal establishments or organizations (as are the HIV organization and the two bars). Moreover, the gay cultural features of the organization of the world require contextualization as gay meets Southern Town. If not strictly gay, there are elements that can be found therein that we now might term "gay." All this information concerning the development of community and the contextualization of gay and homosexual cultures in Southern Town illustrate the idea that community is not a unidirectional process, but an ebb and flow.

It is really access to fresh information about homoerotically interested men and activities that is at a premium in Southern Town. In large part because homoerotic interest is taboo in the status quo, a special value is placed on information about homoerotic interest and activities. Trying to find out who the homoerotically inter- ested men are, how they lead their lives in terms of their homoerotic interest, and what settings they frequent are important parts of life for men in search of both short- and longer-term relations of sexual and other types with other men who profess interest and/or (will) engage in sex with other men. Concentrated knowledge can aid the adjustments the homoerotically interested may make (Dank 1971). Others in South- ern Town can help one learn most of the things that would be helpful to know about the local world of men's homoerotic interest. Otherwise, a man would have to use trial and error. As Johnny Finley put it, he would need to know how to discern which men at the park are "dipping worms what ain't fishing." Of course, a combination of learning from others and discovery by trial and error happens in reality, but the more exposure to the former the better.

Two exemplars illustrate the service of these two modes. The first is someone like me: the somewhat knowledgeable and older man who moves to town and already has a sense of where to look and how to proceed. (The "how to proceed" to a new-comer from the big city might not be apparent unless he had given it quite a bit of forethought, as I did on my stay.) The second is the young man growing up in South-ern Town sheltered from information about homoerotic relations there (and else-where, for that matter). This young man may hear rumors among his school peers (usually a jest about the bar). His search will largely depend on his own ingenuity and may well lead him out of town. Floyd Gilbert (white, twenty-nine) sneaked an *Advocate* during a high school band trip to Atlanta and arranged from the personal advertisements in that magazine immediately following his high school graduation to move more than 1,500 miles away to another state to live with two older men with whom he had developed a correspondence. Shortly thereafter, Floyd moved back to Southern Town because the relationship he had set up through the mail did not work out.

George Spry (white, twenty-one) moved away from Southern Town to attend col-lege in Atlanta, where he resided when I talked with him. George did not know that there was a gay bar in Southern Town until I told him. Before moving to Atlanta, George had peeked at gay magazines during trips to Atlanta with his family, gleaned whatever he could about gay life from television, and otherwise did not pursue homo-erotic activities in Southern Town. George bided his time in Southern Town until he moved away to college in Atlanta, where he expected to have a gay life.

The sort of knowledge that would work to the advantage of gay men in Southern Town would be that of the bars, the parks and tearooms, the parties and households, the friendship groups and cliques; and that of how to read the highly coded personal advertisements (found on the cable television and in the daily newspaper) and the demeanor and activities of the homoerotically active and interested men in town— for instance, the argot used, sources of status among them, divisions among them, et cetera. It would be advantageous to know that many homoerotically interested men go out of town to attend gay bars, cruise men at parks and at bookstores, and so on, and to learn where those places are located. Most important would be access to the word-of-mouth networks of homoerotically interested men that exist in Southern Town.

A Networking Community

The key to getting along and getting laid in a place like Southern Town is being in the loops where men exchange information. Friends provide introductions and fix up men with other men in the region. As Andy Park (white, twenty-seven) put it, "In a small town you need to have a lot of friends." And Jack Maxwell (white, forty-four) describes a Southern Town introduction: "Met one person through Southern Town community theater that just had the guts to say: 'Are you gay?' 'Yeah.' 'Well, Friday night I'm giving a party, come, I want you to meet some people.' And from those peo-ple you meet more and you meet more and you meet more, you know. But until that first encounter, it's a lonely existence in a little small town like this."

When I asked men in Southern Town to provide advice on "getting along and getting laid" there, they most frequently told me that being friendly and honest ("not putting on airs") was of paramount consequence. (The "friendly" part was often cited as more important than good looks, money, and/or a "big dick.") Because everybody who is anybody to the sexual market of men in the locale will eventually know you, it is to your advantage to cultivate amiable relations by being as friendly and honest with everybody as possible. "Speak to everybody! Care!" says Jack Maxwell (white, forty-four). Amiable relations mean access to information about sites, sources, and men. (This is somewhat different from gay life in the big city, where there is more anonymity and first impressions based on appearances may matter quite a bit more than friendliness and veracity.)

Not only is friendly a strategy to follow in getting into the information networks, but it is also the major strategy for feeling out, recruiting, and locating new members in the homosexual marketplace. Men frequently tout face-to-face relations among men in everyday life as a major mode by which they garner sexual partners and relations in Southern Town. Since there are few ostensibly gay scenes in Southern Town, and perhaps most of the homoerotically interested men lead lives that impede attending the gay scenes that do exist, men rely on verbal and nonverbal approaches to discover others with interests similar to their own. For instance, the men cite cruising (trying to make eye contact and detect interest) around the Southern Town Mall and at straight bars in town as productive ways to meet men, even more than going to the gay bar. Randall Harris (white, thirty-five) points out that there is "more time to ogle in a small town." Charles Ericson (white, thirty) explained to me how working as a waiter kept him in the mix where he could scrutinize the range of men in town (and they him). I call this approach to getting along and getting laid in the smaller town "networking," because the "net" is the sites and sources, the structure, of the community, while "working" is the process of accessing and developing that community.

"Working" is a popular term used by homoerotically interested men in Southern Town to refer to chatting up a man to detect his level of sexual interest and cultivating others, in addition to making oneself appear interested (by cruising in a bar or a park or wearing clothing or using language indicative of interest). For instance, one could work a man seen at a store and work a park, a bar, and a bathroom. The metaphor of work conveys the seriousness of face-to-face contacts and their central place in everyday life for homoerotically interested men in Southern Town. The work of the homoerotic social role is to discover homoerotic places and people.

Two Sides of Familiarity: Scrutiny Versus Renown

Ironically, the familiarity among residents of a town the size of Southern Town is what men told me they most like about small(er) town life. This observation is confirmed by Black and Rhorer (1995). There is something reassuring, they told me, about seeing everyone in everyday life: at the stores, driving down the streets. There is a certain overlap or redundancy in contacts with others. For example, one might well come to know quite a bit about the bank teller's other roles, statuses, relationships, and habits from seeing him or her in these other situations and contexts day in and day out. There is a sense among the people of coming to know the others well.

> The people that I have known and came back, who have moved from Atlanta, say, for example, and returned, for some reason, lost, you know, the closeness of what . . . people have here. I mean people may not be real happy about it, and I don't think very many people are, but at the same time they feel a certain closeness. I mean, even the people you might not hardly even speak to, you know, that you've known for years and years and years—there's that closeness there. You know that maybe we are not the best of friends, but I could probably still tell you something or cry on your shoulder and you might would actually care. And I think maybe you lose that maybe when you move away. (Floyd Gilbert, white, twenty-nine)

Not only are there rewards that result from being so exposed to other people; there are rewards that come from being noticed too. "People are starting to recognize me around town. I feel a part," Scott Hutto (white Hispanic, twenty-six) told me.

Density and Friendships: Levels of Acceptance

One consequence of the everyday redundancy and density of social contacts in Southern Town ("tight-knit" is a popular local term) is the formation of friendships. Associations happen quickly. It will not be months or weeks before one sees a given person again. One will likely see that person again tomorrow. Many, like Jack Maxwell (white, forty-four), say that in a smaller town these are "deeper friendships, longer-lasting friendships."

In lower Manhattan, there is something like a gay city the size of Southern Town and with a much larger gay population. Interaction can be quite dense among those who live and work in Greenwich Village (see Levine 1992). There is a microcosm of interaction there in the gay ghetto, and the familiarity resulting from that can be pleasurable. There are also more gays to interact with inside the gay ghettos. Because of the small numbers in Southern Town, though, there is not a plethora from which to choose. The tendency is to accept what is there. Ronald Akers (white, thirty-eight) describes the gay party scene at Max Freeland's house and in the process the adjustment to difficulties between the gay men (and the tolerance of friends in general):

Ronald. Everybody . . . kind of hung around together. Everybody was like—friends were friends. . . . I don't guess we really did have, like, differing groups. You know? It was just like everybody hung around everybody, and everybody talked about everybody, and talked about everybody's trash. You know. But yet we all kind of liked each other, but . . . talked about each other . . . well, behind your back. That's the way people were. But then you really liked them, regardless of what they did.

David. Why?

Ronald. I don't know. Because . . . they were friends. Assholes, but they's friends.

David. Why would you have assholes for friends?

Ronald. All of my friends that I have ever had have been assholes. I've never had a friend who . . . wasn't an asshole, to be honest with you.

David. Really?

Ronnie. Yeah. And I'm probably an asshole too.

Tolerance under Scrutiny

I wondered why the owner of Reflections tolerated in her bar the man who is so often hyped on crack until I found out that they work together during the day in close quarters in the same store. She has worked there and known him longer than she has had the bar. If she banned him from the bar, she would have to deal even further with his resentment and acting out (which is volatile) during her daytime job. It is within the context of familiarity that "being friendly" assumes paramount importance over appearance ("looks") and economic resources in terms of getting along. Although the renown the individual can incur can be a source of pleasure, the scrutiny that comes with the familiarity can prove troublesome. Everyday scrutiny is such that I could feel the watchful eyes of others whenever I went into a restaurant in town. Rules of conduct seem pregnant with significance in such dense watchfulness. For instance, the expectation that I defer to my elders was ever present in ways that I have never experienced in, for instance, New York City. One can become too big a fish in the fishbowl of Southern Town.

Affinities?

There is not an institutionally complete gay community in Southern Town. There are a few formal and informal institutions for meeting other homoerotically interested men in the Southern Town area. The less formal ones are really friendship networks that provide a variety of support and information. Some are domestic networks, like those centered on Chrissy's house, where there are clear material exchanges. All such sites are places where men congregate and share things besides the possibility of same-genital acts. These scenes are consequential for their impact on the way homoerotically interested activities take place in Southern Town. Again, there appears to be more supportive relationships among the homoerotically interested in Southern Town than the men involved actually notice (while the tensions they note between them do exist).

These relationships contain cultural elements, such as a distinctive argot, that indicate mutual feelings of belonging and help to assuage feelings of negative self-worth. It is evident in examining life for homoerotically interested and active men in Southern Town that some of these men believe that they share a common situation and have common feelings (reactions to the situation). In that sense there is community. Because the organization of homoerotic life occurs rather informally by word of mouth, the community in Southern Town is a social networking organization in which elements of the gay culture are deployed and developed.

There does not seem to be much in the way of a common orientation of action toward the collective pursuit of economic, political and social advantages (Neuwirth 1969), a Weberian definition of community. What is gay is in Southern Town partly relative to its local appearance. Ronald Ingram (African American, thirty-nine) had the following to say about gay as a cultural trajectory for African Americans in Southern Town:

> I've noticed also that . . . when it comes to the black and white situation, most white guys are very open with it. They're more open. It's more open and it's more accepted in the white community. And I don't know why that is. . . . People would think that maybe it's that way because . . . the white society is more open and more educated on the subject . . . and the blacks are still very conservative and thinking, "Ooh, . . . God's gonna punish you . . . something bad's going to happen to you." . . . A black man is supposed to be a man. And a woman is supposed to be a woman. It's okay . . . for lesbians or it's okay for two women to love each other. But for two men? Oh no. And a black man? Uh-uh. [No.] He is supposed to be a man. He is supposed to . . . because there's . . . not that many black men left, . . . most of them are dead or in prison. So the ones that are out there, it's "shame on you for being gay." You're not thought of as being a man. You are something less than a man.

I need more data to know the extent to which homoerotically interested African American men in Southern Town embrace gay culture. Still, Jerome Gordon (African American, thirty-six) feels that "it is more acceptable in the white life than it is blacks. For a long time, though, I thought that it was basically a white thing because you never did see many blacks. Even when you went to the clubs, you didn't see too many blacks there, maybe one or two."

Yet the fact that there is an identifiable African American gay bar in the town may be an indication of the movement of black thinking in a gay direction. The existence of the bar is more certainly attributable to the racism and segregation in Southern Town. Bob Stadtler (white, thirty-five), who spent his three-year tenure in Southern Town socializing almost exclusively with homoerotically interested African American men, reasons that movement in a gay direction among them can be attributed, first, to HIV/AIDS forcing them to look to each other for support and, second, to the burgeoning of gay culture and visibility itself, which has been able through its flowering to incorporate some of the margins.

The term "gay" in Southern Town was most frequently used interchangeably with "homosexual" but substituted as being more current and less derogatory terminology.

Though men sometimes embrace the term "gay" as self-description, they seldom explicitly recognize gay as a cultural status and strategy. While they are more or less aware of the gay culture and use the words to describe themselves, their actual sexual lives are unique to the local situation. "Gay" in the sense of a homoerotically interested man who is neither ashamed nor secretive exists in Southern Town, if rarely baldly articulated. A sense of gay pride radiates along personal social networks. This is how gay culture is transmitted, rather than through the mass media. It is perhaps a slower but more personal dissemination that may have more sustained effects. The Southern Town situation makes it clear that pursuit of gay interests advance incrementally in everyday life, situation by situation, person to person, and one social network at a time. The situations in Southern Town and Atlanta also make it clear that the homoerotically interested (at least in the region) have constructed a round of activities and structures that can meet their leisure needs and advance their interests in an evolutionary manner. Such a community does not require their full commitment. This community, like many ethnic communities in the United States, is one of "limited liability" (Suttles 1972).

Notes

1. Pseudonyms for actual people and places are used in this essay to protect the confidential relations that I agreed to in conducting this study.

2. A distinction between social and political involvement in gay community is one that Kippax et al. (1990) use in their Australia-based study to contrast nonmetropolitan with metropolitan men who have sex with men. Those outside the cities tend to avoid gay political involvement even more than those inside.

Works Cited

Applebome, Peter. 1994. "In Selma, Everything and Nothing Changed." *New York Times*, 2 August, A1, A12.

Black, Kate, and Marc Rhorer. 1995. "Out in the Mountains: Exploring Lesbian and Gay Lives." *Journal of the Appalachian Studies Association* 7: 18–28.

Dank, Barry. 1971. "Coming Out in the Gay World." *Psychiatry* 34: 180–197.

Delph, Edward. 1978. *The Silent Community: Public Homosexual Encounters.* Beverly Hills: Sage.

Gagnon, John, and William Simon. 1973. *Sexual Conduct—The Social Sources of Human Sexuality.* Chicago: Aldine.

Harry, Joseph, and William DeVall. 1978. *The Social Organization of Gay Males.* New York: Praeger.

Herdt, Gilbert. 1992. "Introduction: Culture, History, and the Life Course of Gay Men." In *Gay Culture in America: Essays from the Field,* ed. Gilbert Herdt. Boston: Beacon.

Herdt, Gilbert, and Andrew Boxer. 1993. *Children of Horizons: How Gay and Lesbian Teens Are Leading the Way out of the Closet.* Boston: Beacon.

Kippax, S., J. Crawford, R. W. Connell, G. W. Dowsett, L. Watson, P. Rodden, D. Baxter, and R. Berg. 1990. "The Importance of Gay Community in the Prevention of HIV Transmission."

Social Aspects of the Prevention of AIDS Study. Sydney: Macquarie University (Social Aspects of the Prevention of AIDS Project).

Levine, Martin. 1992. "The Life and Death of Gay Clones." In *Gay Culture in America: Essays from the Field*, ed. Gilbert Herdt. Boston: Beacon.

Neuwirth, Gertrud. 1969. "A Weberian Outline of a Theory of Community: Its Application to the 'Dark Ghetto.'" *British Journal of Sociology* 20: 148–163.

Stack, Carol. 1974. *All Out Kin: Strategies for Survival in the Black Community*. New York: Harper and Row.

Suttles, Gerald. 1972. *The Social Construction of Communities*. Chicago: University of Chicago Press.

Whittier, David. 1997. "Social Conflict among 'Gay' Men in a Small(er) Southern Town." *Journal of Gay and Lesbian Social Services* 7, 3 (1997): 53–71. (Also found in *Rural Gays and Lesbians: Building on the Strengths of Communities*, ed. James Donald Smith and Ronald J. Mancoske. Binghamton, N.Y.: Harrington Park, 1997.)

———. 1995. *Gay Life in a Southern Town: The Social Organization of Male Homosexualities Outside the "Gay Ghetto."* Ph.D. diss., State University of New York at Stony Brook.

Part II

Striking Out/
Striking Back

Bonnie R. Strickland

Leaving the Confederate Closet

Some forty years ago, I joined the great migration north. The Ohio State University clinical psychology program was already into affirmative action. The faculty had to assume that a kid named Bonnie Ruth from a school only slightly more imaginative than its name, Alabama College, was African American. Ohio State had a good record of graduating black scholars and scientists, but I was neither. In fact, I was probably the first person from the Deep South that most of the faculty and students had ever met. Of course, I had never met any Yankees either. If the program was committed to diversity, they found it in me, although I wasn't exactly what they had in mind. But then, I'm beginning to think I never was what others expected. And I usually don't know what to expect of myself.

I still have two memorable items that I took on that journey, a book, *Clods of Southern Earth* by Don West, and a small Confederate flag that I keep on my desk at home. I don't know why I have the flag where I can see it every day. Perhaps it simply reminds me of where I came from and where I could return. But I suspect that the reasons aren't that simple and are as complex as the southern culture that spawned me. The flag reminds me of growing up in a South that was torn across boundaries of black and white, male and female, pride and shame, hospitality and hate. Raised in a southern city (Birmingham, Alabama), distinguished still by the vehemence of its violence and the "Redneck Riviera" of the panhandle of Florida, how did I find my way to the urbane, sophisticated, gentle Pioneer Valley of Massachusetts? The first of my family to go to college, how did I become a professor in a five-college system at a major university? Reared in racism, prone to violence, and steeped in religion, how did I join a scholarly world dedicated to humane values and the freedom of ideas? Immersed in an extended family of more cousins than I could count, what prepared me to read and write and study alone among the Yankees of whom I had

An earlier version of this essay appeared in Beverly Greene's *Ethnic and Cultural Diversity among Lesbians and Gay Men* (Sage, 1997), pp. 39–62, copyright © 1997 by Bonnie Strickland. Reprinted by permission of Sage Publications, Inc.

always been suspicious? Most of all, how did the dark secret of being different, of crossing sexualities and loyalties and sin and salvation, shape my life? On this snowy winter morning in New England, with a Confederate flag on my desk, how did I come to be half a century, two thousand miles, and 40 degrees from home?

Ask a southerner what time it is and you will be told how to build a clock. We are storytellers reaching, perhaps, too far into the past to inform the present. We grow up with a powerful sense of place, living on the land with fierce loyalties to family. So this is my story, telling it the best I can about my life as a southerner and a lesbian.

Both my mother's and father's forebears were predominantly English debtors and prisoners who sailed to the southern United States on the condition that they would never return to England. My forefamilies never lingered in the gracious coastal cities but rather seized the great southeastern frontier, confiscating the inland Appalachians from the Cherokees, the red clay of Georgia from the Creeks, and the sandy shores of southern Alabama and Florida from the Seminoles. Escaping the tyranny of one government, they replaced it with another—their own, which included eventually mobilizing an army to defend their independence.

I will not argue the true causes and consequences of the Civil War (I certainly never learned them in the Alabama history that I was required to study as a schoolgirl). I will simply note that I was raised in a land still bitter over losing the "War of Northern Aggression," humiliated at having been occupied by foreign troops, and unwilling to forgive a faraway federal government remembered primarily for the savagery of its rampage across a rural landscape and the rampant corruption of Reconstruction. Although I grew up during World War II, the War between the States was more real to me than the fighting in Asia or Europe. I saved my Confederate money; I knew of the daring horseback escape of my great-great-uncle after he was captured by Yankee soldiers. I remember my daddy, drunk and crying, telling me about my great-granddaddy being wounded by a rifle ball as he knelt for a drink of water from a creek at Chickamauga. I hated Yankees with a passion that left all other minority people models of trust and compassion. Living in a totally segregated society, I had little personal contact with black citizens. I did have a large number of Jewish friends and finally met a Catholic when I was a high school junior. To my knowledge, I never knew a Republican—nor did I want to.

My mother was the twelfth of thirteen children in a family that made a living from the Apalachicola River. Her father ran a general store but spent most of his time on the river with my uncles cutting cypress logs, cultivating Tupelo honey, and making illegal whiskey. If there was any law in those swamps, it was enforced by my grandfather, an undertaking that eventually led to his being jailed for murder along with one of my uncles. Death and violence were a natural part of living on this frontier, not the ferocity of alligators and snakes in the swamps, or the panthers and bears on the shores, but the accidental human cruelties of gunshot wounds and burns from open fires. Once I counted close to fifteen violent deaths that occurred in my extended Florida family—mostly from shotgun wounds and drowning. My father, the second of three sons, lived in the community eventually made famous by Fannie Flagg in *Fried Green Tomatoes at the Whistle Stop Café*. It was a typical railroad family: my grandfather worked on the trains, and his sons were expected to do the same. Typical, as well, was the fact that my grandmother suffered from "nervous breakdowns." In the South, we seldom ask which side of the family is mentally ill; we simply compete as to whose is the most crazy. My father's family easily won this one. My grandmother's episodes were characterized by her tearing off her clothes and running through the neighborhood in a frenzy. She would be hauled off to the asylum until she calmed down and then returned to the family.

My mother met my father at a party in Birmingham in l934 during the depths of the Great Depression. It was love at first sight; they married within three weeks, and my twenty-four-year-old father took his eighteen-year-old bride to live with his family. My grandmother, already taking care of four grown men, didn't particularly welcome the woman who had seduced her second son. In fact, at one point, my mother woke to find my grandmother standing over her bed with a knife. Their rather ambivalent relationship resolved somewhat as my mother joined my grandmother in cleaning, cooking, and assuming her role as a caretaker for men. When my mother became pregnant with me, my grandmother asked that if I were a girl, I be named for her. She died two months before I was born, but my middle name is Ruth as she requested.

As my mother approaches her eighty-fourth year, my birth and her labor with me increase in duration in her remembrance. She now maintains that I was in the birth canal for thirty-seven hours. If she lives to be a hundred, her span of labor will exceed all known medical history. My mother says that finally the doctor told the waiting family that he could save one or the other of us but not both. Naturally, they chose her; the physician delivered me with forceps and handed me, misshapen and not breathing, to a waiting nurse. Using the highest technology of l936, she first dipped me in cold water and then in hot (or vice versa). I began to cry, no surprise under those conditions, and have been generally healthy ever since.

My mother maintains that my daddy was set on a boy and that he had no intention of taking a girl child home from the hospital. With great concern, she asked him how he felt about having a girl. He was holding me and looking down at my crooked head and the port wine stains on my face. He announced happily that he had no idea that I would be "so pretty." I was my father's child from that day on. My brother was born four years later, but my father had evidently forgotten his wish for a boy. According to my mother, he did not even go to the hospital to see his namesake. The ardor of their love at first sight had quickly cooled when they took a second look. Their fights were stormy, and my mother regularly left my father and returned to Florida. Thus began my trips between the river swamps of my mother's family and the streets of Birmingham with my daddy.

Growing up in the panhandle of Florida was a young boy's dream. Life was noisy and active and outdoors. I had cousins of every age—lap babies, yard babies, teenagers, and grownups. We were all happily parented by innumerable aunts, uncles, and grandparents. My great-grandfather had run off with his pregnant wife's sister, and my grandmother was the first progeny of this union. This seemed to begin (or extend) a family tradition in which the men were always philandering and the women coming home with extra babies. We never quite knew who belonged to whom, but since we were all welcomed and well loved, it didn't seem to matter.

When I visited Florida, I stayed at my grandparents' home close to the Apalachicola River, which drains hundreds of square miles of swampland and empties into the Gulf of Mexico. The house, probably built in the late 1800s, had a dogtrot—a wide hall running through the middle from the sandy, swept front yard to the outside pump and smokehouse in the back. There was no electricity or indoor plumbing, and I still remember the chilly outhouse on winter mornings, baths in a #2 washtub at the pump, and the metallic taste of water from the dipper in a basin next to the kitchen door. I also remember alternately cuddling and kicking various cousins as we giggled and finally fell asleep stacked in bed head to foot. Before dawn, we'd often jump in the back of my Uncle Jennings's pickup truck to go grubbing for fish bait. He'd find a field of scrub pine and palmetto, drive a stob into the ground, and rub another stick over it. We would run around picking up the worms that came to the surface, drop them into old tin cans, and deliver them by early morning to the bait stores.

The family grew most of its food. With my cousins, I slopped the hogs, fed the chickens, and even learned to wring a chicken's neck, a not particularly useful talent for these days. We had cows for milk and beef, and meat was supplemented with wild game, including turkey, boar, deer, squirrel, and coon. Of course, we always had freshwater fish and occasionally alligator meat and turtles. When we didn't eat it fresh, the meat was cured in the smokehouse, which also held the gator skins that Uncle Jennings poached. Some nights a cousin and I, with lights on our heads, would float the swamp banks looking for frogs, gigging them when we would catch their eyes in our lights. We skipped the gators, with eyes spaced too far apart to be those of a friendly frog.

At times, some aunt or uncle would drive as many cousins as were around the few miles to the Gulf. We would scamper through the freshwater bays feeling for oysters with our bare feet or float facedown looking for scallops. But the times I remember the best were the long, lazy summer days I spent alone in a flat-bottomed bateau with a rifle. I'd walk down a sandy road that led to the landing, picking blackberries along the way. I'd throw some bait and a fishing pole in the boat but would mostly float with my fantasies. I'd watch the sun slant through the Spanish moss, lighting the dust motes in the water so that they danced like golden flakes. Jesus bugs walked silently on the water, bees swarmed around bright blossoms, cranes and herons scattered through the palmetto bush, and lazy turtles sunned themselves on fallen logs. I knew every slough and waterway and daydreamed that the cypress knees and Tupelo trees were ornamental hedges on the liquid lawn of the house that I would eventually build. All of my uncles built their homes near the river, and I assumed that I would do the same. Like them, I would live off the land—well, at least the water.

Life in the city of Birmingham was very different. My brother and I were the only grandchildren in a family of men. My grandfather cooked holiday meals; my father and his brothers would take us downtown or to watch them play baseball. We would go to the train yards, where I would be hoisted into the engine to blow the whistle. Uncle John also read important books to me and let me read to him. We produced our own plays, and he let me have the best parts. We had electricity and a radio, and it was at their home that I heard about the attack on Pearl Harbor. Although the men had only finished high school, they read books and seemed to have a sense of wonder about the world—perhaps their attempt to escape the trains that they rode back and forth between the yards of Birmingham and the small-town stations of Alabama.

Growing up in the South, I came to know any number of interesting and benignly eccentric folks who might now be called gay or lesbian. In the 1940s, however, the term "lesbian" was reserved for a minor Greek poet, and few of us were reading the classics. When World War II began, eager to reclaim military honor, southern boys, black and white, joined up in vast numbers, although they were not particularly eager to share their barracks and bunkers with Yankees, Republicans, gay men, or each other. southern girls had little to do but plant victory gardens, sleep safely protected from invasion, and dream of the boys who would be coming home. My dreams were also of the war hero, but it was me, easily vanquishing the enemy and returning in triumph to the breathlessly waiting southern belles. I think that I always knew that I preferred girls as my romantic interests. At age six when I began first grade, I promptly fell in love with my teacher, a woman, and I have been enthusiastically returning to school every September for more than fifty years.

The fall I entered the third grade (I skipped the second and have always wondered about that teacher), my mother left my father for good. We moved to the south side of the steel mills across the street from a public park with tennis courts and a library. The librarian, as attentive and attractive as my teachers, told me that "books were my friends" and gave me my first paying job, assisting her. My other neighborhood institution, the Southern Baptist Church, was continually committed to saving and keeping me from sin through innumerable meetings and organizations. I was a Sunbeam and a G.A. (member of the Girl's Auxiliary), although I would have much preferred to be an R.A. (a member of the Royal Ambassadors—the equivalent group for boys). I attended Sunday-morning and -evening worship, Wednesday-night prayer meetings, the Baptist Training Union, Vacation Bible School, and church camp. I was also quite taken with becoming a missionary and traveling around the world to save the heathen. I had no idea why the heathen would want to become Southern Baptists, but I liked the idea of traveling.

In spite of the best efforts of the church, I still found time to sin. I cheated on Bible drills, beat up my little brother, and lusted in my heart after other girls. Although I had no experiences of the flesh, I surely wished for some. I searched the Scriptures for anything I could find on sin and sexuality, especially homosexuality. Much was made of "Men shouldn't lie with men," but I thought this meant that guys weren't supposed to sleep in the same bed together. The Bible was a little weak on women except that Ruth could forsake all others and live with Naomi. I did get the distinct impression that every kind of sexuality, whether of the spirit or the flesh, was sinful, and I resigned myself to everlasting hell. This in spite of the fact that the whole of my rather limited sexual activity was having been fondled by a church deacon and the man who ran our neighborhood dry cleaners.

My mother tried in vain to curl my hair and dress me in frilly clothes, a struggle that succeeded only for some best forgotten piano recitals. Boys had all the fun and wouldn't be caught dead in a dress, an attitude I fully endorsed. While I couldn't change my physical sex, I could at least act, think, feel, and pretend that I was a boy. Boys were my preferred playmates, colleagues in adventure, and best friends. Girls were rather exotic creatures who needed to be pampered, protected, and impressed.

My boyish competition knew no bounds. I spent hours in the backyard pounding a leather punching bag, shooting basketball hoops, and methodically hitting a tennis ball back and forth against the house. I learned to box and played war games in the hot summer evenings after supper, never distracted by television because there was none. My mother worked from eleven in the morning till eleven at night, so my brother and I were mostly on our own. I was supposed to do the grocery shopping and cooking, but I would usually show up at a neighbor's at suppertime, little brother in tow. Southerners invariably want you to eat with them, and my brother and I gave them opportunity to bring new meaning to the word "hospitality." One neighbor also taught me to play tennis on the park courts. I eventually was nationally ranked and won a state title at Birmingham's most prestigious country club. My mother, having heard me practicing the piano for years, knew immediately that tennis was a better investment and paid for lessons from the club pro.

Perhaps in contrast to most southern boys, I also enjoyed school and found another avenue of competition. I struggled to be the best in class, whether through grades, spelling bees, drama, poetry reading, or essay writing. At home, I built crystal radios and brewed rather exotic explosive concoctions with my chemistry set, detonating them in the backyard. No doubt in my attempts at science, I was rapidly becoming a public menace. I gave up looking to the heavens for God and decided to become an astrophysicist instead of a missionary, exploring the planets instead of people's souls. Actually, I would have preferred to be an astronaut, but they existed only in science fiction. School and books and science gave me a potential escape from what I perceived as the dreary world of my hard-working parents. My mother was a cocktail waitress, for a time in a gay bar, and my father a brakeman on the trains. I yearned for a life beyond the soot of the steel mills and the sludge of the swamps, picturing myself a medical scientist in a clean white lab coat finding a cure for cancer, or an astronomer discovering a new star. But I knew in my heart that the closest I would ever get to the stars was in a sports arena. I thought about a career in professional tennis, especially after another kid from the South, Althea Gibson, became the first African American to win at Wimbledon. I knew I could join the military like my cousins and other poor southerners, black and white, but girls were more likely to be military wives than soldiers, and I couldn't picture that as my path to philosophy, poetry, and science, or to other women. Higher education was a completely foreign concept to me. I didn't know anyone who had ever gone to college except librarians and schoolteachers.

My Uncle John seemed to be one who had been able to cross boundaries and bring diverse worlds together, although at some cost. Uncle John had been drafted at the beginning of World War II. The family thought he was fighting in Europe when we learned that in basic training, he had taken his rifle apart and refused to put it together again. He further refused to talk to anyone. The army resolved this dilemma by pronouncing him paranoid schizophrenic and sending him home to the V.A. hospital in Alabama. On one of his visits to my grandfather's home, my mother invited him to come over and see us sometime. The next day, he packed an old metal suitcase, walked across town, and moved in with us. I don't think this is exactly what my mother had in mind, although she was always inviting people to come live with us. At that time, my cousin Charles from Florida was staying with us and attending public schools in Birmingham. Uncle John simply joined the long parade of cousins, aunts, uncles, housekeepers, friends, and neighbors who were part of my immediate family from time to time.

Uncle John was with us for a few glorious weeks. He made me a gift of his baseball shoes, which I still have, showing me how to clean the cleats and various other baseball intricacies known only to the initiated. Uncle John often thought himself to be the manager of the New York Yankees—they were always winning then—and considered me another budding baseball star, conveniently ignoring the fact that I was a girl. He would also sit at a cardtable on the front porch and write long letters to the president of the United States. If Uncle John could direct the president as to how to run the country, I had no doubt that he could turn me into a major sports figure. This happy state of affairs lasted until one evening when my cousin Charles didn't come home for supper. Close to midnight, my mother found Charles hiding. He explained that Uncle John had threatened to bash his brains in and boil them in a dishpan for supper. Charles decided to avoid the evening meal, and mother decided that Uncle John needed to go back to the hospital.

Losing Uncle John interrupted my baseball training, and about that time my mother embarked on her efforts to discover and/or develop some sense of femininity in me. She thought I should bathe and wash my hair more often. For a while, she tried to model glamour, describing the proper use of cosmetics and constantly asking me if her face powder were caked. How would I know? I could easily calibrate the ratio of oil to gas for a two-cycle engine but had absolutely no idea of how to apply powder and lipstick, nor did I want to learn. One of the most fearful moments of my generally fearless life was a time when I had to deliver a telephone message to my mother who was under the hair dryer in a neighborhood beauty parlor. I still remember the feeling of panic as I opened the door, an illegal alien entering a woman's world.

My mother was particularly distressed when I was named center on the ninety-pound YMCA boys' football team; she renewed her attempts at a sex change—mine.

She announced that I could no longer play with the boys in the park. Actually, she would have been thrilled if I "played" with boys the way most girls did, the shy giggles, the flirting, the flattery. But my play was the rough-and-tumble touching of young males still more interested in physical contact than sexual innuendo. I sat on the steps of our front porch looking across the street to the park, a familiar but now distant shore to which I could not return. Hurt and helpless, all boyish bravado vanished, I sobbed like the sissy girl my mother wanted me to be.

As my lucky life would have it, however, I found a grownup women's softball team with lots of folks who looked like me. The women, most of whom worked in the mills, cross-dressed and were as good at brawling as they were at softball. Because I already knew how to play ball, I enthusiastically applied myself to a new endeavor, fighting. Skilled in boxing, I now learned more specific techniques of bare-fisted combat—keys between fingers, well-placed knees, and so on. Like most southern boys my age, I learned to cover any feelings of fear and affect a fierceness that I actually came to enjoy. Physical competition was clear to me; I understood the dictates of brute strength and could gauge the caliber of my opponents, including the police who were often called to break up our softball fights. I knew the thrill of contact and the benefits of cease-fire. Indeed, the long-term physical abuse that I visited on my little brother ended abruptly one day when he flexed his muscles and slammed me through a door. No parental interference, no psychotherapy and/or mediation, just immediate conflict resolution and simple justice through one well-placed punch. I knew how to hit people, but I didn't know how to hug them.

My sullen, silent conflict with my mother continued. I begged her to let me leave home and live somewhere else. She suggested the girls' reformatory but, barring that, insisted that I stay with her until I graduated from high school. I pleaded to live with my father, who had remarried. My brother and I met him weekly in downtown Birmingham. We would walk through the streets, the change jingling in his pockets, and visit the dime stores to look at the toys. Before we got on the bus to go home, we would have a banana split at Lane's drugstore. I don't think he ever knew how much those visits meant to me or how much I adored my stepmother. At one point, it was arranged that I might move in with them, a plan that crashed around me when my stepmother thought it better that I didn't live with my father. She could tolerate his drinking and womanizing, but she didn't think that I should have to. I escaped to softball where my teammates appreciated and applauded my athletic skills, and to high school where my interests were girls, sports, and cars, in that order. I dated boys from school, and although we were too shy to talk about girls, we spent long hours working on cars, discussing high school football and our beloved minor league baseball team, the Birmingham Barons.

Another resource for me was that eternal lesbian savior, the gym teacher. Louise Pope happened to be straight but took a special interest in me and how well I did in school. When I barely missed being inducted into the National Honor Society, she went roaring into the principal's office to demand an explanation. Aside from Uncle John, no one else had ever seemed that interested in my grades. Mrs. Pope changed my life. Although I had no plans or money for college, she simply applied to her old school for me. I signed the applications enthusiastically when I received a physical education scholarship, which she arranged, and realized that I would be attending an all-women's college.

The day I graduated from high school, I left home and rented a room in north Birmingham so I could take a summer job at what we would now call an inner-city public swimming pool. Here again I had other run-ins with the police, as my new friends at the pool were being constantly interrogated about their assaults, shoplifting, and various other questionable adventures. One guy I dated for a while, Pete, was convicted of vehicular homicide and statutory rape (not with me). A few years later, I visited him at the state penitentiary, grateful but confused that he was behind the brick walls of the prison while I strolled the brick walks of Alabama College.

Attending college meant coming home to a loving family. My first weekend, I was invited to a Baptist Student Uunion retreat that was held at the campus lake house and developed my first college crush on a prayer date. Then one of the seniors tucked me into bed, leaned over, and kissed me goodnight (although only on the forehead), a completely new and joyous event for me. I happily settled into a warm world where I was financially independent and well taken care of emotionally. Scholarships and a job waiting on tables gave me funds to cover my tuition, fees, room and board, health care, and laundry. During the summers, I lived on campus while I worked as a lifeguard and taught swimming at the town creek. I had a paper route and delivered movie announcements for the local theater. I never returned to my mother's home. I had found a new family of women that satisfied my every longing; I would stay in school the rest of my life.

Surrounded by women students and women faculty, it never occurred to me that men were necessary or useful in the life of the college. We ran our student government (I was elected recreational director), wrote and produced our own plays, dissected cadavers, learned opera, and generally completed the usual academic requirements and extracurricular activities with a sense of self-sufficiency and pride. My junior year, I was devastated to learn that my school would become coeducational to increase enrollments and avoid financial disaster; I preferred bankruptcy.

The addition of men to the student body threw my college life into disarray. I now had to compete with men for a woman's time, and I was no longer cast as the male romantic lead in our theatrical productions. I tried dating some of the male jocks. We hiked the hills around the college, swam the creeks, and explored caves and the old mines that had played out years before. Once, on an outdoor adventure, as we were about to stumble on an illegal still, a bearded man with a shotgun blocked our path. We quickly decided on another direction—one of the few times that I was delighted to be with a guy instead of a girl.

In college, I discovered women, reading, and writing, in that order. In the South, one does not admit to being intellectually inclined, nor did I ever discuss my divergent sexual patterns. I did spend a great deal of time wondering in what ways I was similar to and/or different from others. I was comforted by the fact that southerners are actually very good about accepting the peculiarities of family members, friends, and people they like. As far as I could tell, most unusual activities on the part of people I knew personally didn't seem to get them into too much trouble, except for my Uncle John who kept being carted off to the hospital and my Uncle Cliff who was killed by a tax revenue agent. Still, I was increasingly curious about how someone comes to be the person she or he is, especially me. I gave up my earlier questions about the faraway worlds of stars and galaxies and began to wonder about people rather than planets. Sports also became less precious to me. My physical education classes were fun, but classes in campcraft gave me no clues as to why my grandmother became psychotic, fly casting no hints as to whether families needed fathers. Volleyball and synchronized swimming taught me something about getting along with others but little of the dynamics of interpersonal interactions.

Physical education majors didn't usually go on to graduate school but the two faculty (50 percent female) in our Philosophy, Psychology, and Religion Department encouraged me to pursue psychology and apply to graduate school. Professor Herb Eber, whom I had met on the tennis courts, convinced me that a year in graduate school might not be as much fun as coaching high school sports but would be a chance to travel, and a year of adventure in a foreign culture. I had never been farther north than Tennessee. Once again, a teacher filled out the applications for me. Professor Eber assured me that assistantship support would match the full-time salary that I would receive teaching physical education. He also assured me that I could always return south if I didn't like psychology and living with Yankees. The idea of four more years of school was compelling, even if I had to move north. At that time, I didn't realize that the further one went in school, the fewer women one encountered, as either teachers or students.

Attending the clinical psychology program of the Ohio State University was another dream come true. I was in classes with famous faculty, and the university was a premier football and basketball powerhouse. Jules Rotter and I played tennis, and he supported me on a research assistantship. These were the heady early days of research on locus of control and need for approval. Graduate students were expected to involve themselves immediately in research and to aim for an academic position. Further, the Ohio State clinical program, especially through Rotter's efforts, prided itself on the diversity of its students and its large proportion of women. Surrounded by Yankees and Republicans and fitting no known minority category, I immediately found a black southern woman to room with. We both had double names, spoke the same language, and ate the same food. I only felt discriminated against once, when Rotter denounced the hundred thousand "noodle heads," which included me, that filled the football stadium every Saturday afternoon.

Having been in school for nineteen of my twenty-five years and having received my Ph.D., I was now faced with another life dilemma. I could remain in school by changing majors once again or by finding a job in academia. A faculty position in clinical psychology was clearly tempting. As a teacher in psychology, I could spend my life reading, writing, and talking about human behavior. Perhaps I could finally learn why my Uncle John had become schizophrenic and whether I would as well. I was troubled, however, that being lesbian had already marked me as mentally ill, and I was distressed that clinical psychology seemed to designate any number of differences as disorders and deficiencies. While not quite diagnosable, being a woman was no big help either. I was considered for faculty positions at several major universities only to be told that although my record was very good, they had decided to hire a *man* instead. Little did they know that they could have hired me and never noticed the difference. Professor Rotter finally found me a job at Emory University. I welcomed the chance to return south, where I reverted to my first language and could stay outdoors all year.

My public and private lives were distinct and disconnected in my early years in Atlanta. The suburban manicured elegance of the university with its well-mannered students was a far cry from the noisy downtown streets where demonstrations, predominantly by black protestors, launched the civil rights movement. I longed for another kind of integration that merged the classroom with the lessons of the streets; I didn't realize until much later how torn I felt about the lack of integration of my professional and personal lives. My teaching, research, and clinical practice never overlapped with my social world of playing on yet another women's softball team and partying with my predominantly lesbian friends and lovers. With few exceptions, my work colleagues and close women friends never met. My partner's picture was *not* on my office desk, and my friends preferred the sports pages over my research articles. I attended faculty events with handsome, charming gay men who were judged by my colleagues to be high-quality husband potential. My faculty, like my family, was happily matchmaking, benignly indifferent to the fact that I would rather have a wife than be one.

Atlanta was a mecca for gay men and lesbians, although the term "lesbian" was never used, and "dyke" was an expression of contempt. The big city of Atlanta offered large closets of opportunities for gays and lesbians from all over the South. It was not only the center of the civil rights movement but home to a homosexual population whose members never considered taking their concerns into the streets. I fell in love, dated, and became friends, usually in that order, with a large circle of lesbians. We remain close friends to this day.

This social group has been together and expanding for almost forty years. A woman falls in love with someone new and after a few months of bickering with her ex, and the rest of us, rejoins us with her new lover. Well, perhaps the term "bickering" is not strong enough, especially since one of our group shot out another's windshield after this woman had run off with her long- term partner. Nonetheless, the weekly poker games and bowling tournaments continue, although we fifty- and sixty-year-olds are more likely to play golf than softball; eighteen holes are a lot easier to get around than three bases. We are building our retirement homes close together, and when someone becomes sick or ill, women compete to take care of her. Because our social circle includes physicians and plumbers, we can usually attend to any contingency. When I visited Atlanta during the spring of 1996, I stayed with an old true love and her partner of over a decade. Late one evening, after her partner had gone to bed, we sat comfortably with me watching the news and her working on a crossword puzzle, like the old married couple we could have been. We still delighted in each other's company and talked about our past adventures, including the only time in Atlanta that I was accosted by the police. She and I had climbed Stone Mountain, young lovers happily on a picnic far away from the crowds. We spread out a blanket on a rock outcropping, sunbathing, confident of our privacy. Suddenly, two police officers in a helicopter descended on us like thunder. I don't know who was more surprised. They averted their eyes, stumbled around, and finally chased us away, saying that we were out of the picnic-area bounds.

Living as a lesbian in the South in the 1960s, even in enlightened Atlanta, meant living in the closet and worrying about the police. On a university faculty, I was especially careful about being known publicly as homosexual. Actually, this was true of most of my friends, whether they were schoolteachers, realtors, or insurance agents. Gay bars were raided regularly, and police kept records of gay men and lesbians through automobile license plate numbers. Although I managed to avoid most encounters, my friends would tell me of being at parties in private homes and escaping through windows and down back alleys when the police arrived to arrest them simply for socializing with friends.

We restricted most of our activities to softball, basketball, poker, and occasional private parties. Many of my lesbian friends lived near each other in the new apartment complexes that were being built in the suburbs of Atlanta, and we planned our own, exclusive social and sports events. One friend, Sylvia, having access to tennis courts where she lived, held a HOTT (Homosexuals Only Tennis Tournament) complete with "official" ball girls, line judges, umpire, and photographer. Large lesbian audiences surrounded the courts, and winners were celebrated with a champagne party. When one of the group was picking up the T-shirts imprinted with the initials, she was asked what they stood for. She thought quickly and responded "Hell of a Tennis Tournament." It was a hell of a tournament. My doubles partner and I won and moved into a new partnership of eighteen years.

By this time, I had bought a home not far from Emory that became a center of subversive activity, not only for my lesbian and gay friends but for clergy and student demonstrators involved in the civil rights movement. I never actually marched, but I would pick up the protestors at the end of the rallies in my Mustang convertible. We would retreat to the Quaker House, banners blowing in the wind, where I attended my first underground mass led by Philip Berrigan. I also met Dr. Martin Luther King Jr. and eventually sadly helped arrange volunteers to assist with his funeral. With word of his assassination, Emory students—not known for their liberal proclivities—became instant members of the Southern Christian Leadership Conference. They staffed phone lines, baby-sat the King children, and draped large identifying placards on their expensive sports cars so they could drive through the streets of Atlanta and pick up visitors as they arrived at the airport and bus station.

The years at Emory were rich and rewarding. Although the administration never quite knew what to make of me, I will always be grateful that they hired a woman on the faculty and even asked me to be dean of women for a time. As dean, I delighted in those aspects of administration that not only allowed me to be a recreational director again but introduced me to women students across disciplines. For many, I was their first and only female university administrator and/or professor. Some were lesbian, although we never discussed this aspect of their lives, or mine. Rather we talked about their interests in careers and professional pursuits. Like my mentors, I sent a number off to graduate school, whether they wanted to go or not. Many have become distinguished in their own right. I treasure our continued contact, and those who are lesbian and I sometimes review our closeted pasts and wish that we could have been more open.

Bright young women, lesbian or straight, did not have an easy time growing up in the South in the l960s, even though the conservative and parochial attitudes of Atlanta and Emory were bastions of liberalism in contrast to the intolerance of the rural Southeast. Recalling the last time the Yankees had some advice for the South, white southerners had built their barriers of bigotry against social change, refusing to accept integration and aghast at the thought of a woman's movement. I chaffed under the conservative bounds of Emory apathy; the terms "gay" and "lesbian" were unknown, and Emory students affirmed the war in Vietnam. Promotion and tenure had been difficult to come by for me; my woman partner, a high school basketball coach, had a salary almost equal to mine. In the early 1970s, I also spent a sabbatical leave in Hawaii (where my only continuing education was scuba diving). I began to wonder if there might be life beyond Emory and the South, although I really couldn't imagine leaving Atlanta and my friendship network.

On a job interview at the University of Massachusetts at Amherst in the spring of l973, I pushed my way through the student union, surrounded by the aroma of drugs I had never smelled at Emory. Student in tie-dye staffed tables filled with flyers to sign up for almost every major or minor social movement. The community of Amherst had held a nine-year vigil against the war in Vietnam. The president of Amherst College had been jailed along with hundreds of student and faculty demonstrators who had shut down the five colleges. UMass was and is a "people's university," with most of the students, like me, first-generation college. I joined the Psychology Department, which was already comprised of more women and minority faculty than had ever been hired in the history of Emory.

My partner (from Alabama) had no intention of moving north until she visited me during the fall of my first semester. Seeing the beauty of New England (before the brutality of winter), she decided to join me in the Pioneer Valley. We were a faculty couple warmly welcomed by my colleagues and dean.

Without a doubt, being lesbian, female, and southern, I have been belittled and discriminated against at UMass. In fact, students walked out of the first classes that I taught when they heard my southern accent. Like most universities, UMass is plagued by institutional sexism, homophobia, and other prejudices. I prefer, however, to recall a charming incident of acceptance. The five-year-old daughter of my next-door neighbors asked her mother, a social psychologist in my department, why I didn't have a "daddy" living with me. The child's mother carefully explained that my partner and I loved each other, just as she loved the child's father. The youngster, having never seriously considered this possible arrangement before, frowned for a moment and then cheerfully announced that when she grew up, she would marry her best girlfriend (another faculty couple's three-year-old daughter).

My partner and I settled into life in the Valley, a community rich with a history that began well before white Europeans settled these shores. I finally learned something about the first War of Independence. And I was delighted to discover that I lived close to the site at which Daniel Shay led the only other armed rebellion against the government of the United States. I was even more intrigued to learn about the sites of the Underground Railroad and about Sojourner Truth, who joined a long line of strong women who to this day live in the Northampton area.

I also found a new family of friends and faculty that increasingly became a true blending of my public, professional, private, and personal lives. I began to teach courses in the psychology of women and to conduct research in women's health. For five years I served as department chair, which allowed me to be a recreation director again. I planned department socials, only one of which was ever closed down by the police. We organized a sports program and proudly cheered our co-recreational volleyball team to a university intramural championship. We also had a co-rec tag-football team of some renown because one of our male faculty had to be regularly removed from the games for fighting. Our women's intramural football team shared not one whit of this competitive spirit; we never won a game (our season average score was -2). We did, however, compete with the other members of our team; when one of our players sent our own linebacker to the infirmary with a concussion, I knew it was time for me to go back to softball.

I joined a team in a feminist league, where we spent more time deliberating the nature of politically correct competition than playing. Some of us secretly called ourselves the Politically Incorrect Girls (PIGS) because we wanted to keep score and liked to win. In spite of our competitive stance, however, we never came close to fighting, even with our arch-rivals, the Hot Flashes. Rather, we held homecoming celebrations complete with lesbian queens and a majorette with hair under her arms. As best I can recall, the state troopers were only called once, when a woman's team held a sit-in on second base while two men's teams played each other, thinking they had scheduled the field.

In the spring of 1992, I hitched a ride toward the Cape with some of my department colleagues who were attending an undergraduate curriculum meeting at another university. The director of our Undergraduate Studies Committee asked if I would consider teaching a new course on health psychology. Feeling rather generous of spirit, as I was on my way to Provincetown, I offered to teach lesbian psychology. You would have thought I had endowed a building. The members of the Undergraduate Studies Committee and the department chair, none of whom were gay or lesbian, jumped at the chance for such a course offering. The secretaries helped type the syllabus, the provost's office found funds for an additional teaching assistant and helped shepherd the course through the faculty senate (without a dissenting vote). The Chancellor's Task Force on Gay, Lesbian, and Bisexual Issues was ecstatic and the chancellor himself quite pleased.

The first time I offered "The Psychology of Differences: The Lesbian Experience" (affectionately called Dyke Psych), I had thought that mostly lesbians would sign up for the course. In fact, I mentioned to the class that I had hoped to have all lesbians. The class members—lesbians, bisexuals, straight women, and three men—attacked as one. I apologized profusely and begged to start again, knowing immediately that I would have to redefine differences and reach new heights of sensitivity about straight people and sexual minorities.

We read about Greek goddesses, Boston marriages, and contemporary lesbian couples. Our guest lecturers were lesbian poets, writers, mothers, and transsexual performance artists. We found that every part of psychology had something to teach us, from human development through sexual differentiation to prejudice, social change, and our fears of the radical Right. We may have overemphasized interpersonal attraction and emotional intimacy, in that we all talked openly and earnestly with each other about our social and sexual selves in a homophobic and sexist society. We discussed our differences but talked more about our similarities. We shared our weaknesses but more often celebrated our strengths.

Class members kept personal journals and worked on group projects of their own choosing. One group, mostly straight, having identified a new arena (for them) of social injustice, wanted to hold massive demonstrations on behalf of gays, lesbians, and transgendered persons. They may have secretly wished to close down the campus, but they sponsored a Gay Awareness Day instead. The day's events, held on the steps of the student union, were enormously successful, with speakers, lesbian music, tie-dye lavender T-shirts, and several hundred home-baked pink triangle cookies. The student newspaper headlined the happening with amazingly positive editorials and press coverage. Students of every sexual persuasion seemed to enjoy the idea of a new civil rights movement for social justice.

Several student groups, using class members, produced videos, including one on gay and straight women's reaction to lesbian music. Another video portrayed the story of a straight male who wakes in a completely gay and lesbian world. As a partner in a heterosexual marriage, he can't get a job, rent an apartment, or enroll his children in school. Another group project was a replication of research showing that male, highly religious, politically conservative students, especially those who did not know a lesbian personally, were significantly more prejudiced toward lesbians than were students without these characteristics. Five undergraduates, all straight, presented these findings at a national psychology convention. Their poster, a serious collection of tables and statistics, was decorated with the multicolors of the gay flag. Dazzled by its brilliance, more than one conference participant remarked on the only psychedelic poster they had ever seen at a professional conference.

Each time I teach the class, we end with a dinner party at my home. We watch the class videos and at one party were entertained by a live lesbian band. At another party, which was held in December, the straight boys and butches first argued about, and then helped each other put up, the Christmas tree; students of every religious and sexual persuasion decorated it.

Having always been drawn to the water, my partner and I built a lakefront home six miles from UMass and a further six miles to Northampton (Lesbianville, USA). We also have always had a home on the white sandy beaches of the "forgotten" coast of Florida, close to my relatives and the swamps. A few years ago, we decided to separate, and she moved back to the redneck Riviera. She's family; I love her dearly and I try to visit often. Also, like my mother, I love to have people come to visit and stay as long as they can. Once in Atlanta, my "little sister" from college called and asked if she could come over to talk about some romantic problem. Jane arrived with her dog, Ginger, and stayed for a year and a half.

Jane and I first met when I was seventeen and she a year younger. We always joked about her being my oldest and dearest living friend, but at age fifty-eight, she is dying of cancer. She lives in a suburban Atlanta neighborhood with at least four lesbian couples within two to three doors of her. Since she has been ill, she has been continually surrounded by her birth sisters and her extended lesbian family. Some months ago I went to Atlanta to see her. Known for her parties, Jane, as usual, arranged a gathering of old friends to visit while I was there. As she became tired and went to bed early, I climbed in with her, holding her until she fell asleep. None of us welcomes pain, and most of us fear death. But, like Jane, I rest comforted in my advancing years by the clear and constant care of an extended lesbian family. They have been with me as long as I have known how to love, and they will never leave me.

At this time in my life, I live happily in the beautiful Pioneer Valley. I still enjoy outdoor sports—hiking, biking, swimming, and sailing on the lake in the summer. During the winter, downhill ski slopes are close by, and I keep my cross-country skis on my deck to ski on the lake or the wooded trails around my home. In fact, I've been taking breaks from working on this chapter to go cross-country skiing with my chocolate Labrador retriever, Murphy Brown. Somewhat impaired in winter sports, another consequence of being southern, I am further handicapped when Murphy romps happily through my carefully groomed tracks and tries to retrieve the skies, with me on them. I also enjoy soaking in my outdoor hot tub, a far cry from those #2 washtubs of my past filled with water heated on a woodstove. At night, Murphy and I curl up in bed together, joined by my three cats. They're comforting and cuddly, but I'd rather have a friendly human face on the pillow.

My social life is crowded and my Yankee friendship network wide. I've even started going to church again after forty-two years of considering the term "Christian lesbian," or vice versa, an oxymoron. I attend Congregational services (only an hour a week) and am always warmly welcomed by the lesbian minister as well as a deacon who looks like the quintessential white-haired Yankee of a Norman Rockwell painting. He seems genuinely glad to have me in church along with other out lesbians from the community. His handshake shows no hint of sexual interest—nor does the preacher's, for that matter.

After three decades in academia, I have discovered what I do best: sabbatical. Once my partner and I went around the world on standby. I have visited Thailand and Tibet and learned not to call people "heathen." On my last sabbatical, I cruised the Mediterranean, shopped in Morocco, and rafted through the glowworm caves of New Zealand. This last winter break, I climbed temples in Burma, explored Ankor Wat in Cambodia, and hiked the rural highlands of North Vietnam. Occasionally, I meet with psychologists and talk with women's groups, but I mostly enjoy the excitement of foreign adventures with enthusiastic traveling companions.

Having left the South and the closet, I still return as often as I can to Florida. Several lesbian friends originally from Atlanta also live in beach homes right next to mine. We feel accepted by and a part of our small community of 1,200 people. In fact, one of our straight friends warned the new Methodist preacher that she better be open to and affirming of the lesbian and gay folks in town if she wanted to be successful in the church.

The last time I visited, my ex and I went next door to see our friend Sylvia, the same Sylvia who arranged the HOTT tennis tournament some twenty-five years ago. She bought my house when I left Atlanta and now lives retired and happy in another home she bought from me on the beach. As usual on a Saturday night, her home was filled with straight people from the community and lesbian friends from Atlanta. The same woman who picked up the HOTT T-shirts so long ago strummed her guitar, and lesbian and straight alike, we sang old songs that bridged our growing up years of the 1950s and 1960s. I thought about my cousins a few miles away, preachers and poachers, some just out of jail for fishing the bay for drugs instead of shrimp, others well-off folk who developed the Tupelo honey business in Florida. My Uncle Jennings is too frail to go oystering these days, but three generations of his children, grandchildren, and great-grandchildren still take him fishing.

Having always wanted to be a southern gentleman, I still sometimes feel like a stranger in New England and occasionally envy my brother his storybook life. Named after my father with the initials of Robert E. Lee (from whom every southerner claims to be a direct descendant), my brother completed college on a full-time tennis scholarship and, with the help of military benefits, became a dentist and opened a practice in the South. He married a beautiful southern debutante, and they built an elegant home with swimming pool and lighted tennis court. Perhaps most importantly, they've raised two lovely daughters. My nieces were recently presented to society at their debutante cotillions. The South has become more enlightened, but they still "came out" as the gracious southern belles they are—not as lesbians.

Even though my brother has a lovely wife and the joy of daughters, is nationally ranked in Master's tennis, and seems to have recovered fully from the childhood physical abuse I perpetrated, I would not change my life for his. At one time, I might have welcomed the comfort and safety of society's acceptance in exchange for the feeling of being different. But I have learned, finally, that sometimes being strange is more a blessing than a burden. My life as a lesbian is full and happy. I believe that I could live openly now almost anywhere. But as a displaced southerner whose accent betrays me at my every word, I still feel torn between the North and the South. I think of those long, lazy southern seasons that shaped me, blurring boundaries and the sharp edges of sexuality. And I look at my Confederate flag and long for faraway family, friends, and old lovers. I wish we were all together.

Charles I. Nero

Black Gay Men and White Gay Men: A Less Than Perfect Union

Liberal and nationalist politics has consistently been imagined as a union between black and white men. However, I challenge the idea that masculine sameness is, should be, or can be the basis for equality and justice. In a racist state, "white tribalism" has always been a force for cohesiveness more powerful than masculine sameness.[1]

Progressive Politics and the Myth of Masculine Sameness

The union of black and white men is a myth both old and persistent. In a superb essay, the historian John Saillant located this union in the very origins of the American republic. In the latter part of the eighteenth century, several white male abolitionists in their fictions depicted homoerotic unions between black and white men to show their fundamental sameness and hence the equality of African American and white men. When white men depicted in vivid detail the beauty and desirability of the black man's body, the purpose, Saillant states, was to use "physical equality to hint of political equality, while homoeroticism hinted of the likeness and benevolence that might join black and white."[2]

In the twentieth century, this idea of masculine sameness as the basis for equality has been propelled into our consciousness by a white-dominated media. In literally scores of Hollywood films and television movies, black and white men discover that they are essentially the same. Benjamin DeMott has called this enactment of interracial masculine sameness a "friendship orthodoxy," and in Hollywood film, it is a prevailing force for bringing about peace, harmony, and justice.

Clearly, the friendship orthodoxy is the underlying guide for the movies that made Sidney Poitier one of the top ten box office attractions of the 1960s. In movies like *The Defiant Ones, In the Heat of the Night*, and *Guess Who's Coming to Dinner*, an always dignified Poitier played a black friend so loyal that even the most hardened racist men came to love and respect him. Since Poitier's box office reign, it has become a Hollywood truism that every African American male who has gained box office appeal has had to demonstrate at some point in his career that he can play the friend of a white man.[3] Of course, the opposite is not true. The box office success of white male actors does not depend on their demonstrating a capacity for friendship with an African American male. White males who do play friends of African American males in Hollywood films seem to gain a certain appeal as good "liberals." However, being perceived as a good liberal has never constituted the sole criteria for employing white actors in Hollywood. No white actor's box office appeal depends solely on playing a friend to an African American, but every black actor's appeal seems to depend on being perceived as friendly to white men on film.

Although I have focused on film thus far, and its representation of white/black male friendship, the same can be said of the early philosophy of gay liberation, in which masculine sameness was a guiding principle. Some have argued, for instance, that the baths represented gay democracy at work. According to this view, all desires were equal in the baths. But what may have happened in the baths was not carried out in the streets. Despite this belief in equality and democracy, gay gentrification of neighborhoods throughout the United States has been mostly a white phenomenon.

New Orleans is an example. In a miniversion of the greatest creation of wealth the history of the world has ever known, when millions of white Americans after World War II were given access to government-subsidized real estate ownership, a similar case, on a much smaller scale, occurred among white gay men in the 1970s in the city of *laissez le bon temps rouler*. Through a network of white gay men's relations and friendships, as well as connections to the political system of the city, the Faubourg Marigny was gentrified. White gay men of different social extractions—professionals, artists, small businessmen, shop assistants, and even waiters—were capable of pulling important resources from the city and the state. Black gay men, however, were not invited to participate in this process. The result was that white gay men became owners of real estate that almost instantly became highly desirable, thus establishing them among the solid middle class of New Orleans. I will come back to this case later in this essay.

Gay White Men, Gentrification, and the Exclusion of Black Gay Men

Since Foucault's claim that the "homosexual" is a creation of the nineteenth century, scholars working in a variety of fields have examined the relationship between gay identity and societal forces. One of the most influential works to follow Foucault's claim was John D'Emilio's essay "Capitalism and Gay Identity." D'Emilio argued that it was only by the second half of the nineteenth century, "when individuals began to make their living through wage labor, instead of as parts of an interdependent family unit, [that it] was . . . possible for homosexual desire to coalesce into a personal identity–an identity based on the ability to remain outside the heterosexual family and to construct a personal life based on attraction to one's own sex."[4]

The relationship between economics and gay identity that D'Emilio outlined has attracted the attention of numerous scholars. In 1994 the Center for Lesbian and Gay Studies of the City University of New York sponsored a conference on the subject. Many of the essays were later gathered in the collection *Homo Economics: Capitalism, Community, and Lesbian and Gay Life.* Two of those essays paid attention to the formation of gay communities. Jeffrey Escoffier outlined an economic history of gay communities since World War II that included what he called the "Territorial Economy" of the late 1970s, which was "marked by the spread of gentrification and neighborhood development."[5] As Escoffier suggests, gay neighborhoods not only meant the presence of bars, retail establishments, and political organizations, but the extremely important factor of home ownership, the most significant means for accumulating capital in the American post–World War II economy.

The second study in *Homo Economics* that treats gay communities is Lawrence Knopp's "Gentrification and Gay Neighborhood Formation in New Orleans: A Case Study." In this essay, Knopp provides much critically needed information about the history and methods by which one gay neighborhood developed. Knopp's study is important because it challenges the usual myths about gay neighborhood formation. According to these myths, gay men fleeing oppression in small towns across North America moved to cities like New York, San Francisco, New Orleans, and Toronto. There, thanks to the anonymity of the city and the ability to derive an income apart from a family structure, gay men found more tolerant environs and affordable housing in the inner cities. Once established, these gays, mostly men, initiated community renewal projects. Knopp's study of gentrification in New Orleans provides a sophisticated examination of the formation of a contemporary gay neighborhood.[6]

I am particularly intrigued by Knopp's study because I grew up, attended school and college, and worked in New Orleans. Having come out as a gay man in New Orleans, I was familiar, and sometime intimately so, with some of the occupants in the neighborhood and surrounding environs Knopp described. In the critique of Knopp's study that follows, I make two points. First, I keep the issue of race in focus by noting consistently that this gay neighborhood was almost exclusively white. Second, I indicate a contemporary so-called progressive scholar's inability to account for the role of racism in gay neighborhood formation.

Knopp focused on gentrification in the Faubourg Marigny, a small but densely populated area adjacent to New Orleans's famous French Quarter. Knopp attributes gentrification of the Faubourg Marigny to three events: "the movement of a small number of predominantly gay middle-class professionals to Marigny during the 1960s"; "a movement for historic preservation in the neighborhood, organized primarily by gay men"; and "the arrival of speculators and developers, who again were mostly gay, in the mid-to-late 1970s" (47). Whiteness (and concomitantly the exclusion of black men and to some extent lesbians) mattered in all three events.

Regarding the first of Knopp's list of events that led to the neighborhood's gentrification, the gay middle-class professionals who moved to the Faubourg Marigny in the 1960s were men hired to work at the newly created University of New Orleans. Knopp does not identify them racially, but race matters here. Whiteness was an implicit criterion for employment at the University of New Orleans. The UNO was founded in 1958, while segregation was still legal, as Louisiana State University at New Orleans; until the late 1980s, most black professionals in higher education did not get jobs at University of New Orleans. Instead, most African Americans employed in higher education in New Orleans worked at one of the city's three historically black universities— Dillard University, Southern University of New Orleans, or Xavier University.

Race was also a significant reason these early gentrifiers selected the Faubourg Marigny.

Knopp speculates that the gay professionals preferred the Faubourg because its multicultural social history "made it easy for liberal whites to settle there without feeling that they were applying racist standards in their decisions" (49). Knopp notes that these men preferred the Faubourg because they enjoyed the neighborhood's proximity to the French Quarter and its gay institutions, and because they rejected living in the more heterosexual family-oriented suburbs sprouting up near the University of New Orleans. The Faubourg's multiracial history included its being a nineteenth-century community of free people of color and, during the late 1960s, being primarily composed of Irish and Italian whites fleeing to the white suburbs because of the in-migration of African Americans. While Knopp's speculation about liberal white attitudes may have some validity, I think it is important to keep in mind that a confluence of racial and economic issues may have been as important as not appearing racist. These professionals selected the Faubourg because it was not the adjacent predominantly African American Treme neighborhood. Although the Treme neighborhood was comparable in style to the Faubourg, it also contained a housing project and a population of African Americans considerably less well-off economically than those in the white ethnic working-class Faubourg. Given the city's historical racial discrimination in bank lending practices as well as in the insurance industry, I am sure that it made more economic sense to buy property in a neighborhood that was marked by the Federal Housing Administration as white ethnic rather than black.[7]

Concerning the second in Knopp's series of gentrifying events, by emphasizing historical preservation, white gays joined their interests to those of the white elite. Historical preservation has a long history in New Orleans that is very much associated with the local elite. The Vieux Carre Commission, which regulated development in the French Quarter, was established by members of the local elite in 1936. The initiator of the movement was a white gay architect who lived part of the year in San Francisco's gay Castro. According to Knopp, this architect purchased property in the Faubourg in 1971 and used his connections with other, presumably white, middle- and upper-class gay men to encourage gay gentrification of the Faubourg. These men created the Faubourg Marigny Improvement Association, and they emphasized historic preservation. The FMIA cultivated its members' connections with city officials, most notably the city planning commission, successfully lobbied the mayor and city council for land use regulations, and held candidate forums at election time. The success of the FMIA had notable consequences beneficial to middle- and upper-class whites. Local politicians and new zoning regulations made historical preservation a priority in the Faubourg, with the very practical result that bank financing and insurance became easier to get.

Knopp's third-listed event concerned the speculators and developers who really brought about the gay gentrification of the Faubourg with their focus on developing a market for all kinds of housing in the neighborhood among gays. Brokers encouraged "as much in-migration, home-ownership, and renovation in Marigny as was humanly possible, regardless of the in-migrant's class status" (53). The targets were white gays who were middle and upper class, as well as those employed in the low-wage service sector. For instance, one gay real estate broker made aggressive efforts among young, low-waged, gay service-sector workers from the French Quarter who would otherwise not have had access to the housing market. I know from personal experience that most of these young gay men were white, because most of the workers at the bars, restaurants, and shops were white. When I lived in New Orleans, it was a truism that the gay service sector never hired black men and seldom any other men of color. The bars were especially notorious for hiring white men and for excluding black men from entrance.[8]

In order for gay in-migration to occur, it was necessary to develop, Knopp states, "the social and economic potential of the gay community" (53). Actually, the resources of the gay community melded with those of the white banking community. One real estate firm used a series of maneuvers, many of which were illegal, to help members of the local gay community to secure financing for virtually the entire purchase price of the home (53–54). The consequence was that white gay men, regardless of social class, received access to housing and the wealth that accrues from home ownership, and that black gay men were systematically excluded from participating.

Instead of a rigorous exploration of race as a factor in gay culture, Knopp's explanations seem flimsy. The gay neighborhood in Knopp's study was overwhelmingly white and male, but Knopp gives the following extremely weak explanation for the this racial composition:

> Gay identity in the United States is skewed in terms of class, race, and gender, i.e., that while homosexual desire and behaviors are multiclass and multiracial phenomena involving both women and men, the self-identification of individuals as gay is more of a white, male, and middle-class phenomenon. This is because it is easier, economically and otherwise, for middle-class white males to identify and live as openly gay people than it is for women, non-whites, and non-middle-class people. (46)

This explanation is a cop-out, even though white gays often proffer one like it. For instance, the entry "Ghetto" in Steve Hogan and Lee Hudson's recently published *Completely Queer: The Gay and Lesbian Encyclopedia* contains the following remark: "A distinctive factor of black lesbian and gay life has been that a higher percentage of African American lesbians and gay men live outside gay and lesbian ghettos than their white counterparts."⁹ Statements such as these by Knopp or by Hogan and Hudson fail to consider perspectives, testimonies, and theoretical writings that call attention to the ways in which white identities, including those of gay whites, are maintained by excluding people of color. Marlon Riggs called attention to this exclusion in his epic documentary film *Tongues Untied* when he announced that he was leaving San Francisco's legendary Castro because he discovered that

> In this great gay mecca,
> I was an invisible man, still
> I had no shadow, no substance.
> No history, no place.
> No reflection.
> I was an alien, unseen, and seen, unwanted.¹⁰

Brian Freeman, an African American and a founder of the performance group Pomo Afro Homo, confirmed Riggs's observations in the 1997 documentary *The Castro*. The testimony of Riggs and Freeman calls our attention to the galling hypocrisy implicit in a progressive rhetoric that loudly proclaims that homosexuality is "multiclass" and "multiracial" except in the very communities in which people openly construct and live gay lives.

Scholarship such as Knopp's, while progressive in sexuality issues, is dismally conservative in race issues. This type of scholarship does not consider, on the one hand, that race has a history among gay people and, on the other, that gay people exist in a racist society.

The history of race among gays must account for what the sociologist Patricia Hill Collins calls "controlling images" of black gay men. The significance of these controlling images is twofold. They are far from humanizing representations, and they serve as guides that may influence policies and other forms of public decision making. Hill Collins notes, for example, how public policymakers continually evoke the controlling image of black women as wanton, libidinous jezebels in the ongoing welfare debates. In another example, the legal scholar Regina Austin has sketched quite powerfully how the jezebel image figures prominently in juridical decisions that negatively impact black women. The public image of black women has a correlate in its image of black gay men.

Arguably, the dominant culture's most powerful controlling image of black gay men is "the impostor." In numerous works, particularly dramatic works for both the stage and film, urbane black gay men populate narratives of revelation. The sole purpose of these narratives appears to be the discovery by whites of the black gay man as fraudulent, as an impostor. The prototype for the black gay impostor is Shirley Clarke's documentary *A Portrait of Jason*. At the beginning of *A Portrait of Jason*, the eponymous protagonist appears to be an elegant and witty dandy. Jason wears thick glasses, a blue blazer, and beige slacks. As the film progresses we witness Clarke supplying Jason with drugs and alcohol. By the conclusion of the film, we see Jason as a pathetic hustler and a con artist.

In the cult classic *Next Stop, Greenwich Village,* Antonio Fargas plays Bernstein, the only black person in a group of 1950s bohemians. Continually, the white Greenwich Village bohemians speculate about Bernstein's social origins; by the film's conclusion, it is revealed that he grew up in the housing projects. In John Guare's award-winning play and subsequent film *Six Degrees of Separation,* a "Black impostor intrudes on a white family by pretending to be a college chum of their son's."[11] Paul, the black impostor, who also pretends to be the son of Sidney Poitier, is revealed as a gay con and professional hustler.

In the hit film *The Crying Game,* Dil, the black female love interest, turns out to be a male. The thrill of the documentary *Paris Is Burning* was "realness," how well poor and marginalized black and Latino gay men could convincingly pass as women, professionals, and students. In the landmark drama *The Boys in the Band,* Bernard plays a black friend to a group of witty and articulate white gay men. By the drama's conclusion, we learn that his mother is a domestic worker for a rich white family in Detroit and that Bernard still carries a torch for the son of his mother's employer.

This controlling image of the black gay man as impostor sharply contrasts with the image that gay men have cultivated since the 1920s. In *Gay New York: Gender, Urban Culture, and the Making of the Gay Male World,* George Chauncey astutely observed that middle-class gay men in the period of 1920–1940 used a highly mannered and ambiguous sophistication to differentiate themselves from working-class fairies and the stigma that accompanied them. Chauncey states, "While the [more often working-class] fairy intended his style to mark him as a sexual invert, however, the [more often middle-class] queer intended his style to deflect such suspicions."[12]

Scholars studying the material origins of gayness must begin to examine the ways that controlling images such as the black gay man as impostor function. I suspect that when white gay men in New Orleans emphasized historic preservation as a bridge between themselves and New Orleans's white elite, they also played out the controlling image of the impostor to exclude black gay men.

White-oriented researchers of gay neighborhood formation must also acknowledge that racist policies that have regulated housing in this country affect gays, too. When gays form neighborhoods, they participate in economic institutions that for decades have been openly hostile to African Americans and many other people of color. The Federal Housing Authority (FHA) is a notable case.

Begun in 1934 to stop bank foreclosures on home mortgages, the FHA began the discriminatory practice of redlining. Appraisers took maps of cities and assigned areas in them colors ranging from green as the most desirable to red as the least desirable for FHA loans. Racially mixed neighborhoods or those tilting toward black were redlined; those in white suburbs were assigned green colors. The FHA's most basic sentiment was that racial segregation was necessary to maintain property values. The FHA's *Underwriting Manual* openly stated that "if a neighborhood is to retain stability, it is necessary that properties shall continue to be occupied by the same social and racial classes," and recommended that "subdivision regulations and suitable restrictive covenants" were the best way to ensure neighborhood stability. Although restrictive covenants were declared illegal in 1948, the practice of racial segregation in housing continued. Levittown in Long Island was typical of the effect of racial segregation. Begun after World War II as a mass-scale suburb, by 1960 not one of its 82,000 residents was an African American.

Not only was the state hostile to African Americans, but the banking industry was, as well. Banks routinely denied African Americans access to mortgage money. In a 1991 study of 6.4 million home mortgage applications, the Federal Reserve concluded that bank lending practices were racist. Some of the findings are startling. The poorest white applicant was more likely to get a loan approved than an African American in the highest income bracket. In Boston, African Americans in the highest income levels faced loan rejections three times more often than whites.

In general, banks were reluctant to lend in minority communities, and the Federal reserve study shows that racism in lending follows blacks wherever they want to move and no matter how much they earn. A 1993 *Washington Post* series supported the findings of the Federal Reserve study. In Kettering, a black suburb in Prince George's County, Maryland, the average household income is $65,000 a year and the typical home has four or five bedrooms, a two-car garage, and a spacious lot. Despite the upper income levels of the African American residents, local banks granted proportionately more loans in low-income white communities than they did in Kettering or any other high-income black neighborhood. Banking biases are particularly harsh for the working class and lower-middle-class African Americans, often leading many to go to finance companies for housing repair loans. These finance companies are the equivalent of loan sharks, with interest rates as high as 34 percent and huge balloon payments. Foreclosures are typical.

White-oriented scholarship on gay economics, and particularly on gay housing, does not address the degree of this hostility toward African Americans, but it should. This routine hostility toward African Americans provides important clues concerning the material reasons we continue to see gay as primarily a "white male identity." We know that homosexuality is multiracial and multicultural, but we must begin to examine the material practices that keep white gays visible and that deny visibility to gay men of color. If scholars are really serious about gay economics, then they must begin questioning what the exclusion of people of color means in material terms.

Frederick R. Lynch's study of suburban gays is a prime example of a scholar's failure to even raise the question of what excluding people of color might mean to white gays. Lynch found that suburban white gays consciously and routinely exclude people of color from their friendship networks. These white gays in the suburbs "rejected any comparison of homosexuals with minority groups such as blacks or Latinos." A group of white gay couples who worked in middle- to upper-level white-collar positions with an age range of twenty to forty-two maintained racially rigid boundaries so that "only white middle-class persons were even considered for membership." What is appalling about Lynch's study, which took place over four years, is that it never seems to have occurred to Lynch to ask his respondents why racial exclusivity was so important to them. After reading this study, I don't know—and I am not even sure that Lynch asked his white male respondents—if racial exclusivity was related to achieving their primary goals of "jobs/careers/income, a middle-class suburban home or condominium, a lover, and the 'suburban good life.'"[13] Actually, I begin to think that the answer to such questions is so obvious to anyone of white orientation that the questions never arise.

Gay Men and the Myth of Masculine Sameness

Given the frequently ironic and camp behavior of gay men, one might think that interracial male sameness, particularly given its homoerotic origins, might become a reality in the gay community. This is far from true, as I have hoped to show in this essay. Clearly, racial tribalism—or more specifically, whiteness—played an integral role in the Faubourg Marigny's transformation from an ethnic white working-class enclave to a gay neighborhood. I suspect that tribalism has played a significant but unspoken role in the creation of every other gay neighborhood in North America, and I might even add in South Africa, that is predominantly white and male. These neighborhoods that are produced by in-migration do not become white by accident. I will admit that it may not be the intention to create an all-white gay neighborhood, but systemic and institutional racism seems to prevail as a force far more powerful than masculine sameness.

As a last word, I want to make it clear that I am not suggesting that gay men argue for masculine sameness between white men and men of color. Instead, I will conclude by pointing out that at the same time that some white gays were accumulating wealth via gentrification, some black gay men were imagining alternative unions. A striking example appears in the late black gay poet Donald Woods's poem "Sister Lesbos" for Audre Lorde:

> With the smell of last night's love on our lips
> our paths collide
> Sister Lesbos seeking new love.
> Gold studs in the square of your ears
> boots like mine.
> My directions are full of smiles and approval
> Sister and brother, brother and sis
> smelling love for ourselves
> on mornin' lips
>
> I call you sister distinctly, loudly
> We are family of a real kind
> fruits of the flower pushed sun-ward
> through wide cracks in concrete.
> March on sister, giving brothers poems
> and your sisters that warm love.
> What we've shared

is the strength
to be apart
what we seek
is the strength
to be together.
Liberation to love ourselves
fiercely, in the family way.[14]

Woods's poem was included in the pathfinding *In the Life: A Black Gay Anthology.* Published in 1986, *In the Life* was the brainchild of Joseph Beam, who served as the anthology's editor.

One of the remarkable factors about this anthology, as is evident in Woods's poem, is the profound influence of black feminism and black lesbian feminism on many of the contributors. Beam, who would become one of the founders of the National Coalition of Black Lesbians and Gays and an editor of its journal, *Black/Out,* had himself been deeply influenced by black feminism and black lesbian feminism.

Beam announces the influence of feminism on his work in the very first sentence of the introduction to *In the Life* with a reference to the representations of whites and blacks in film and literature: "All the protagonists are blond; all the Blacks are criminal and negligible"—a clear allusion to an earlier anthology of black feminist writing that boldly announced the rationale for black women's studies. Further, Beam wrote, by 1983 he had grown weary of reading literature by white men, none of which, he states, "spoke to me as a Black gay man." Beam wrote that this white literature "offered the reflection of a sidewalk." Beam turned away from this literature and, instead, read "exclusively, work by lesbians and Black women," because "at the very least, their Black characters were credible and I caught glimpses of my reality in their words." Beam read some of the most brilliant women writing in the 1970s and early 1980s. He writes: "I was fed by Audre Lorde's *Zami,* Barbara Smith's *Home Girls,* Cherrie Moraga's *Loving in the War Years,* Barbara Deming's *We Cannot Live Without Our Lives,* June Jordan's *Civil Wars,* and Michelle Cliff's *Claiming an Identity I Was Taught to Despise.*"[15]

While reading Joseph Beam's papers, I got more glimpses into how important black feminism had been to him. Beam wrote that Barbara Smith's magnificent anthology *Homegirls* had served as the principle for organizing and structuring *In the Life.* Like *Homegirls,* Beam's anthology included a variety of genres: poetry, drama, short stories, photography, and artwork. Beam divided the anthology into six sections that reflected various aspects of living as a black gay man. Beam also did not want to present a monolithic black gay identity, which is most obvious in the section "Speaking for Ourselves." This section contains interviews with the contemporary black gay science fiction writer Samuel R. Delany; Bruce Nugent, a gay elder and a writer associated with the Harlem Renaissance of the 1920s; Blackberri, a poet, singer, and culture worker; and "Emmett," a black gay factory worker who lives in the rural South.

Joseph Beam's essay "Brother to Brother: Words from the Heart" is arguably the most well known contribution to the anthology. The essay was prominently featured in *Tongues Untied* and is the source of that documentary's famous intertitle, "Black men loving black men is the revolutionary act." The essay has a profound sense of urgency, no doubt influenced by Beam's readings of Audre Lorde's *The Cancer Journals* and her collection of essays and speeches *Sister/Outsider* and Julie Blackwomon's *Revolutionary Blues and Other Fevers*. The particular urgency was the sense of self-destruction as well as the viciousness of racism and chronic unemployment that Beam observed among so many black gay men.

Joseph Beam and many of the contributors to *In the Life* gave us a radical vision of black masculinity. This vision rejected the white-created images of hypermasculine black men or black men as frauds and impostors. Beam's political vision reveals that a union of black gay men and black feminists is a highly productive one. As black people, we need continue to imagine unions between black gay men and black feminists as part of a progressive and liberating politics. In much the same way that Lorde called upon straight black women to see in her a sister, Beam called for a sense of caring among black men. "Black men loving Black men is an autonomous agenda for the eighties, which is not rooted in any particular sexual, political, or class affiliation, but in our mutual survival. The ways in which we manifest that love are as myriad as the issues we must address."[16]

Notes

1. I deliberately use the phrase "white tribalism" instead of either "racism" or "white supremacy." Although "white tribalism" is synonymous with the two terms, "racism" and "white supremacy" have become too emotionally loaded to be used in polite discourse. Today, no one is a racist. Even Ku Kluxers, as David Duke proclaimed when he ran for the U.S. Senate, are merely showing their racial and cultural pride. Furthermore, "white tribalism" has a couple of advantages. First, the term clearly announces that I am focusing my critical lens on white people. As an African American gay man, for too long a member of groups who were the subject of study and speculation, I find it empowering to refocus the anthropological gaze onto whites. Second, "tribalism" has enormous explanatory potential by drawing attention to practices of inclusion and exclusion. For instance, tribalism goes a long way toward explaining miscegenation laws that forced whites to marry within the tribe, or financial practices such as redlining that excluded African Americans from access to bank loans and housing but awarded these privileges to whites.

2. John Sallaint, "The Black Body Erotic and the Republican Body Politic, 1790–1820," *Journal of the History of Sexuality* 5 (1995): 426.

3. In the 1970s, the actor was Billy Dee Williams in *Brian's Song* and the last two entries in the *Star Wars* trilogy, as well as Richard Pryor in *Silver Streak* (1976), *Greased Lighting* (1977), *Blue Collar* (1978), and *Stir Crazy* (1980). In the 1980s and 1990s Eddie Murphy dominated the box office, playing characters who eventually befriended white men in the wildly popular *Beverly Hills Cop* (1984), *Beverly Hills Cop 2* (1987), *Trading Places* (1983), *48 Hours* (1982), and *Another 48 Hours*. Before Lou Gosset won an Oscar as the tough Sergeant Foley who brings Richard Gere to manhood in *An Officer and a Gentleman* (1982), he had played James Garner's buddy in the *The Skin Game* (1971), a comedy set during the period of enslavement. In the 1990s Wesley

Snipes went from playing a frightening black drug kingpin in *New Jack City* to Woody Harrelson's slick basketball partner in *White Men Can't Jump*. Playing black soldiers in the Civil War who die in the arms of their white colonel, Denzel Washington and Morgan Freeman were both nominated for Oscars in *Glory;* Washington won. Freeman was nominated again for an Oscar in *Shawshank Redemption* as a convict who becomes the best friend of a white fellow convict. In *Philadelphia*, Denzel Washington scored one of his biggest triumphs as an ambulance-chasing lawyer who successfully defends a white gay man dying of AIDS wrongfully terminated from his employment. Samuel L. Jackson received an Oscar nod in *Pulp Fiction* as the black half of a team of assassins.

4. John D'Emilio, "Capitalism and Gay Identity," in *Making Trouble: Essays on Gay History, Politics, and the University* (New York: Routledge, 1992), 8.

5. Jeffrey Escoffier, "The Political Economy of the Closet: Notes Toward an Economic History of Gay and Lesbian Life Before Stonewall," in Amy Gluckman and Betsy Reed, eds., *Homo Economics: Capitalism, Community, and Lesbian and Gay Life* (New York: Routledge, 1997), 124.

6. Lawrence Knopp, "Gentrification and Gay Neighborhood Formation in New Orleans: A Case Study," in Gluckman and Reed, eds., *Homo Economics: Capitalism, Community, and Lesbian and Gay Life* (New York: Routledge, 1997), 45–63. Page numbers cited in the text that follows refer to Knopp's essay.

7. I grew up in a working-class African American neighborhood, and during the late 1960s I witnessed an insurance representative misrepresent my parents' home. The representative said our property was littered with beer cans and that neighbors reported that my parents regularly gave raucous parties. Although this representative lied, the insurance company denied our family coverage. My parents regularly tell this story, and it is a part of our family's folklore about experiencing institutional racism.

8. In his 1989 documentary *Tongues Untied,* Marlon Riggs showcased the widespread practice of carding, a practice of demanding from black men an inordinate amount of identification to enter bars. It was not unusual for the same club bouncer to let white men enter a bar without asking for identification and to immediately stop black men at the door to request identification. One black gay man in *Tongues Untied* tells the story of how a bouncer asked him for five pieces of picture identification. I have yet to meet a black gay man who is unfamiliar with carding.

9. Steve Hogan and Lee Hudson, *Completely Queer: The Gay and Lesbian Encyclopedia* (New York: Holt, 1997), 18.

10. Marlon Riggs, *Tongues Untied* (San Francisco: Frameline, 1989).

11. Otis Guernsey Jr. and Jeffrey Sweet, *The Applause/Best Plays Theater Yearbook of 1990–1991* (New York: Applause Theater Book Publishers, 1992), 309.

12. George Chauncey, *Gay New York: Gender, Urban Culture, and the Making of the Male Gay World, 1890–1940* (New York: Basic Books, 1994).

13. Frederick R. Lynch, "Nonghetto Gays: An Ethnography of Suburban Homosexuals," in Gilbert H. Herdt, ed., *Gay Culture in America: Essays from the Field* (Boston: Beacon, 1991), 185, 189, 180.

14. Donald Woods, "Sister Lesbos," in Joseph Beam, ed., *In the Life: A Black Gay Anthology* (Boston: Alyson Publications, 1986). Reprinted by permission of Alyson Publications.

15. Beam, ibid., 13.

16. Ibid., 242.

Donna Smith

Same Difference:
My Southern Queer Stories

One of the stories that I tell about myself begins something like this: In 1982, I moved to San Francisco to become gay, and there I found out that I was southern. Of course, this story is not literally true, but it does reflect an emotional truth, for it was not until this move to San Francisco that I felt gay and southern; it was there that I began to experience a gap between where I am from and who I was becoming—a gap that gave new meaning and self-consciousness to both identities. Behind this story is a question that has often been put to me about how—given my heritage as a white woman from Pawnee, Alabama, with a deeply religious, fundamentalist Christian as my mother, a housewife and rural mail carrier, and with a policeman as my father (a job that placed him on the front lines of Bull Connor's war to preserve Jim Crow in Birmingham)—how I became a lesbian feminist academic. This story traces my attempts to answer this question and to negotiate this gap, both perceived and real, between my southern and queer selves.

Stories always lie, however, if only through reduction. This story about my having moved to San Francisco to become gay is as telling through what it conceals as through what it reveals. For I had moved to New Orleans to be gay as well, three years before this move to San Francisco. Awarded music scholarships to several schools, I chose Loyola in New Orleans in part because I had heard that there were lots of gay people there. It was in New Orleans that I came out to myself more fully, went to my first lesbian bar, told select others that I was lesbian, and lived with a lover for the first time—all quintessential coming-out experiences. So I've had to ask myself, Why doesn't New Orleans serve as the jumping-off point for this coming-out narrative? Why was I so eager to get to San Francisco that I worked as a waitress for almost a year in order to finance this move, serving drunken tourists at the New Orleans Hilton to a perpetual soundtrack of Dixieland jazz? The answer to these questions begins to illuminate how myths of the southern and the queer have operated in my life and my stories.

In the three years I lived in New Orleans, my knowledge of gay culture grew expo-nentially. I devoured the lesbian and gay periodicals in the Faubourg Marigny Book-store, marveling at the evidence of lesbian and gay bookstores, small presses, com-munity centers, and guesthouses they documented—at the spectacle of lesbian feminist music festivals attracting tens of thousands of women from all over the coun-try. These lesbian and gay cultural institutions were springing up everywhere, but pri-marily in big urban centers on the east and west coasts, with San Francisco firmly established as the cultural center. Of course, New Orleans too had gay restaurants, gay religious groups, gay cultural organizations, and scads of gay bars—gay people were visible everywhere to those who could read the signs—but in my mind, it came up wanting. After three years New Orleans, I had decided that it was too touristy, too provincial, and ultimately, too southern. I was ready to move on, and San Francisco seemed the logical destination.

Also important is the fact that, by 1982, I had grown weary of playing the "open secret." I wanted to live fully out, which meant coming out to my parents back home, and somehow I couldn't imagine doing so while still living in the South. My desire to be out symbolized my rejection of the script that had been handed me at birth, or the general familial and societal expectations that I would marry and have children—that if I worked, it would be in a traditionally female occupation like nursing or teach-ing that wouldn't interfere with child-rearing duties and church work. As a female with half-conscious feminist leanings and as a dyke, such a radical break from social expectations seemed to require movement, and great distance. Unconsciously, I felt that this transformation could only take place in San Francisco.

In fact, San Francisco was firmly established in my mind as the gay mecca before I ever left Birmingham, Alabama. While still living at home in my late teens, I began to monitor news programs such as *20/20* for gay content: reportage of any gay issue tended to begin with stock file footage of leather-clad men walking down Castro Street, bare-assed in chaps, hand in hand. These programs alerted the nation to how pervasive this disease of homosexuality had become in San Francisco: viewers were informed that parents were afraid to let their young sons walk home from school alone because of the unbounded cruising of gay men. During this period, I happened to catch the evening news on the day that Dan White murdered San Francisco mayor Moscone and city supervisor Harvey Milk. I was stunned: in the same moment that I learned that an openly gay elected official existed, I learned of his death. Five months later, I watched news coverage of the riots that followed the Dan White verdict after his conviction, not of first-degree murder but of voluntary manslaughter, and a mere eight-year sentence was handed down. Images of gay men overturning and burning police cars outside San Francisco's city hall filled the television screen—my first sight of queer anger.

To my mind, San Francisco exemplified a queer visibility that if generally pejora-tive, was also highly intoxicating. It seemed to differ qualitatively from the open secret of queerness I witnessed in New Orleans. There, a strong gay presence was treated as local color and tolerated as long as it contributed to the exoticism of a city that existed on tourism. Normal conventions could be suspended, but they weren't ever fundamentally challenged in this party town. In contrast, the organized political presence of queers in San Francisco, embodied by the figure of Harvey Milk as martyr, represented a potential validation of gay lives I had never thought possible.

Like many young people, I was attracted to the variety and stimulation offered by a truly cosmopolitan city. However, my point is not that there weren't real differences between New Orleans and San Francisco, but that the meanings I attributed to these differences weren't totally logical. My move to San Francisco was made not only for practical reasons, but under the influence of two overlapping myths. Like all myths, these contain just enough truth to appear self-evident: the first, that the South is more racist, more sexist, more homophobic—more oppressive in general, than any other region of the country—and the second, that San Francisco is the gay mecca. Where the former diagnosed the disease, the latter provided the remedy.

It's easy to see why I felt queer in San Francisco: within a month of my arrival, I was working and living in predominantly gay and lesbian space. Through a posting on the bulletin board of Artemis Cafe, a lesbian coffeehouse on Valencia Street in the Mission district, I found a room in a dyke household on Guerrero, just blocks away from a lesbian bar and a lesbian feminist bookstore. These were new and exciting innovations to me—places one could enter in broad daylight and see other dykes. Although lesbians were far from the majority in this narrow corridor of the Mission district between Valencia and Dolores Streets, neither were we an uncommon sight on the streets. Our neighbors in this long-established Latino community were generally tolerant of the smattering of white, mostly middle-class, downwardly mobile young lesbians infiltrating this small corner of the Mission, too occupied with their own survival to concern themselves unduly with us.

Initially, San Francisco fulfilled all my desires for radical difference. Even the landscape seemed to comply with my expectations, underscoring how far I had moved from home: dramatic vistas of ocean and bay, hillsides that turned svelte gold rather than deep green in the summer, cool and foggy mornings year-round, the foreign scent of eucalyptus. For years, I was repeatedly unsettled by these benign variations, as if the terrain of the lower Appalachian foothills had been etched into my genetic code as defining "nature." But the more dramatic contrast was in the people; growing up, I had rarely encountered other than white and black people, but here persons from all parts of East Asia, Mexico, Central and South America were readily visible, living in distinct neighborhoods. Eventually, I would come to see that San Francisco was as segregated as Birmingham and New Orleans, its patterns just more checkerboard, but at first, it seemed like a multicultural haven.

Finding a job in a city where everyone wanted to live was more challenging. After weeks of diligent searching, I finally found work at a gourmet deli in the ritzy Pacific Heights district, paying half of what I had made in New Orleans. All exiles of one sort or another and mostly queer or queer-identified, my co-workers reflected the city's diversity: Carlos, an artist and mathematician from São Paulo, and his lover, Aaron; Victor, our French chef who had settled in the States with his American wife;

Ahmed, an art student and political refugee from Iran, where his father had been a judge under the shah's rule; and Elizabeth, a bisexual woman from Detroit who had hoboed all over the country for several years before settling in San Francisco with her Asian American lover, who owned a pricey hair salon up the street. They were very protective of me as the newest arrival to the city and became my new work family.[1]

Yet if I arrived in San Francisco with notions of a mythical queer solidarity that would override all other cultural differences, my relationships with my new roommates soon curbed this idealism. All highly politicized lesbian feminists, two were in the women's studies program at San Francisco State, and the other worked as an apprentice for a welder. I've told stories about my experience in this household that make it sound like a Dykes to Watch Out For cartoon strip that gently satirizes the seriousness of lesbian feminist culture. Indeed, these women were much further along on the lesbian feminist evolutionary chart than I. The day I moved in, one was at work sewing her own Kotex-like menstrual pads out of seaweed—I tried to swallow my amazement. One of the requirements for membership in this household was to have been in therapy, a process they were all deeply engaged in; my few months of counseling in New Orleans just qualified me. Katherine, the welder, kept a blow-up doll in her room as a punching bag on which to act out latent aggressions. What seems to me now a fairly wise move, given her general pugnacity, just seemed profoundly weird then—I had not yet been fully socialized into the therapeutic culture. Weeks into my stay, I was told that the Calvin Klein jeans I wore to my interview caused great debate and almost knocked me out of contention.

But this version of my experience in this dyke household is reductive and self-serving. It masks the fact that these young dykes were genuinely welcoming of me, and that I found many of their political commitments admirable, if a bit intimidating. That I felt very much an outsider in this household and only lasted there about four months says as much about me as about them. For it was as I began to see myself through their eyes that I began to wonder about what it meant that I was from the South—about what difference this difference made.

How could I describe my experiences without revealing myself as hopelessly provincial, without reifying their stereotypes of the South? Which stories would I tell, and which would I omit, and what would be the implications of those tellings and omissions? How would I describe Pawnee, the little community I grew up in ten miles north of downtown Birmingham, where most of my neighbors were at least distantly related, if not immediate family? As I recreated Pawnee in my memory, this place I knew like the back of my hand, its landmarks assembled themselves like a Grandma Moses painting—a primitive cartography of Bottom Road, Middle Road, Back Road, Gurley's Holler, the Rock House, the Reservoir, the Spring, Buzzard's Den, centering around Pawnee Missionary Baptist Church. Would I pretend that I wasn't deeply moved by the messages I received at this church and by the community I found there, a church that my grandmother had founded, my great-uncle had built? Would I reveal that I had been saved three times, baptized twice (somehow it never would stick)?

Would I omit the fact that this was an all-white community, surrounded on two sides by the all-black communities of Zion City and Ketona? Would I disclose the fact that I was in my late teens before I ever saw a black person drive through Pawnee, though we took shortcuts through black neighborhoods daily, on our way to the grocery store or the shopping mall, where we were waited on by all-white clerks? Would I note that I had attended a white-flight Christian academy for two years after a court-ordered desegregation plan had us attending New Castle, an all-black school in Ketona, less than two miles from my home?

Ultimately, I revealed very little about myself, preferring to emphasize what they could see, what I imagined we had in common. Bringing my roommates into this world I came from, even imaginatively, seemed as impossible as envisioning my family in my new world. My reticence undoubtedly contributed to my unease with them, and theirs with me.

This is, at one level, an age-old dilemma, characteristic of all whose opportunities and ambitions lead them away from their home cultures. But for me, the lens of southern history and southern myth magnified it, as did my experiences growing up in Birmingham, Alabama. Already, I was familiar with the typical response of "Wheeew ... !!!" when I divulged that I was from Birmingham, as if that wordless reaction said all that was worth saying. While I resented this effect, there was no denying Birmingham's history.

Furthermore, I too held their assumption that the South was more oppressive than any other region of the country. In this city I came from, good and evil had been drawn in stark terms: Bull Connor versus Martin Luther King Jr., fire hoses versus small school children. These images were historical record, indelibly etched into the memory of anyone in range of a newspaper. The difference was that before, I had held this view as an insider and never felt it reflected negatively on me, personally. Now I was experiencing for the first time the weight of the nation's collective judgments about the South; I was being perceived as a southerner and would represent the South for my new friends. Had I been born to liberal white middle-class parents in the South, I might not have felt such an urgent need to work out the ethics of my background. But this history lived very close to home, embodied in my father, whose work as hands-on enforcer of racial apartheid had literally fed me. What did this say about me? I increasingly wondered. Though I couldn't have articulated these feelings or questions at the time, they were collecting around the edges of my consciousness.

Shortly after I arrived in San Francisco, I met Andrea, a woman who would have a profound impact on my experience in California. Our relationship forced me to articulate these questions, to begin a process that would radically transform my ideas about race and region. I had ventured forth alone to check out Amelia's, then the happening lesbian bar in the city, located just a few blocks from my flat. Tall, androgynous, her features classically handsome rather than pretty, I thought Andrea cast a very striking figure in the gray tank top and camouflage fatigues she was wearing that night. Of course, she would have probably caught my eye anyway, since she was one of the few black women in the bar. As she passed by me through the aisle of women lining the bar, a Calistoga water in her hand, I asked her if she planned to join up. Andrea laughed congenially at my bad joke, and we began a conversation that eventually moved to an all-night coffeeshop up the street, as we exchanged the basic information about ourselves.

As we talked then, I learned that she was thirty-five, which made her twelve years older than I, and from a lower-middle-class family in New York City—from Washington Heights in Harlem, to be exact. After attending college at Hampton Institute in Virginia, she'd followed her best friend out to San Francisco, where she became deeply immersed in the antiwar movement. She'd been to Indonesia and to Africa, had tramped all through Central American and back several times, and on a dime. She told me how she'd held lots of jobs, but the one she loved most was teaching at a school run by the Black Panthers for several years during the late seventies. Her discussion of the complexities of the Black Panther party, as well as her descriptions of Washington Heights as a safe and interesting place to grow up in the 1950s, exposed all my stereotypical assumptions, making clear how little I knew about racial politics. I flashed back to a memory of sitting around the dinner table in my parents' kitchen as we watched the evening news on television, and the striking appearance of Angela Davis on the screen. This segment began with that infamous footage of Davis walking into court with a raised fist, her hair styled in the defiant and huge Afro. I recalled my mother's response to my sudden interest, her disdainful remark: "You know she's a Communist!" I tried to imagine my mother's reaction to my dating a black woman, much less one who had been even tangentially associated with the Panthers; it wasn't a pleasant thought.

When I arrived in California, I held the same attitude toward race relations felt by most whites of my generation—those of us who grew up in the 1960s and 1970s. I felt that the revolution had been won, in the main, and saw racism as being limited to individual acts. With the arrogance of extreme youth, I thought that I could escape the sins of my parents' generation through good intentions and right actions. In other words, if I was nice to individual people of color, if I pretended that color didn't matter, I'd be all right. Becoming involved with Andrea and getting to know her history required me to rethink these notions.

Ironically, I found it easier to talk about myself with Andrea than with my new white friends, perhaps because she had no need to distance herself from the bigotry of white people. Also surprising was that our mutual southern roots—hers just one generation removed—seemed to provide some commonality. When she described her parents, her mother from Georgia and her father from Florida, she did so in phrases and stories that sounded uncannily familiar. Andrea had traveled to Georgia regularly as a kid in the late 1950s, and she told me stories about those scary, seventeen-hour-long car trips when there were few places a black family with New York license plates could safely stop. She also noted how her own ideas about the South had changed through the years. Growing up, she had assumed that white people in the North were okay—that the real bigots were in the South. Black folks who stayed in the South she assumed to be either stupid or foolish. Her experiences at Hampton

Institute, a historically black college that attracted African Americans from all over the South, discredited this view, as did the increasing racial violence she witnessed in the North as a young adult.

That night, Andrea promised me a walking tour of San Francisco, the first of many to come in the next couple of months, as we became running buddies. Early on, she also told me that she had been diagnosed manic depressive, having experienced two manic episodes in her twenties, but that these incidents hadn't occurred in years and she didn't expect them to return. She seemed terribly sane to me, so I wasn't put off by this revelation, too ignorant of the disease to realize that her optimism was in fact characteristic of it.

Four months into my move, Andrea and I took a week-long road trip together, north to Washington State and back down the California coast on Highway One. This trip solidified our relationship, which slid into an easy companionability neither one of us wanted to break. As had happened before, I fell in love with someone I wanted to become. Andrea's big-city background and her age gave her a sophistication I felt lacking in myself. More important, she wasn't overly invested in that cool reserve I was finding so very alienating in San Francisco youth culture. That trip was passed with unending stories about ourselves—our home, families, friends, and lovers, the meanings constantly changing as we integrated new information and perspectives with the old. By early winter, she asked me to move in with her; as it seemed silly to keep my room in the flat on Guerrero Street since I was so rarely there, I did. Long after the effects of her illness had taken their toll on our relationship and we had ceased to be real lovers, we remained best friends, living together until I left California for graduate school.

Several months after my arrival, I held a sidewalk sale in the Castro outside Cafe Flore, ridding myself of all my conservative, slightly femme dress clothes to raise a little cash. What self-respecting San Francisco dyke would ever need scoop-necked blouses with Peter Pan collars, blue-and-white-striped searsucker slacks? In a gay boys' barbershop on Castro, I got a modified flattop and for weeks afterward was shocked to see my reflection in storefront windows—with my hair cut short, I looked much like my father. From army surplus stores and garage sales, I created a uniform of baker's pants or jeans, v-necked wool sweaters over tees, bomber jacket or trench coat, PLO (Peruvian Liberation Organization) scarf and desert boots, more suitable to the urban dyke–warrior image I wanted to cultivate. Sunday evenings, Andrea and I would go teadancing at the I-Beam—a gay club on Haight Street made famous during the heyday of disco. We'd arrive and immediately peel down to shorts and tees, maneuvering around the drag queens competing for mirror space in the women's restroom. On the dance floor, we'd sweat it out for several hours amidst a hundred gay men in cutoffs and Doc Martens to gay anthems like Diana Ross's "I'm Coming Out," Sister Sledge's "We Are Family," or Sylvester's "You Make Me Feel, Mighty Real." With the bass beat thumping in my chest, it was easy to imagine that I had arrived, if late, at the heart of the queer/sexual revolution.

If in those first few months in San Francisco I attempted to recreate myself, to distance myself from my provincial southern roots, my coming out set in place a chain of events that catapulted me back home emotionally. I didn't come out to my parents forthrightly, however; I just kind of backed out of the closet, leaving an increasingly broad trail of breadcrumbs in that summer before I moved to San Francisco. My father's response to this news exemplified both his personality and our close relationship. He wrote me a letter confirming that his love for me had not changed, but he did offer some advice, noting, "I didn't like carrots and peas at your age either, but I do now, so keep an open mind." Though patronizing, as parents often are in dealing with young-adult children, his comparison of my sexual object choice to food tastes inserted some levity into this unfolding drama. For my mother's response was a different story.

I thought I had prepared myself well for this event, becoming financially independent and moving to the far side of the continent, but still, I was taken aback by the viciousness of her response. At the same time my parents found out that I was lesbian, they found out that I was involved with Andrea. I was never able to untangle which part of this news mother found most upsetting. For a couple of months, I received three and four letters a week—hate-filled missives, really. In one of these letters she asserted my criminality, observing that my father "had to arrest so many of them [homosexuals]." In another, she informed me that Andrea would "slit my throat for a buck," exposing a racist paranoia I hadn't known or wanted to admit that she possessed. Yet another letter simply returned a snapshot I had sent home shortly after I moved to San Francisco—a picture of me playing tourist, posing in front of the monkey cage at the zoo. My face had been X'd out so fiercely that the ballpoint pen she used rippled and tore through the photo paper. What was most maddening was that she framed these hateful letters in the language of fundamentalist Christianity, beginning and ending with her love and her prayers that I would turn from my sinful ways to find peace and forgiveness in Jesus: "It's not too late. I want to help. I love you, Mom."

Shell-shocked by these letters but relieved to be 3,000 miles away, at first I tried to shrug them off and carry on as usual. I didn't want mother's madness to spoil the pleasures of my new home. At the same time, I felt somewhat badly that my coming out had created such havoc in the family, and that my father and my siblings—also supportive, were having to deal with the fallout up close. Reportedly, much of mother's anger was directed at my father for not backing her opposition, and this was surfacing longstanding problems between them. After thirty-three years of marriage, my parents separated for several weeks. Years later, during an argument with my father over queer politics in which I had accused him of fence sitting, he replied defensively, "Your mother and I almost got a divorce over this!" Maybe you should have, was my silent response, though I was unable to imagine it.

Intellectually, I knew that mother's reaction was not about me—that her own demons were surfacing—but emotionally, this separation was impossible. Barely conscious of what I was doing, I stopped eating for several weeks, living on coffee and cigarettes. Like those people compelled to self-mutilate, I needed some physical release, and this one at least resulted in my becoming absolutely skinny for the first time in my life. Throughout this period, Andrea's calm support provided a much needed anchor. She forced me out on walks and urged me to carry on with my plans for school. My applications to Berkeley and San Francisco State were coming due, but I was finding the pages and pages of forms and the detailed financial aid documents to be assembled overwhelming; Andrea made a coffee date to help me sort through and complete them.

Sometime that fall, she had written her own mother about me, enclosing a photograph of us. Then in her seventies, her mother was still living in Harlem on Riverside Drive, and her response to our relationship was a marked departure from that of my own. She wrote back immediately, informing Andrea that she was glad to hear she had found a "friend," but pointedly remarked on the photograph: "That child's not happy." Later, after Andrea had revealed more of how my own mother had responded to our relationship, her mother gave Andrea some sharply worded advice. "Pay no attention to those peckerwoods!" she responded, using the language of her Georgia childhood.

After several months, I finally summoned the will to put a stop to my mother's letters through the suggestion of the free therapist I had begun seeing at the Pacific Center, a gay and lesbian counseling service. Putting them all in a big manila envelop, I included a curt note instructing mother that if I ever received another one of these, I would cut off all communication. The letters stopped; I had won a temporary victory. Gradually, it felt hollow, though, for I then had to come to terms with the fact that my deep anger at my mother revealed my continuing love for her and desire for her approval, which I then found humiliating.

My mother's behavior exacerbated questions about the South just beginning to surface for me, and I wondered if her southernness was in part responsible for her extreme reaction. At one level, there seemed to be nothing particularly southern about it—parents everywhere often feel justified in the most vile behavior upon learning they have a gay or lesbian child and will use any weapon at hand. Yet mother's blatant racism as well as her narrow-minded religiosity epitomized everything that I found abhorrent in this region. The few friends with whom I felt close enough to confide seemed to be absorbing this information through the frame of region as well. I was highly ambivalent about our mutual tendency, however; dismissing mother as just another southern nutcase seemed to dissolve her of moral agency, and above all, I wanted her held accountable.

I hadn't heard from mother in almost a year when I received another and entirely different kind of letter. In it, she apologized—not for her response to my being lesbian, but for the entire way that she had raised her children. In it, she was more self-reflexive than I had thought her capable. She begged forgiveness for her inability to express her love in any ways but materially, and in the moral language of dos and don'ts—behavior that she now realized was often cruel in its effects. She explained that she had raised us as her mother had raised her, thinking that if she provided for us physically and taught us to work, she would have done a good job. It was her own sense of insecurity and desire for approval, she wrote, that had led her to demand an unattainable perfection from her children and herself. And she expressed her own sense of loss at not allowing herself to enjoy her own children: "I so wish I could go back and relax—play games with you kids, so wish I had stopped my rushing around and talked to you," I recall her writing.

It was a painful letter to read, not only because I knew that it was sincere, but because it presented the specter of reconciliation but didn't go far enough to realize it. For mother still didn't believe that my being lesbian was a morally acceptable choice, and her "not in my house" rule had not changed. This rule meant, as I interpreted it, that while I could visit my parents' home, my lovers and friends wouldn't be welcome, which, as far as I was concerned, meant that I wasn't welcome. Most of all, I was far from ready to forgive; having located my anger, I nurtured it as I would a newborn.

Gradually, however, the drama of my first year in San Francisco subsided, the newness of the city faded, and I settled in. Accepted into U.C. Berkeley as a transfer student, I began in the fall of 1983. Much of my emotional energy was still spent trying to absorb and integrate all the changes that had taken place, but being a student gave me a much needed focus outside myself. The education that I sought and received at Berkeley met a visceral need to bridge the gap between my past and present, both of which were raising so very many questions.

The next three years were a period of intense discovery. For instance, it was at Berkeley that I discovered that I was considered working class. Being southern was a part of this mix, for most Californians saw the South as working class and poor in general. Applying for a tutoring job at the Student Learning Center—a program that provided academic support to minority groups—I was asked to define my class background. Unable to do so decisively, I was asked about my parents' occupations and whether or not they had attended college. Perhaps to all the world it was obvious that the daughter of a mail carrier and a cop would be considered working class, but this was news to me. I had grown up in a big new ranch-style house set on ten acres of land; my siblings and I were always dressed nicely, we had music lessons, we took educational vacations every summer. In the world I came from, these were considered the trappings of middle-class success.

But I also remembered that my father had built this big house over three years of weekends with the help of his father, his brother, and my mother; that he had torn down an old boardinghouse on the south side of the city to get the lumber. I remembered that it was built on land my mother had inherited—her family having been land-poor in her generation, but quite wealthy several generations before, owning 3,000 acres in the northern valley. And I also remembered that her great-grandfather, a Civil War veteran, had been a U.S. congressman in the late nineteenth century, and I knew that this distant but privileged past gave mother's side of the family a limited currency among those who remembered. When mother's heritage came up for discussion, my father often told a story that purportedly traced his lineage. "There was a fire at a whorehouse down on Fourth Avenue, and somebody threw a baby out the window," he would joke.

Although I was uncomfortable with these assumptions being made about my region and class and confused about how to actually describe them, I began to realize that in truth, I had not experienced many of the privileges my peers, mostly children of professionals, took for granted. I recalled conversations overheard while standing in a long line outside Zellerbach Auditorium during enrollment—eighteen-year-old freshmen comparing the relative merits of the Greek isles they had visited during their summer vacations. I too had taken a European vacation after high school graduation, but I had waited tables full-time for eight months to fund it. At that moment, I was worried about how I would buy my books for these classes and had just enough change in my pocket to take the train home, back across the bay to the tiny studio apartment I shared with Andrea in the Mission.

By 1983, feminist studies and perspectives were institutionalized (though still marginal) at Berkeley, and the notion that the personal was political was in full flower. This idea appealed to me. It seemed crucial to figure out what meanings to attach to my own experiences, to answer the many questions, not yet fully articulated, floating around the edges of my consciousness: What did it mean that I was now thought to be working class? Why was the high school that I attended obviously substandard in comparison to those attended by my peers? Why was the South in general poorer than the rest of the nation? Had it been the poverty of my mother's childhood that so negatively affected her self-esteem and her relationship with her children? How had my experiences growing up in Birmingham, Alabama, site of some of the most entrenched resistance to the civil rights movement, affected me? What did it mean that my father, always my strongest parental ally, had fought on the wrong side of this battle, and how should I interpret his silence around this experience? What did it mean that my primary relationship was with a black woman? If my years at Berkeley didn't answer all of these questions, they at least gave me the tools to seek the answers on my own.

During my first semester at Berkeley, I picked up a class as elective, quite by accident, that would change my worldview entirely. It was a Third World literature class, which explored the deep biases at work in the Western European literary canon, taught by Paula Gunn Allen, a Native American poet then teaching in Berkeley's ethnic studies program. A deeply gifted teacher, Allen seemed to communicate on several different levels at once. Reviewing my notes at home, I would often find that they made no sense to me, even as I knew the harmony and order of her analysis in her presence; perhaps I didn't have enough hooks on which to place these new perspectives.

When Allen gave us the freedom to respond personally to one of our readings, I chose Pat Parker's *Movement in Black,* a book of poems in which Parker explored her experiences growing up Southern Baptist, working class, black, and lesbian in southwest Texas. I strongly identified with Parker's themes of border crossing, or the difficulties she experienced negotiating her lesbian feminism in her home culture, as well as the strain of negotiating her race and regional heritage in the predominantly white, middle-class lesbian feminist community in which she found herself. This essay

I wrote so long ago has stuck in my memory not only because it resulted in my first and only A+ as a student—a grade that went a long way toward helping me feel I could compete at Berkeley—but also because it was my first attempt to explore my own experiences as southern and lesbian. As I tried to sort out how region, race, class, gender, and religion intersected in my own experience as lesbian, I was beginning to do southern lesbian and gay studies without realizing it.

I've since lost this essay, but I do remember the two images with which I introduced my subject. The first was a memory of myself at about age ten or eleven, staring out the window of my parents' bedroom one Sunday evening, having just returned home from Baptist Training Union. What so riveted me was the image of a huge cross burning down in the valley next to the Robinwood Drive-In Theater. Terrified, I summoned my mother, half-fearing it was a sign of my inherent sinfulness (I was going through a period of taking religion very seriously). "That's probably just the Klan, protesting the dirty movies they've started showing down there," she responded. The word "just" and what it suggested was more chilling than the image of the burning cross; I had never before seen evidence of the Klan or known anyone to admit to such knowledge. The second image was then current—of Andrea and me shopping in the Mission on Market Street, poking around in one of the stores that sold standard work clothes, like the dickey pants popular with the Latino teenagers in our neighborhood. I spied some overalls and joked to Andrea that maybe I should buy them and "get back to my roots." "Why don't you just get a white sheet?" she quipped in return. Ghoulish humor was one way we dealt with racial difference in our relationship.

During the next several years, I entered into a kind of textual southernness, immersing myself in the history and literature of this region. Interestingly, I experienced most of my support for this work in Berkeley's ethnic studies program. In courses taught by Barbara Christian, I read the works of James Baldwin, Richard Wright, Zora Neal Hurston, Toni Morrison, Alice Walker, and many other black writers for the first time. I was shocked to find so much in common with the in-group experiences of African Americans these writers' portrayed so brilliantly and then shamed by my shock, as if in my ignorance of these groups' actual lives, I had been unable to fully envision the humanity of people of color. These writers' acute analyses of the structural nature of race, class, and gender oppression gave me the flip side of America's ideological coin. While their analyses were liberating, giving more coherence to the world I actually lived in, I also found the implications of their analyses unsettling. If racism was structural in nature, if it was built into our institutions, functioning much more in subtle ways than through obvious acts of bigotry, then I couldn't escape it by individual will. I carried white privilege with me, whether I wanted to or not. This new perspective required that I explore the effects of my own acculturation into racism—how it lived in me in the present.

Without having a name for this process, I was beginning to engage in what we in academia would now call "deconstructing whiteness," and this was not a particularly comfortable process. "How does my privilege shape my relationship with Andrea?" I had to ask myself. What made me willing to speak to her first, before any of the white women in the bar, that night I met her? Did I assume that she, one of the few black women in this predominantly white dyke club, felt as out of place as I did, and was I thus less afraid of risking rejection with her? Was she my insurance card against being perceived as the typical southern white racist? The more I learned about racial politics, the more I realized that our relationship had to be marked by the myriad of differences made by race, culture, and region. But I also knew that it didn't feel useful or accurate to characterize our relationship as simply a working out of white guilt on my part, or of black resentment/anger on the part of Andrea. Beyond that acknowledgement, I wasn't sure where to go.

It was also at Berkeley that I discovered the existence of southern lesbian feminists and through them learned about longstanding, southern white antiracist traditions—information that led me to reconsider my assumptions about what kind of life it was possible to live in the South. Randomly exploring the periodical stacks in Berkeley's library, I came across old copies of a lesbian feminist journal published in North Carolina called *Feminary* and was simply stunned. I had never imagined that there were organized lesbian feminist communities in the South. This journal's contents made clear that they had been active since the late 1960s. While browsing at Cody's bookstore on Telegraph Avenue, I stumbled upon Mab Segrest's 1985 collection of personal and literary essays, *My Mama's Dead Squirrel*, in which she sketches out a southern white lesbian literary tradition from the early twentieth century. Through Segrest's work, which has been so foundational to southern queer studies, I located the works of Lillian Smith, Minnie Bruce Pratt, and numerous other southern white lesbian feminist writers. Clearly, I was seeking models of resistance; I needed to know that there were other southern white lesbians and feminists out there who had transgressed their culture's conventions, to see physical evidence of their/our existence. It seemed the ultimate irony that I had had to travel all the way across the country to learn about these movements.

All through my years in California, my father maintained regular contact, providing consistent emotional support that I depended on greatly. Unlike mother, he was respectful of my relationship with Andrea, treating her with genuine warmth when he would call to chat. Dad's preferred method of communication was by audiotape, though, his favorite toy being a microcassette recorder. With anthropological zeal, he kept it with him constantly and recorded everything from phone conversations with relatives and friends (often without their knowledge) to conversations around the dinner table at family gatherings.

Sometimes, these tapes simply narrated his movement through his day. "I'm on Tarrant Highway now, heading home. I just passed the ABC plant, the water tower, Gurley's Insurance—you know, they've gone out of business. Here's the Waffle House, city hall, that new Chinese Restaurant. I'm coming up on Jim's office [his brother, the insurance agent] now, and I see his car out front. Think I'll pop in and have a cup of coffee with him."

In other tapes, he'd update me on local politics. "The mayor's race seems like its running more on the merits of each individual, which is real good. Arrington predicts he'll get 20 percent of the white vote, and Katapodis—pollsters predict he'll get 3 percent. It's not quite that way with the council race. There's been quite a few racial slurs thrown in that one. In fact, one councilwoman's car was firebombed out in the eastern section."

As Dad's familiar voice conjured up the everyday sights of home, these tapes gave me much pleasure, and I was touched that he took the time to make them. He wanted me to reciprocate the effort, but I rarely did, feeling awkward talking into the recorder and uncomfortable imagining how my parents would receive the realities of my life. While the tapes were a visible sign of his continued love and support, they also had the effect of rooting me—of making it very difficult for me to just write off my family or reduce their lives to stereotypes.

Only twice during my five years in California did I go back home for a visit, and both visits were quite tense, as I began to figure out what kind of relationship I could have with my family as a whole, given the deep rift between my mother and me. During one trip, I had a conversation with my father that would force me to rethink our relationship entirely. I had just completed a course on the civil rights movement and had finally gotten up the nerve to ask him about his experiences during that infamous summer of 1963. He responded defensively to my questions, resenting what he saw as my a priori, knee-jerk radical position. Dad argued that contrary to popular perception, the movement in Birmingham was not nonviolent, that rocks and pieces of pavement were being chucked at officers—that they were outnumbered and at times afraid. He told me how scary it had been to be called out at 2:00 A.M. to arrive on the scene of a bombing and find himself the only white person present—a mob of angry black folks gathered around. He described how the "northern" press took a photo of him "just trying to get handcuffs on a woman" that made it appear that he was clubbing her on the head—a photo that appeared in one of the major news magazines.

I was taken aback, wanting to hear him say anything but this, thinking, But you had guns, firehoses, clubs! Bull Connor even had a tank, for Christ's sake! Instead, I changed the subject and sat silently, trying to absorb the realization that this father who had never hit me with anything but a rolled-up newspaper, and that in play, had undoubtedly acted in ways that I hadn't wanted to imagine. In that moment I began to realize how dad's total silence around his work had functioned to protect my image of him as a peacemaker, and how much I wanted to retain this image, against all facts. No doubt, it was an uncomfortable moment for him as well, as the devoted daughter, so dependent on his love and affection, asked the impossible question How could you?—a question no parent wants to hear.

My Southern Baptist heritage had given me an almost old-world view of the universe as a place in which the individual alone is accountable directly to God for his or her actions. Against this background, it seemed patronizing to assume that my father, for instance, hadn't known what was wrong with his lack of stance against segregation, even as it seemed too much to expect—ridiculous, really—to think that he could have so easily stepped outside his culture and taken risks for which he had no fallback. I recalled Dad telling me how he became a cop quite by accident in the early 1950s when ACIPCO, the steel company for which he worked, kept going out on strike. My mother was pregnant with his first child, and he felt he needed a steady paycheck. In the summer of 1963, he was thirty-five years old and had four children. How was I to deal with questions of accountability and justice in relation to my parents, when I began taking into my analysis what I had learned about all the ideological and material forces of race, class, gender, sexuality, and religion—the power of which I was just beginning to be aware.

This new understanding of the structural nature of oppression required me to rethink my relationship with my mother as well. Increasingly, I realized that in our family dynamic, my father had always held the good-guy position, which was basically unfair. At some gut level, I knew that my tendency to demonize my mother was made all too easy by our culture's general devaluation of all things female. When my anger toward my mother abated to the point that I no longer saw her as evil personified, then I had to deal with her history and its effects. And I began to realize how much her silence around her childhood had been designed to protect as well. Growing up, I had only heard the most benign snatches of stories about mother's childhood—the "we were poor but hardworking and happy" version. As she and I began to try to communicate across our major differences, bits and pieces of another, much harsher, story began to surface, usually at the end of major arguments. What emerged was a story of mental illness, violence, poverty, and emotional abuse. My grandfather, mother's father, had died before I was born, and I never heard much about him. When mother described her life with him, I knew why.

My mother was born in 1930, after my grandfather had returned from three years' incarceration in the state mental asylum, having been placed there by his brothers and sisters after he had threatened to kill his whole family. Mother described behavior in her father that would probably classify him as paranoid schizophrenic today: he accused the neighbors of poisoning his well, his brother of stealing from him; he beat my grandmother regularly, until her oldest children became big enough or brave enough to stop him. My grandmother was left with the task of being the sole provider for her six children during the depression. They lived in a house that was formerly a dairy barn, that lacked proper insulation or indoor plumbing until the late 1940s. Though I had never heard the details of this story before, it felt uncannily familiar. I had of course grown up with its effects; though not verbalized, this story had been told in silence and action.

When I came out, my mother had access to no public discourse, either moral or legal, that would make me socially acceptable. I came to see how her tactics—or her emotional abusiveness—though powerful, were the tactics of the weak. She had devoted her tremendous energy to giving her children the tools to pass seamlessly into the middle class and beyond, through our training in how to be smart, polite, straight, Christian, and white. That she envisioned this training as safety—safety at the very least from poverty and its debilitating effects on the spirit—is clear. She didn't want us to inherit her fears, or the limits she experienced.

In her mind, my being lesbian and willing to tell cast me outside this mythical protected circle. Taking for my lover a black woman gave me a hypervisibility, in fact, for why else would we be together? No one could say we were sisters. For someone so conscious of trying to please, producing a daughter so willing to thumb her nose at social conventions—conventions that she saw as useful and protective—must have been mystifying. She felt it was her job as the mother, as the enforcer of cultural norms, to steer me back into that circle. I am thankful that she has since given up this effort, and I have given up the effort of staying angry with her.

Gradually, my anger itself began to seem like a kind of privilege, and my impulse to judge my parents so harshly a desire to distance myself from them—from both their choices and lack of choices—for I feared that they negatively reflected on me. It was about the loss of my innocence upon realizing that there was no separation, that I was thoroughly of this region, that the values and beliefs of the working-class or lower-middle-class white Protestant culture from which I came lived in me. It was about realizing that the complex of attitudes toward race and class that I inherited still lead me to react with fear when encountering someone who looks poorer than I, or of a different color, and require me to fight my immediate assumption that they are dangerous. It was about realizing that it was now my responsibility to reeducate myself, and that this reeducation will be a lifetime's work, never ending.

In 1987, I left the Bay Area and moved back South. In part, this was a practical decision: I wanted to continue the scholarship I had begun as an undergraduate on southern women's history and literature in graduate school, and some of the best programs in southern studies were in the South. But of course, my scholarly interests were also personally motivated. I had become fascinated with the southern radical political traditions I had discovered and wanted to not only study these traditions, but to locate and participate in them—to see if it were possible to be myself on my home turf. Perhaps more importantly, I was homesick: I missed having a closer, more casual relationship with my sisters and brother and their families, and increasingly, I felt that I needed to work out a better relationship with my parents. None of this seemed possible from such a distance.

When I returned home, I still held the assumption that it was going to be more difficult to be an out lesbian in the South. Instead, I've had a number of experiences living in Atlanta in the ten years since that have challenged this notion. For instance, when I arrived at Emory for graduate school, I never thought it would be possible for me to get a doctorate degree as an out lesbian feminist whose scholarship focuses on queer southerners. I never dreamt that Emory would change its attitude toward its queer members so profoundly, and over such a short time. I never thought that it would extend equal protection and benefits to its queer faculty, students, and staff, create an Office of Lesbian, Gay, Bisexual Life, or fund a queer studies program. I never thought that I would find myself a student activist, pushing the university to make these changes.

Neither did I imagine that I would find myself marching down Peachtree Street on Gay Pride Day with Atlanta's Lesbian Avengers, in nothing but a push-up bra and cut-offs, pausing in front of the First Baptist Church only long enough to moon the goonish security guards placed outside by its notoriously homophobic pastor, Rev.

Charles Stanley. I never thought I would see members of St. Mark's Methodist, located across the street from Stanley's First Baptist, set up a water table on their front steps underneath a banner declaring that everyone was welcome at St. Mark's. Silly stuff, you might say, but symbolically very powerful. Of course, change never comes without cost, and at times that cost has seemed very high. But we pay that cost wherever we live and do our work. For me personally, the costs have been balanced by the reward of seeing change happen here, by the rewards of seeing my own and others assumptions about what is typically southern exploded.

But it would be highly reductive if I told these queer stories only, without also describing the radical changes I've witnessed in my own family—without telling my new southern stories. It would be a distortion to not also describe my surprise at this vision: that at my father's retirement party (from his second career working seventeen years as a security officer for the Birmingham city school system) was present his entire work family, all African American, sitting in uneasy alliance with his blood family on my parents' patio, their relationship with him clearly easy and affectionate. Neither should I omit the fact that on my last visit to my parents' home, I saw that my mother had placed on the refrigerator, along with the photographs of her white grandchildren, a photograph of my brother's grandchildren, Brian and Corwana, both African American. Neither should I fail to describe how all of my family has provided me consistent emotional and material support in my career as an out lesbian feminist academic creating scholarship about southern queer experiences. Without telling these stories too, I risk being read within stereotypes of the South that fail to reveal complexities.

While I can't embrace a simple, celebratory response to my southern queer experiences, neither do I think it useful to ignore these positive changes. To do so allows the South to be portrayed as hopeless. It requires us to write off this whole region of the country as not worth the effort, even as it dishonors those homegrown radical traditions for social justice that have been so important to our survival. For queers from the South, it keeps us thinking that we have to run off to New York, or as I did, to San Francisco, to be queer. Writing this essay on my southern queer experiences has required that I reconceptualize the telling of my own stories, not as an act of shame or betrayal, but as an act of faith. For if the devil lies in the details, so do faith and hope.

Notes

Acknowledgments. The support of friends, family, and colleagues was crucial to the year-long process of writing this essay. Mary Anne Adams, Judith Byrne, Becca Cragin, Danny Clinton, Carlos Dews, Herb Green, Lori Grigsby, Juliana Kubala, Erin O'Briant, Brooke Perry, Aaron Taub, Edrica Webb, and Celeste Weaver each provided me with encouragement and insightful close readings. In particular, I am indebted to my brother and sister, David Price Smith and Virginia Ruth Smith, for blessing this project with their unwavering emotional and material support, and for their critical perspective on successive drafts.

1. All personal names used in this essay are pseudonyms.

James R. Keller

Tennessee Williams Doesn't Live Here Anymore: Hypocrisy, Paradox, and Homosexual Panic in the New/Old South

Columbus, Mississippi, is the birthplace of Tennessee Williams. In a recent move by the city, the house of the playwright's nativity was purchased from the Episcopal Church, upon whose grounds it had rested, and was moved one block north to Main Street where it was established as a Mississippi Welcome Center. In its new location, the house has been given a complete face lift. It has a brand-new foundation and a new colorful paint job, making it the nicest building on Main Street. It is brightly illuminated with spotlights at night, thus calling attention to itself. The building occupies a formerly vacant lot that has been newly landscaped with a well-manicured lawn and new sidewalks that make the structure easily accessible to tourists and residents alike. In front of the house, the city has erected a sign, identifying the building as a historical landmark and claiming the Tennessee Williams legacy as Columbus's own. The sign displays the following inscription:

> The First Home of Tennessee Williams. One of America's leading playwrights. Tennessee Williams was born here March 26, 1911. He received the Pulitzer Prize for "Streetcar Named Desire" and "Cat on a Hot Tin Roof." Both stories set in the South.

The sign is interesting for what it does not say. Information vital to the identity of America's premier playwright and yet repugnant to this small southern town has been carefully omitted and highlighted at the same time. Tennessee Williams was a homosexual, a fact that he made no effort to conceal and a fact that, I am told, created quite a

This essay originally appeared in *Studies in Popular Culture* 19, 2 (1996): 303–318. Reprinted with permission of *Studies in Popular Culture*.

scandal among Columbus's residents. Yet many years later, Columbus does not fail to exploit its connection to Williams. One would like to believe that this move reveals the community's growing tolerance toward sexual diversity, but this unfortunately is not true. Columbus is a profoundly homophobic community, harboring an intolerance and militant hostility fueled, of course, by the ubiquitous influence of the Southern Baptist Church. Indeed, at the same time that the city has chosen to honor a homosexual by moving his birthplace onto Main Street, it has initiated legal reprisals against the local gay community, which it seems intent upon driving right out of town.

Columbus has still another claim to fame. It is the birthplace of the national Memorial Day. The holiday is said to have begun in one of the local cemeteries after the Civil War where the soldiers of both the North and the South were buried alongside each other. The local ladies indiscriminately decorated all of the graves—both northern and southern—to honor the war dead, and it is out of this gesture that the national holiday was born. The association between the community and the nation's chief war holiday reveals the most potent influence upon the local social consciousness. Columbus is a military town, facilitating one of the country's pilot training bases, and it is in the military camp that the community's sentiments lie.

Columbus's two claims to fame replicate one of the most vexed issues in American society today—the presumed incompatibility of homosexuals with military service. Whereas the American military has always been hostile toward homosexuals, the extent to which it was willing to pursue soldiers with alternative sexual identities has varied over the past century. Of course, the antigay element of the debate would have us believe that the policy, partially overturned in 1993, finds its origin in Leviticus, a sentiment that conveniently ignores history. During the debate over gays in the military, Columbus was relatively quiet, not because it was indifferent but because it continued to observe the culturally imposed silence upon the issue of homosexuality in spite of the national uproar. However, as Foucault has taught us, we as a culture have devised multiple covert discourses for talking about sex, even as we tell ourselves that we are sexually repressed. From this perspective, it is probable that Columbus's profound hostility toward Pres.ident Clinton is, at least partially, fueled by his stand on gays in the military. Those ubiquitous bumper stickers revealing yet another Bush supporter may be a clandestine means of protesting Clinton's breach of the silence on homosexuality without actually breaching the silence again with protest.

The Tennessee Williams house has not enjoyed its renaissance because of the increased social tolerance of the community but because the playwright's reputation has been sanitized by time. The historical marker commemorating the building recognizes *Cat on a Hot Tin Roof* and *Streetcar Named Desire* as Williams's most important works, but, of course, it does not mention that homosexuality is symbolically central to both of these plays. The catalyst behind Blanche Dubois's nervous breakdown is the discovery of her husband in bed with another man. It is the contrast between her sister's husband Stanley (a former soldier) and the memory of her own deceased husband (a queer and boyish poet) that defines the spectrum of manhood in the drama. Blanche has both repressed the painful memory of her husband's sexual transgression and also highlighted it through the pursuit of her own sexual object choices. She continues to pursue males who are explicitly referred to as boys; the most memorable of course is the young schoolboy whose seduction resulted in her dismissal from her job. Blanche openly condemns her dead husband at the same time that she pursues and validates him through surrogate lovers and through her repudiation of Stanley's notion of manhood.

In *Cat on a Hot Tin Roof*, Brick is torn apart by his obsessive guilt over his latent desire for his friend Skipper, another queer suicide. The action of the drama surrounds Maggie's effort to coax her husband back into her bed after long absence, but Brick is more intent upon drinking until he hears the click in his head that shuts out the world. Brick's savage denials of any homoerotic attachment between himself and Skipper serve at once to repudiate and confirm the accusations made against him. The play suggests that the close relationships between males, resulting from what our culture considers manly activities, reveal repressed homoerotic impulses, yet since our culture defines masculinity as a repudiation of homosexuality, it is important for Brick to carefully police the division between his sentiments and those of an admittedly gay man such as Skipper. Despite his repressed homoerotic desire for his buddy, Brick is plainly the most homophobic individual in the play; it is vital to his masculine self-image that he repudiate any implication of forbidden passion. However, despite his energetic and even hostile denials, his continued self-destructiveness, manifest in his alcoholism, his indifference toward the family legacy, and his rejection of his wife's seductive overtures confirm his deep attachment to Skipper.

In a subtle way, the historical marker's commemoration of Tennessee Williams's two most prominent plays provides a clue to the proper interpretations of the cultural processes that brought the Tennessee Williams home to Main Street at a time of increased hostility toward gays and lesbians, hostility that at times borders on panic. Just as Blanche and Brick attempt to drive the memory of same-sex desire out of their consciousness, they only succeed in validating those sentiments that they attempt to negate. While Columbus collectively and conveniently forgets Williams's sexual identity in the process of honoring his life and work, it revives its hostility toward the homosexual community with a renewed vigor; the antigay campaign includes police harassment and entrapment, vituperative newspaper editorials, and telephone campaigns sponsored by the religious right.

In the past few years, the harassment of gay men, at the national level, has been characterized by a discourse of difference that pits hegemonic masculinity, represented by the military man, against the homosexual, who is stereotyped as the refutation of masculinity. In the opposition between military man/gay man, the former is favored to such an extent that the civil rights of the latter can be legally abridged just because they make the former uncomfortable. This phenomenon is part of an ongoing effort to relegate homosexuals to a position of second-class citizenship.

The national debate over gays in the military concluded with a policy that left no one satisfied and prompted some surprising admissions about gender relations from the military leadership. The resolution to the national uproar is perhaps the most vexed policy in recent memory, don't ask; don't tell; don't pursue. With this compromise, the military leadership acknowledges that it can cope with gay men and lesbians within the ranks of the service but cannot endure the knowledge of their presence. Even more astonishingly, the military leadership complained that it would not be able to maintain discipline among the common soldiers if homosexuals were permitted to admit their sexual preferences publicly. This is perhaps even more unsettling than the previous admission, because here we discover that an institution whose very existence is predicated upon discipline is so vulnerable to the vicissitudes of social change that it is threatened by collapse if the average soldier believes another is looking at his bum in the shower. The military leadership further argues that the heterosexual soldier would not be able to respect a superior officer who is gay or would not be able to trust his peers when their unit is under fire. It had been the assumption of most that discipline under these circumstances is maintained by fear of punishment and/or death. Paradoxically, the new military policy, lifting the ban but not the silence, implies that maintaining a false identity makes a gay man worthy of respect and trust. Thus the military plainly values dishonesty over integrity and sincerity.

The military base is a privileged space whose boundaries represent the split between traditional and compromised masculinities. The refusal to allow openly gay men in the service constitutes an effort to designate a social space within which men can still be traditional men without fear of having their socially constituted gender identity undermined by the presence of those who seem to contradict it. In other words, the gay man must lie about his sexual identity so that the heterosexual male can continue to believe that gender identity is dictated by nature rather than social conditions. The military as an institution then attempts to create a space in which hegemonic masculinity can be fully facilitated. The institution as a whole denies admission to anyone who undermines the ideal. Even the women who are a part of the institution must conform to what our culture defines as masculine, not in their sexual object choices, but in their behavior. Indeed, most of the arguments against women in combat begin with the premise that females are not sufficiently male. A woman in the service must be able to compete with men on men's terms because the masculine identity and the military identity are coterminous. She must act like a man (except, of course, in sexual expression) in order to avoid undermining the confidence of her fellow soldiers.

So closely allied are heterosexuality and masculinity in military ideology that, paradoxically, a straight woman, by virtue of her sexual preference, is more likely to have the necessary masculine qualities than a gay male or a lesbian. For males, the price of admission at the restricted American military bases is a willingness to exploit women sexually. The close male bonding that occurs between soldiers in battle must be safeguarded and guaranteed by the mutual desire to possess the female. That guarantee is maintained at the military recruitment offices, where, in the past, sexual identity has been carefully policed in order to assure the average military man that it is safe to bond with his mates.

The same social processes that are currently working themselves out on the American military bases have begun to replicate themselves in other segments of American culture. In fact, the trend is to restrict overt homosexuality to a smaller and smaller area within the culture and, specifically, a private area. This amounts to a concerted effort to silence the Gay Rights Movement, returning it to its pre-Stonewall obscurity and vulnerability. Perhaps one of the most revealing examples of this agenda is the recent effort by the religious right in Florida to prohibit the annual gathering of gays and lesbians at Disney World. The Disney administration refused to take a side in the dispute, arguing that it had no way and no desire to exclude any particular group from the premises. The religious right responded by offering legal advice on various techniques for excluding undesirables from the park. The Right suggested that Disney could prohibit open displays of same-sex affection provided they were also willing to prohibit open displays of heterosexual affection. Once again, the stipulation for inclusion within the public space is secrecy. Provided the homosexual remains closeted, s/he can be included.

Perhaps the most notable figure in the debate is the Reverend Phelps of Topeka, Kansas, who made a special pilgrimage to Orlando to protest the presence of gays and lesbians at the theme park. Phelps gained notoriety by demonstrating at the funerals of gay men, dead from AIDS, telling the mourners that the deceased are in hell. Another example of the process is the recent effort by Congress to deny federal funding to schools that characterize homosexuality as normal. The legislation is part of a trend that seeks to deny tax money to any practice that may prove beneficial to gays and lesbians, a trend that conveniently forgets that queers are taxpayers too. These social practices ultimately backfire, because at the same time that the opposition tries to silence gay activism, it makes that activism the object of prolonged public attention; moreover, it acts as a catalyst for unity, the consolidation of gay power, both financial and political.

The same cultural practices identified at the national level have begun to define local social relations. The split between public and private space and between conscious and unconscious, the binary opposition between military man and gay man, has begun to (re)segregate a community that previously accepted integration only by compulsion. Of course, the objects of exclusion have changed. In effect, Tennessee Williams has been assigned a closet in his own house. His prominence on Main Street relies entirely upon the sanitizing of his image, the unspeakable remaining unspoken. The new Mississippi Welcome Center does not so much welcome as marginalize and exclude those who have a close affinity with the playwright.

A debate at Mississippi University for Women initiated one of the worst local flare-ups of the controversy regarding the place of gays in American society. The university invited one of the nationally prominent figures in the gays in the military issue, Tom Panacea, to participate in a debate with a local retired colonel. The forum had been planned entirely for the interest and benefit of the students and faculty. However, that did not stop the community from getting involved. The public outrage bordered on panic; the silence had been broken. The president's office at the university was deluged with calls from angry citizens who were evidently part of a telephone campaign by a local ministry. The final tally was approximately three hundred calls in just two days. They included such memorable suggestions as that of a store owner who instructed the university to consult local businessmen before it schedules any controversial presentations. Another caller accused the university of inviting Panacea to campus to teach the students how to be homosexuals. Still another suggested that the program was legitimizing homosexuality, and when informed that the forum would include the opposing point of view, the caller added that just to invite the man to town was an implicit endorsement.

The evening of the program brought several surprises, not least of which was a bomb threat. I guess one of the local residents felt it was his/her civic duty to hinder the debate at all costs. However, after the building was checked, the event went forward as scheduled, largely without incident. There were only a few protesters during the forum, yet they were not allowed inside because the limited seating was reserved for students and faculty, and even many of the students had to be turned away. Only one of the protesters remained committed to his cause throughout the program and was still holding his vigil outside when it concluded. He carried a sign that indicated (we hope) that he had never attended a university: "Homosexual not with my tax dollar." My first impulse was to hand him a nickel and ask for change, but instead everyone, myself included, just ignored him. The real winners of the evening were the students, who adopted a very mature attitude toward the discussion, showing respect for both speakers despite the unequal skills of the presenters. It turned out that the retired colonel was not entirely committed to the task of defending the military ban.

At the end of the event, the coordinators were quite happy that the program had gone off without incident, had been covered by local television, and had demonstrated the politeness, maturity, and broad-mindedness of the student body. However, what was done was not yet done. The next day Mr. Panacea attended a class in the Humanities Division, a class that included a discussion of his struggle and his commitment to military service. This was followed by a polite question-and-answer session and an uneventful dispersal of the group at the end of the period. Panacea's presence in the classroom was dramatically distorted in the media. The most unfounded account of this latter event held that freshmen had been herded into a room and "forced" to watch a video on how to be a homosexual.

Interestingly, it was Panacea's participation in this class discussion that created most of the controversy, because it dissolved the safe distance between the queer presenter and the unblemished student body, and in the minds of religious hysterics, the discussion resembled programming. Anger over the address resulted from the assumption that students should have the opportunity to ignore any information that conflicts with their prejudices and their religious conditioning. This popular sentiment neglected to consider the ever present detractors who are available to undermine any effort by gays and lesbians to make an honest and positive portrayal of themselves. However, the hysterical response of the community presumed university students to be more impressionable than they are. I am sure that the local parents would be proud to know that their children brought all of their biases into the room with them. Although the majority were respectfully silent, one walked out and another muttered obscenities under his breath.

Interestingly, the public conversation that followed did not dispute whether or not the forum should have taken place but, instead, whether or not it was appropriate to hold the event on campus; some maintained that it should have been held downtown in the civic center. Of course, had the event been scheduled at the civic center, it would never have taken place. The implicit argument of the opposition was that homosexuals should be excluded from public space, specifically the university, and should have no opportunity to influence college freshmen, to invest them with the most dreaded of sentiments—social tolerance. More and more, the issue turned to a dispute over the nature of a university. The agenda of the detractors was to exclude gays and lesbians from public property under the implicit assumption that any particular taxpayer who objects to a program should have the right to shut it down. (There goes the MX missile and SDI.) At one point, local homophobes sent a letter demanding that the administration fire all faculty members believed to be gay. Of course, the letter also included a list of names. If the administration had circulated that letter among the faculty, I am sure that the latter could have taught the perpetrators the meaning of "libel" and "litigation." But the administration graciously suppressed the document. Perhaps the most vituperative and certainly the most persistent voice in the debate came from a prominent businessman who wrote many editorials in the local paper denouncing the university and calling for its closure. Since the university is one of the town's principal employers, it is difficult to determine whether this retailer is merely short-sighted or prepared to sacrifice everything for his beliefs; the closure of MUW would devastate the town financially.

In symbolic contrast to the aforementioned fiasco, controversial figure Oliver North was invited to Columbus to speak at the civic center only a short time after Panacea's visit. There were no public protests, no angry phone calls, no bomb threats, and no vituperative letter-writing campaigns. Many people from the university who denounce the senatorial candidate attended the event and listened politely. North was treated with respect and even admiration by the community. In Columbus, Mississippi, he is the type of individual who is licensed to occupy public space. Columbus prefers to validate a man who was convicted of lying to Congress and who knowingly subverted the Constitution of the United States. Here again, we see that the community prioritizes falsehood or silence above courage and sincerity. Mr. Panacea is fighting the federal government so that he can live an open and honest life and be reinstated in his job. In contrast to North, Panacea is waging his battle through the courts, and instead of fighting to justify subversion, he is struggling to be liberated from a secret life. This contrast exposes a "fault line" in the ideology of the community.[1] Overwhelmingly fundamentalist, Columbus characterizes itself as one of the final bulwarks of traditional morality and, therefore, denounces homosexuality as the great evil that threatens America's families, while at the same time the community celebrates and embraces falsehood and political corruption. Of the two men, North has the reputation for bravery and patriotism, despite the fact that he has shown no respect for America's institutions. Moreover, he has the unqualified approval of the religious right, which apparently believes that the only irredeemable sin is the transgression of sexual norms. The Right is perfectly willing to lionize a subversive scoundrel.

North's acceptance affirms traditional notions of masculinity. Politics and militarism are the exclusive province of heterosexual men, so despite his efforts to undermine the American political process, North possesses the criteria necessary for public service—chief among them the desire to dominate and sexually exploit women—whereas Panacea, despite his efforts to participate in the social institution that fashions itself as the arbiter of courage and masculinity, and despite his former success in that institution, is automatically deemed unfit and is excluded. In a discussion following the university forum, one student suggested that it is foolhardy to re-admit a homosexual to the service since he would refuse to fight when conflict arose. So even in his effort to be included in an institution that could put him in danger, the gay soldier is still stereotyped as a coward.

Another local social phenomenon relevant to this discussion involves law enforcement's efforts to exclude queer men from public land. Since Columbus is a small town, there are no establishments that cater directly to the gay community; thus gays have had to compromise, choosing to meet in public places. I do not refer here to public sex. For a number of years, gay men gathered at a local park called the "Lock and Damn," not so that they could transgress local standards of decency by buggering each other in the bushes,[2] but so that there was a centralized location to meet people with the same sexual orientation. Of course, I cannot deny that there were those who, carried away by passion, were compelled to consummate their desires in some private niche. However, gay men were not the only transgressors in this area. Heterosexual couples frequented the location and had the audacity to consummate their affections in the backseats of parked cars and in plain sight. However, when the sheriff's department decided to clean up the place, its attention focused exclusively on the queer subversives. In the words of one young officer, "We understand that there is homosexual activity in this park, and we aim to stop it." What resulted were old-fashioned, pre-Stonewall entrapments, undercover officers who coaxed and seduced and teased until they had enough evidence to arrest the unsuspecting transgressors.

The remarkable aspect of the Lock and Damn purge was that the officers themselves were able to do everything the gay men did, which is to talk about sex, but they were never in danger of arrest themselves. This double standard is based upon the assumption that the officers are being dishonest; they don't really mean what they say. While there is no actual intention behind the officer's words, the gay man, who is the subject of arrest and prosecution, is presumed to be honest and sincere in his words and his intentions. So the whole search-and-destroy mission rests upon a perception of intentionality. The officer escapes the odium of arrest because he, by virtue of his position in the exchange, can be presumed dishonest, whereas the gay man is subject to arrest and public humiliation because he is perceived to be truthful. Here again, this hotbed of fundamentalism values covert action and lies above openness and sincerity, to the extent that the hypocrite is construed to be the defender of community values and the honest man the subject of exclusion and persecution.

In one exchange, a law enforcement officer told a visitor to the park that he (the officer) was from El Paso, Texas, and, indeed, he sat in a battered old car with Texas plates. He said that he had come to town for a few weeks to work at Weyerhaeuser, a paper processing plant in town, that he was staying at the Regency Park Motel on Highway 45 in Columbus, and that soon he would be leaving for Oregon to take another temporary position. Of course, he was actually a sheriff's deputy from Aberdeen. He asked the gay man if there were any places in the area where people went to be private, and he asked about some of the other individuals driving around in the parking lot. The gay man asked him if there were any clubs in El Paso and if he cheated on his wife when he was at home or only when he traveled. Of course, much more passed between them; nevertheless, before long, the officer flashed his badge and explained that he was in the employ of the sheriff's department, that there had been a number of complaints by fishermen in the area who accused the local queers of propositioning them.

The politics of this exchange are quite complicated. The officer was able to make explicit allusions to his desire for a sexual tryst without any aspersion of homosexuality. He suggested that he was waiting for a boyfriend in order to account for his continued presence in the parking lot. He spoke the language of the gay underworld fluently. He smiled and seduced, and yet he was excluded from prosecution and, despite his considerable powers of misrepresentation, was recognized by the court for his veracity in his account of the arrests. He was considered by the courts to be the honest witness because in his exchanges with the many entrapped homosexuals, he was insincere, for if he were not construed in that way, he would be subject to the same prosecution to which he subjected others. Thus the veracity and justice of litigation rests upon the presumption that police officers are liars.

The sting operation in its effort to terrorize gay men, chasing them back into the closet, was only a marginal success, although it did clean out the Lock and Damn boat ramp. The presumption that the division between heterosexual and homosexual constitutes a real rather than a symbolic barrier created what must have been surprising results for the officers involved. They discovered ostensibly straight men soliciting for gay sex; many of the victims of the purge were married. Often, the single attribute sufficient to thwart suspicions of homosexuality (at least to the uninitiated) is marriage. Perhaps one reason the officers were considered above suspicion, despite their involvement in the intimate process of seduction and entrapment, was that they were married men. However, the presence of married men among the transgressors makes the issue of intentionality problematic. If the men who were prosecuted could be construed to be serious in their intention to commit sodomy, despite their marital status, then the officers cannot be presumed to be above suspicion.

The Lock and Damn is controlled by the Army Corps of Engineers, and it too participated in the mission to eradicate homosexual socializing from the public space. It is difficult to view the army's involvement as anything other than a reprisal for concessions made to gay soldiers during the national debate. The "reign of terror" at the dam, as it has been described by a local lawyer, is yet another effort by the far-right fringe to restrict the movements of gay men, to inhibit the infiltration of gay men into traditionally masculine areas of influence. If queers are permitted in an area occupied almost exclusively by men, an area in which platonic male intimacy is a principal objective, they create a problematic environment, because they threaten to associate homosocial bonding with same-sex desire. Through their complaints, the fishermen betray their fear that the presence of homosexuals casts aspersions on their own exclusively male activities; it reminds them of the potentially homoerotic implications of their own world. Thus their masculine integrity requires that they forcefully repudiate any association with queer interests. The presence of homosexuals interferes with the bonding of men in manly activities. As was explained during the gays in the military debate, intimate relations crop up between men in battle, and the presence of homosexuals makes those relationships suspicious. The straight soldier would not know if it were safe to bond with a comrade. The other man might construe the intimacy as a sexual overture. Interestingly, allowing openly gay men to serve in the military would have resolved the dilemma; the straight men would have known exactly whether it was safe to bond. The current policy, endorsed by the military leadership, guarantees continued confusion of intention and reception.

The campaign to exclude gay men from public places has become even more dramatic in recent months. One unsuspecting individual made the long ride out to the boat ramp at the Lock and Damn, drove once through the parking lot, and turned around and left. By the time he reached the edge of town, a car had closed in behind him and was flashing its headlights, signaling him to pull into a nearby parking lot. The driver of the first car turned into the lot of a bait shop and was confronted by an undercover cop, who after much coquettish meandering invited the driver to a room at the Regency Park Motel. Evidently, the driver found the solicitation appealing, so he followed the undercover cop back to the room. When the two men arrived at the motel and before any groping transpired, two more policemen popped out of the restroom and arrested the as yet unoffending driver for attempted sodomy—a felony. After a time, still more people arrived, this time from the Army Corps of Engineers, who charged the victim with still another crime. As they departed from the motel with the sodomite in cuffs, one cop promised to make the victim take an AIDS test. It is uncertain whether at the time the cops knew that they had nabbed a married man whose chief concern was to conceal the arrest from his unsuspecting wife.

The sexual politics of this particular entrapment are quite complex. Consider first the symbolic implications of two adult men hiding in a motel bathroom waiting for a third to lure a sodomite into their midst. Each will then have the opportunity to possess, victimize, and humiliate the captive. The situation resembles a gang rape. Here the boys' club achieves its homosocial bonding by collectively objectifying and symbolically excluding the man who dares to cross the boundary between bonding and erotic desire. Just as the mutual longing to objectify and sexually exploit women constitutes the single criterion for inclusion in male homosocial bonding, the officers involved in the arrest are further defining the parameters of that male world through their dramatic humiliation and marginalization of queer sensibilities.[3] Thus at least subconsciously the officers are treating the gay male as a woman and thus an object of exclusion through desire. They demonstrate their fragile masculinity by competing to be the one individual who most aggressively rejects and degrades the queer.

The operations at the dam exposed a whole buddy network in which one organization encouraged another to participate in the victimization of a particular social group. The initial purge of the boat ramp was perpetrated by the county and the Army Corps of Engineers because the area lies outside the city limits. Apparently, the city police felt left out of the fun. The more recent arrest involved a conscious effort to lure the victim to a motel within the city limits so that local officials could have their opportunity to prosecute, and so that the victim could be charged with the more serious crime of attempted sodomy, which is, evidently, a felony only within the city limits. But the county and the corps were not left out. Although the encounters with the undercover policeman did not take place on the corps's land, the assumption was made that because the victim had driven through the boat ramp parking lot, he too was subject to violations of that space. As it turned out, the victim was charged by the city, the county, and the corps. The extent of this operation we must presume is to signal the gay community that there is no safe place for its members in the city of Columbus, Mississippi.

The issue of veracity comes into play once again. The law enforcement officers, particularly the one who lured the unsuspecting driver into the trap, are excluded from the odium of attempted sodomy only because they are dishonest in their intentions. The subject of the sting operation is the only man who is construed to be sincere. The others by virtue of their positions are necessarily liars and hypocrites, or they too would be subject to arrest. However, the presence of the suspect in the room did not verify his intentions; no one had touched anyone else. The victim was entitled to be just as dishonest in his objectives as the other men. After much legal wrangling, the charges against the man were dropped upon the stipulation that he was banned from the park for one year. Even the conclusion to the case reveals that the objective of the purge was to exclude gay men from a public place, even if they had no intention of violating any laws, since it cannot be said that the victim of the arrest in this case had any homoerotic intentions before being confronted by the cop on private property.

The arrests at the dam were intended to remove gay sexuality from the public view. To force gays back into the closet, where they would conduct their activities in secret. However, the result was to make gay sex even more ostentatious. The names of all the men arrested were published on the front page of the local newspaper, making the private sex lives of these men public knowledge. It is usually at this point that the straight community accuses gays of pushing their sexuality into the collective space. The local businessman who wrote all of the angry letters to the paper after the university debate only succeeded in making the taboo an object of constant attention for months. Furious that the university would give the debate over homosexuality a place in the social discourse of Mississippi, he proceeded to perpetuate that discourse at great length.

Jonathan Katz founded the now defunct organization Queer Nation in response to his realization that there is no safe place in America for queers, no home or job that cannot be taken away at the whim of the heterosexual majority. All public space is heterosexual space, and even the bodily integrity of the homosexual is not protected by the law. Too often, the heterosexual adolescent male considers it his civic duty to beat and/or kill gays and lesbians when they are made known to him, and many of these assaults go unpunished even when brought to the attention of the law. In fact many of the worst violations of the personal and physical sovereignty of gays and lesbians are perpetrated by the police.[4]

The cultural politics of the new Welcome Center illustrate the traditional position of homosexuals in American culture. Queers are symbolically central and socially peripheral. As is the case with Tennessee Williams, the culture is willing to co-opt his fame for its own purposes, to take credit for his work and his life at the same time that it rejects his humanity, assuming that somehow his creative impulses are separate from his sexual predispositions. Williams is symbolically central insofar as he contributes to the nation's cultural identity and to the city's fame, but at the same time he is, in the eyes of local moralists and religious hysterics, suitable only for exclusion from the public space.

The ideological ruptures that have begun to expose themselves in the cultural and social institutions of Columbus, Mississippi, are represented in physical form by that house at the end of Main Street. It is only a facade enclosing a truly empty space; it is the city's conscience. The city's appropriation of Tennessee Williams's birthplace constitutes not a capitulation to queer interests, but a suppression of them, a continued testament to their irrelevance. The house is a decayed house masquerading as a new beginning and a new openness while it continues to perpetuate Mississippi's history of repression, persecution, intolerance, and segregation. The house is an appropriation and rehabilitation of the formerly subversive space, a social process in which power guarantees its success, possessing and transforming transgressive energy. The house's new paint job signifies the sterilizing of Williams's image, making his space the public heterosexual space, his house the bourgeois home. I envision a new and more appropriate sign for the building: "Tennessee Williams doesn't live here anymore, and if he did, we'd run his queer ass right out of town!"

Notes

1. In his book *Faultlines: Cultural Materialism and the Politics of Dissident Reading,* Alan Sinfield defines a "fault line" as the collision between contradictory assumptions within the same ideology (Berkeley: University of California Press, 1992, 9).

2. The issue of public sex is problematic. Queer theorists have demonstrated that what is considered public sex is generally quite well concealed. The participants take considerable effort to veil their activities. Pat Califia, *Public Sex: The Culture of Radical Sex* (Pittsburgh: Cleis, 1994), 71–82.

3. Eve Kosofsky Sedgewick, *Between Men: English Literature and Male Homosocial Bonding* (New York: Columbia University Press, 1985), 21–27.

4. Katz articulates the motivation behind the formation of Queer Nation in a discussion with Frank Browning in *The Culture of Desire* (New York: Vintage, 1993), 26–54.

Part III

Representing
Queer Lives
in Public Space

R. Bruce Brasell

Greetings From Out Here:
Southern Lesbians and Gays
Bear Witness to the Public Secret

And this is like our chance to be here and to like show that we're doing
things. This isn't a New York thing. This is not San Francisco. This is
Atlanta, Georgia. And no you don't have to pack up and move to San
Francisco to be gay.

> Comment from a participant at the Atlanta Lesbian
> and Gay Pride parade interviewed in Ellen Spiro's
> 1993 *video* Greetings from Out Here

Ellen Spiro, at the beginning of her 1993 video *Greetings from Out Here,* after telling us that she moved from the South to New York City and "became a full-fledged gay activist," muses: "But there was something funny about this picture. Here I was being an out dyke, and back home I was still in the closet."[1] The narrative framing of Spiro's documentary uses a trope familiar in contemporary southern literature—for example, Peter Taylor's *A Summons to Memphis* and Gail Godwin's *A Southern Family*—in which an expatriate southerner living in New York City returns home to the South for a visit, a trip usually prompted by a family crisis. In Spiro's case, that crisis was breaking up with her girlfriend of three years and feeling homesick. So Spiro hit the road with her dog, Sam, resolving, "My mission for the next year is to explore southern gay subcultures and to find people who stayed in their small towns instead of joining the anonymous masses of the big cities." Based on this narrative structure, the lesbians and gays Spiro visits in the South become positioned as her family, allowing her an outsider/insider perspective on, in Spiro's words, "the southern world that formed me and to recreate it with my camera, this time from my own queer's eye view."

Spiro's road trip takes her to such diverse events as a gay rodeo in Texas, a Two Nice Girls concert in Austin, a gay Mardi Gras ball in New Orleans, a Radical Faeries'

May Pole festival in Tennessee, a Lesbian and Gay Pride parade in Atlanta, and a women's music festival in Georgia. She visits the diverse homes of Isis, a lesbian who inhabits a school bus in Arkansas; John Blansett, an AIDS patient who lives with his extended family in Mississippi; Chance, a sixteen-year-old dyke who works in a feminist bookstore in Atlanta; Michael Lane, cocreator of *Monk* magazine who occupies a farm with his mother, grandmother, and lover in Arkansas; Allan Gurganus, author of *Oldest Living Confederate Widow Tells All,* who resides in North Carolina; and James Cox, a gay minister who pastors a straight congregation in Alabama.

At first glance, Spiro's video appears to share many affinities with Ross McElwee's 1986 film *Sherman's March,* both at the level of the documentary filmmakers themselves and in the narrative structures they use to construct their documentaries.[2] Both filmmakers are expatriate southerners returning to the South for a road trip on which they bring along their filmmaking equipment. And both documentaries are structured as visual and audiovisual diaries of personal searches: for love in McElwee's case and gay roots in Spiro's case. The South has a long tradition of oral storytelling, whether in the form of tall tales, jests, folktales, personal experience narratives, or anecdotes. Though the South does not have an indigenous commercial-film industry, the culture's emphasis on producing images through words rather than visuals has resulted in a long literary tradition in the area, and both filmmakers partake of this storytelling tradition in two ways: (1) the construction of their documentaries as tales about their personal experiences on the road, and (2) the stories told to us by the individuals the filmmakers encounter on their journeys.

Because both documentary filmmakers are one-person technical crews, they must develop filmmaking strategies for the insertion of their own images into their audiovisual diaries. McElwee accomplishes this by positioning his camera on a tripod and sits or lays in front of it. Spiro stretches out her arm and points her handheld camera directly at herself or at a shiny reflective surface, which sometimes may be a mirror, through which she can be viewed. The filmmakers also use different editing styles that are comparable to their respective mise-en-scene strategies. McElwee relies predominately on long takes, while Spiro uses a rapid-fire editing style.

Though we hear stories and musings from the people McElwee and Spiro encounter on their trips, Spiro, unlike McElwee, interweaves her talking heads with shots of their surroundings, visually contextualizing them within various physical environments and social communities. Though the lesbians and gays Spiro meets tell her personal stories, those experiential narratives function not to isolate them as one might expect but rather to position them within larger southern lesbian and gay communities. Both the images recorded by Spiro and the images described by the interviewees position them not only within distinct southern lesbian and gay communities but also broader straight ones that, at times, are hostile to them.

Spiro's editing strategy results in her video being full of snips and snatches of visual and aural representations of the South. We glimpse landscapes, signs, animals, roadside kitsch, and people, none of which occupy the screen for more than a few seconds before the documentary moves on to another image. And the soundtrack samples the diverse musical styles originating in the South—blues, country, gospel, rock—performed by both straight and lesbian/gay artists. One might expect Spiro's reliance on editing to result in fragmenting the acquaintances she encounters on her road trip. Instead, it finds compatibility with a belief that, rather than whole, the South is composed of many cultures, which make up that imagined community we call the South."[3] Spiro's visual and aural representations of "general" southern cultures envelop the images and music of the southern lesbians and gays in the video, functioning in effect to normalize them as just more "peculiar things" within already peculiar southern cultures.[4]

As its title indicates, Spiro's video belongs to the coming-out genre that dominates gay and lesbian documentary films and videos, although hers differs by its focus on southern cultures.[5] Spiro, in her voice-over commentary, remarks that "what used to be an invisible culture seems to be emerging, and all across the South it seems gay folks are beginning to come out on camera." This concern with public visibility and outness is given explicit expression in the segments of the video on the rodeo and the Mardi Gras ball, which are described as having never been, respectively, "on camera before" or "videotaped for outsiders to see."

Coming out is nothing new to the South. Two cultural manifestations of it occur routinely for high-society patrons and fundamentalist Christians: coming-out at debutante balls and coming out as born again.[6] But compared to the coming out of gays and lesbians, these forms of coming out function differently in southern cultures and have different risks associated with them.

Coming out is a confessional, and its use by lesbians and gays functions, in the words of Michel Foucault, as a "technique for producing the truth of sex" (1978, 68). Foucault defines "technologies of the self" as means by which individuals are able to effect "a certain number of operations on their own bodies and souls, thoughts, conduct, and way of being, so as to transform themselves in order to attain a certain state of happiness, purity, wisdom, perfection, or immortality" (1988, 18). However, "the practices of self" enacted to achieve these states are "not something that the individual invents by himself," but rather "are patterns that he finds in his culture which are proposed, suggested and imposed on him by his culture, his society and his social group" (Foucault 1991, 11). Setting aside Foucault's unfortunate choice of pronouns, coming out is such a practice, such a technique, exercised by lesbians and gays for the formation of their collective selves. Unfortunately, southern lesbians and gays are often encouraged to adopt it as though no acceptable alternatives exist.

I believe lesbians and gays have used a different technique to function within southern cultures for some time, one that though riddled with problems is ultimately very comfortable, leading to their (and sometimes my) indifference toward the in-your-face activism associated with coming out. And Spiro's video, for all its emphasis on outness, does not completely reject this competing technique of the gay self, as shown by her inclusion of the Miss Miller segment, which I will discuss shortly.

And just what is this alternative? Spiro's voice-over leading into the Mardi Gras ball sequence announces: "I'm going to New Orleans for Mardi Gras. I'm about to witness the secret of that flamboyant gay ball tradition." If the gay Mardi Gras balls in New Orleans are a secret, then they are a very public one. Lesbians and gays in the South have been able to participate in the southern social order under the banner of southern eccentricity or, as employed by Carson McCullers in her novels, peculiarity. The association of peculiarity with same-sex desire is a trope that runs through all of McCullers's novels and novellas of the 1940s, whether as a peculiar appearance one exhibits, a peculiar stare one exchanges, or a peculiar thing one inhabits. When this seemingly pejorative term is filtered through one of the main cultural/social institutions of the South—fundamentalist Christianity—the term sheds the negative connotations of odd and strange usually associated with it in general usage and acquires positives ones, for in I Peter 2:9 "a peculiar people" is used in the context of a chosen people acquired by God. So the difference implied by peculiarity is transformed through a biblical reading from a difference based on rejection to one based on selection. Therefore, in southern terms, to be peculiar is to be considered special though odd, unique though strange, as biblical and colloquial connotations coexist in contradiction. Christian peculiarity and southern eccentricity share a common cultural affinity in the South, being religious and secular versions of the same thing.

But even the eccentric and the peculiar have to abide by the unspoken cultural rule of polite behavior,"7 which for lesbians and gays means maintaining the status of a public secret, that which is known but not allowed to be articulated. In the early 1980s, the annual Lesbian and Gay Pride parade in Atlanta, Georgia, contained a paper-bag contingent, a group of individuals who publicly marched in the parade but out of fear of disclosure wore paper bags over their heads. Though this performance could be read within the coming-out paradigm to signify the constraint of the closet, which "we shall overcome," for those familiar with the culture, this contradictory statement of public closetedness is typical of southern eccentricity—just one of those peculiar things, and, I believe, a remnant of, a material manifestation of, that other technique of the self used by lesbians and gays in the South.

Michael Taussig defines the public secret as a "secret which is in fact 'known' but for reasons of power cannot be articulated and creates, in its stead, dissimulation and fabulation."8 As Taussig's definition makes clear, the public secret is a mechanism of social control, and I do not long nostalgically for its uncritical reinscription. For example, it seems appropriate that President Clinton, a southerner, would propose a national policy on lesbians and gays in the military of "Don't ask, don't tell." For what is such a policy except continuation on the national level of what has been the southern approach to lesbians and gays all along, that of their status as a public secret. As D. A. Miller points out, "the phenomenon of the 'open secret' does not, as one might think, bring about the collapse of these binarisms [private/public, inside/outside, subject/object] and their ideological effects, but rather attests to their fantasmatic recovery" (1988, 207). Rather, I mention the public secret to assist in explaining why lesbian and gay activism differs in the South, this difference a result of the negotiation between these two techniques of the gay self–a public secret expected by fellow southerners, and a public revelation (that is, coming out) expected by fellow lesbian and gay activists.[9]

Activists in southern lesbian and gay communities have continually reminded their counterparts elsewhere that because the South is different from the other regions of the country their political involvement cannot be analyzed by the criteria that may be appropriate for those other regions.[10] For example, during the 1988 Republican and Democratic conventions in New Orleans, Louisiana, and Atlanta, Georgia, respectively, the local lesbian and gay communities were estranged from the outside activist groups, such as ACT-UP New York, that converged upon their cities. ACT-UP New York considered the lesbians and gays in the southern cities that they visited unenlightened and apolitical for not embracing their particular style of confrontational politics. This view reveals a belief in universal political strategies, which for southern lesbians and gays means the erasure of regional difference in determining what counts as activism.[11] As the confrontational brand of activism associated with ACT-UP New York waned during the 1990s, lesbian and gay activists at the national level began to follow the lead of southern lesbians and gays, choosing to borrow the signification of the southern black civil rights movement[12] rather than align themselves with the ACT-UP style of activism, whose roots lie in the 1960s New Left movement and 1970s Gay Liberation Front zaps.[13] Both the Campaign for Military Service and the 1993 March on Washington[14] strategically used comparisons to blacks' struggles for civil rights effectively enough to result in a backlash from certain segments of the black communities and the predominately white radical right.[15]

During the 1992 Republican primary, Pat Buchanan aired a political ad designed specifically for Atlanta, Georgia, that ignored the region's cultural peculiarity regarding homosexuality as a public secret and, as a result, failed as a political strategy. The ad, decrying the Bush administration's financing of art that "glorified homosexuality," lifted images from Marlon Riggs's 1989 documentary *Tongues Untied* as proof. Though the documentary, in Riggs's words, "tries to undo the legacy of silence about black gay men" (Simmons 1991, 193), the ad quotes only scenes from the documentary in which white men appear. Ironically, these scenes occur outside the South, in San Francisco, while what was elided by the political ad—the poem that provides the title of Riggs's film—was about growing up black and gay in Georgia.

The ad makers took this position to avoid charges of racism, a sure way of jeopardizing a political campaign in a region in which blacks now constitute a significant portion of the organized political constituency. But the ad makers made the mistake of believing that, just as public acknowledgment of racism had been culturally accepted prior to the success of the southern black civil rights movement, public condemnation of lesbians and gays was acceptable behavior. They did not realize that the status of southern lesbians and gays as a public secret meant that homophobia operates differently on a cultural level than racism.[16]

The use of Riggs's documentary was an opportunistic move by the ad makers to accrue the benefits of a local controversy over the film's airing six months earlier on

Atlanta's two Public Broadcast Stations. Local TV viewers were offended not by the words spoken in the ad about Bush and the National Endowment for the Arts, but rather by the images of supposedly gay men dancing in the streets. Even though none of the men in the clips perform any actions that would cause them to be classified as gay, because the text spoke of "homosexuality" and the visuals showed all-male groups dressed in leather and blue jeans, viewers associated the visuals with "homosexuality." The Buchanan ad ultimately backfired because it publicly showed what was culturally in the South supposed to be a public secret and thereby offended the very constituencies it was designed to reach.

As southern lesbian and gay activists are quick to point out: "What plays in New York doesn't necessarily play in the South. We're not in-your-face. We do our work in a Southern way" (Galst 1992, 54–55). Yet activists claiming this "southern way" never fully explain exactly what they mean, except through a circular logic that assumes that the term "southern" innately contains the explanation within it. In Pat Conroy's novel *The Prince of Tides*, Savannah Wingo writes a children's book titled "The Southern Way" under the stolen name of Renata Halpern, a recently deceased Holocaust survivor. The children's story is Savannah's way of announcing publicly, but in a closeted manner, her family's secret—a brutal attack that included the simultaneous rape of three family members and resulted in the murder of the rapists. In retelling the story, Savannah rewrites the ending of the event to provide a last-minute rescue and, therefore, a happy ending. So the southern way is bound to the southern storytelling tradition and to availing oneself of the cultural acceptance of public secrets by creating socially acceptable fabulations that conceal matters that etiquette requires remain unspoken.

A common refrain heard from southern lesbian and gay activists is that they work "behind the scene." True to the common stereotype of the South as backward, southern lesbians and gays approach activism not through the confrontational politics of mass protest but rather through personal and cultural negotiations from behind. Rather than being in your face, southern lesbian and gay activists can be viewed as being "in your behind." After all, being a pain in the ass can be just as effective at accomplishing change as being in one's face. A key difference between these two approaches is that being in someone's ass assumes a certain level of intimacy between the parties involved that is not usually associated with being in someone's face.

The public secret can be very comforting for southern lesbians and gays because it allows one to participate publicly, though not openly, in community life, even as a couple, albeit with certain constraints. One of the narrative lines running through Fannie Flagg's novel *Fried Green Tomatoes at the Whistle Stop Cafe* is the story of a lesbian couple, Ruth and Idgie, in 1930s Alabama who function within the public secret. The public closetedness of the paper-bagged gays and lesbians in the Atlanta Pride parade shares an affinity with another such image common to the region, which also makes an appearance in *Fried Green Tomatoes*—the white-hooded marchers of the Ku Klux Klan. When the Whistle Stop Cafe is surrounded by robed and hooded Klansmen,

Ruth looks at their shoes to see if she recognizes any of them, and she does. No one will acknowledge the identity of the Klansmen even though in their public closeted-ness they are known. The social function of the public secret, in Miller's words, "is not to conceal knowledge, so much as to conceal the knowledge of the knowledge" (1988, 206).

Such refrains as "we are everywhere" and "we could be anyone you know"—thought of as positive and assumed to be innocent by gay and lesbian activists—can be used to instill distrust and division as well as empathy and compassion. And though in the past the Klan has been able to maneuver the public secret to control people of color and their sympathizers, the public secret has functioned to restrict lesbian and gay visibility. This difference is a result of who has the power to narrate the public secret's fabula as well as a function of the way homophobia and racism operate differently on a cultural level in the South.[17] As racism slowly becomes a culturally unacceptable view in the South, and as laws are enacted ensuring lesbians and gays equal protection, the ways in which these two groups operate within the public secret, if they choose to continue using it, could easily shift.[18] Though coming out and the public secret are vying techniques of the self available for southern lesbians and gays to adopt, these two options are not gay and lesbian options per se, but rather cultural options used by diverse groups within the region to varying effects. And, I would argue, the negotiation of the tension between these vying techniques is what forms the (or a) southern way.

Though *Greetings from Out Here* may be, in Spiro's words, "about those gay people who don't flee [the South] but who stay home and do the bravest thing of all, be who they are, where they are"—in other words, come out—the individuals in the video, as well as the narrative construction of the video itself, do not completely forsake the public-secret formulation. Some of the instances are humorous, such as when Chance, a sixteen-year-old lesbian in Atlanta, after describing the place she works as a feminist bookstore, quickly amends her characterization with, "It's really a dyke bookstore, but they call it a feminist bookstore." And the media spectacle in the mid-1990s surrounding Camp Sister Spirit, a feminist retreat located in Mississippi run by a lesbian couple, serves only to further conflate these two terms in the popular imagination of southerners.

But the most telling intrusion in *Greetings from Out Here* of this other cultural formulation is the sequence of Spiro's encounter with Miss Miller, an elderly woman in Arkansas who runs "a makeshift animal shelter and pet cemetery." After conducting a tour of her pet cemetery, Miss Miller tells us about shooting a man in the foot when he attacked one of her dogs. Miss Miller never identifies herself as lesbian or gay, and Spiro refuses to position her as such either. We are shown a seventy-six-year-old white woman wearing blue jeans, a flannel shirt, and a baseball cap—a trucker image that does not exactly fit with the region's definition of white southern femininity. The inclusion of this encounter in a video about southern lesbians and gays only makes sense if viewed from the perspective of the public-secret narrative. Spiro admits in her voice-over introduction to the sequence that "it's an impressive one-woman show that may or may not relate to my theme." Spiro comfortably accepts Miss Miller on her own terms, leaving behind the act of open acknowledgment essential to coming out upon which the rest of the encounters in the video depend.

Of course, the gayness in the Miss Miller sequence is suggested through the images of gender transgression, in terms of both visual presentation and behavior. As a participant at the women's music festival informs us: "It is kind of true about the South, women tend to be a little more feminine in their ways, in their image. And I like that, I think that's great. But I think there is not as much acceptance of people who are maybe more androgynous." My concern here is with social theory filtered through culture. And within most southern cultures, discourses of homosexuality continue to share the same social space as gender violations.[19] So some southern lesbians and gays, instead of denying the association between these two, are using their homosexuality as a means to rearticulate gender.[20] For example, one of the participants at the Radical Faeries' May Pole festival describes the group of gay men as "challenging assumptions about what it means to be a man and how that fits into the whole way society structures gender." And Allan Gurganus, on the way home from dinner with Spiro at Allen & Son's Barbeque, proclaims: "One of the many advantages of being a gay person is precisely that you're not so defined in terms of gender that you're fearful of communicating across the boundary of gender. And if you have that other capacity, it gives you a kind of power. It's a kind of passport. It lets you travel across boundaries and borders, and it encourages you, and it even insists that you identify with people who are unlike yourself." So, though gayness anchors sexual orientation, the spot marked "You are here," it frees one to travel across boundaries of gender. Its solidification, ironically, creates gender fluidity.

In contrast to the limited societal acceptance available to southern lesbians and gays through participation in the public secret, the practice of coming-out is fraught with the potential of danger and rejection for lesbians and gays. Before going to dinner, Gurganus tells Spiro that "it takes those of us who understand trouble, and who have been left out, to witness to the larger picture. It's the people who are entitled, the people who inherit the earth without question, who can't really see the whole picture, because it's theirs." For lesbians and gays, coming out can often mean being left out, for "out" can mean not only opening up (come out) but also rejection (get out). For southern lesbians and gays to come out means openly acknowledging, in Spiro's words, "who they are, where they are"—in other words, a public disclosure rather than a public secret.

In *Greetings from Out Here*, a Georgia lesbian claims she is "southern by birth, gay by God," and a gay Texan considers himself "blessed for being a gay person," as though it was one of the fruits of the Holy Spirit. James Cox, a black minister "with roots in the civil rights movement" who recently came out, equates the freedom he now feels to be able to speak about being gay with spiritual release from sin and physical freedom from slavery. The segment of the video on Cox closes with this ambiguous statement: "For I thank God that I have come this way and most of all that my living shall not be in vain." Which way? The way of the Christian faith or gay sexuality? Neither Cox nor the video clarifies this point, but for Cox I believe it is both, an example of southern lesbians and gays following the lead of the southern black civil rights movement, defining themselves in spiritual terms, encroaching on the signific.ation of fundamentalist Christianity and its religious dogma frequently used to condemn them.

Counteracting the old iconography of lesbians and gays as a sign of the world's decay and, therefore, harking the approach of the second coming of Christ, this subterfuge of religious verbal imagery and activity by southern lesbians and gays allows them to participate on the same metaphorical level as fundamentalist Christians. Because gays and lesbians too function as the salt of the earth, it can be argued that it is the world that would decay without the presence of their preserving touch, not vice versa. Gurganus's use of the term "witness" brings forth both religious and secular connotations, which often become conflated in usage. "Witnessing" can be either passively observing something or actively testifying to something. And this term with its contradictory meanings, appropriately enough, describes southern activism. The "act" in southern lesbian and gay act-ivism is bearing witness to the open (or in gay and lesbian rhetoric, out) lives of lesbians and gays in the South, rather than accepting the comfortably numb position as a public secret.

In other words, bearing witness can be viewed as a continual outing of the public secret. But "out" is *not* confrontational politics, but rather a negotiation of the cultural space, the place one is assigned within southern cultures. For southern lesbians and gays, activism emerges out of their day-to-day existence, where simply to live one's life openly is a kind of activism.

Notes

Acknowledgments. I would like to thank Heather Hendershot, Chris Holmlund, Patricia Leonardi, David Lugowski, and Chris Straayer for their comments on an earlier version of this article.

1. The world premiere of *Greetings from Out Here* occurred on Thursday, 17 June 1993, at the 1993 New York Lesbian and Gay Film Festival. It aired the following evening on WNET (channel 13), one of New York City's public broadcast stations, as part of the station's *Out* series in honor of Lesbian and Gay Pride week. The video is available from the Video Data Bank at the School of the Art Institute of Chicago, 112 South Michigan Avenue, Chicago, IL, 60603, (312) 345-3550; (800) 634-8544. The Internet site for the Video Data Bank is www.vdb.org. All of the Ellen Spiro quotations in my text are from her voice-over narration in *Greetings from Out Here.*

2. I use the term "film" here to encompass both film and video.

3. Just as there are many southern cultures, there are many gay and lesbian cultures, hence my use of the plurals "cultures" and "communities" throughout this essay. Though "the lesbian and gay community" is a social fabrication, the term is often strategically used for political purposes. Lesbians and gays are not only divided by racial, gender, and economic differences but also by more culturally specific ones such as whether one is closeted or out, activist

or "party girl," assimilated or blatant. And these three classifications can be combined in any permutation.

4. Many of the images of "general" southern cultures used by Spiro fall into the category of "southern camp," and her attitude toward them seems to vary from playfulness and fun to superiority and disdain. In addition, her use of eccentricity (whether sites or people) falls prey to the common problem encountered when this strategy is used. By focusing on the eccentric, southern culture becomes represented as a collection of eccentric people, places, and practices. As a result, the commonality of the culture becomes the uncommonality of all its individual components with the esoteric the rule rather than the exception. Although such an approach breaks down the usual idea of normality, temporarily placing the "normal" within quotation marks as a suspect and highly unstable category, it eventually reestablishes a new normal as that of eccentricity and peculiarity.

5. Only a scant number of documentary films and videos exist that specifically address southern lesbians and gays. In addition to Ellen Spiro's video, one finds *Fighting in Southwest Louisiana* (Peter Friedman and Jean-Francois Brunet, 1991), about Danny Cooper, a rural mail carrier in southwest Louisiana who has AIDS, and *Dear Jesse* (Tim Kirkman, 1997), about Tim Kirkman's return to his native North Carolina from New York City interwoven with an indictment of homophobic North Carolina senator Jesse Helms. *Dear Jesse* uses the same personal diary form that *Greetings from Out Here* uses. Spiro's 1990 video *DiAna's Hair Ego,* about DiAna DiAna, who runs the South Carolina Aids Education Network (SCAEN) out of her beauty shop, tangentially considers southern lesbians and gays. *Where Are We?* (Rob Epstein and Jeffrey Friedman, 1993), about a nonsouthern gay couple's road trip through the South asking the individuals they encounter along the way a series of questions, includes gay men among the individuals the filmmakers interview on their journey. Most general lesbian and gay documentaries have either a short segment on southern lesbians and gays, as in Rosa von Praunheim's 1978 film *Arm of Lovers, or Revolt of the Perverts,* or else an interviewee who is a southerner, as in Arthur Bressan's 1977 film *Gay USA.*

6. The 1995 short film by Bill Oliver, *The Debutantes,* specifically associates coming out with high society and lesbians and gays. The story concerns a young man who, while returning home to attend his sister's debut into Savannah, Georgia, society, contemplates telling his parents that his is gay. Both he and his sister have reservations about their respective comings out.

7. In 1993, Pensacola, Florida, received attention in the national media after some city officials reacted negatively to a portrayal of the city as gay-friendly in a local TV news story on the influx of gay tourists into the city on holiday weekends. Local promoters of Pensacola as a gay tourist attraction "discouraged demonstrations or marches by gay and AIDS rights groups such as ACT-UP," preferring, as one promoter put it, "to keep low-key." As a gay visitor commented, this strategy relies on pride of southern hospitality to win out. As this example illustrates, it seems that the southern cultural rule of polite behavior can be subverted by lesbians and gays to their benefit, but only at the cost of visibility. See "'Gay Riviera' Coming Out of the Closet," *Stonewall News,* 26 July 1993, 12–13.

8. I would like to thank Jan Nathanson for pointing out Michael Taussig's definition of the public secret to me.

9. Although I position the public secret as antagonistic to coming out, I do not perceive them as diametrical opposites, one the inverse of the other. The opposite of coming out is being in the closet, and I do not view participation in the public secret as synonymous with being in the closet.

10. See, for example, Dave Walter, "In Depth: Atlanta's New Activism," *Advocate*, 11 November 1986, 10–11, 20; Liz Galst, "Southern Activists Rise Up: Lesbians and Gay Men Gain Ground by Speaking Out from Below the Mason–Dixon Line," *Advocate*, 19 May 1992, 54–56.

11. I am not against confrontational activism. It is a wonderful form of political theater, and ACT-UP in its heyday made activism hip, sexy, and trendy again, qualities that I believe did not detract from the seriousness of its mission. Why should activism be boring and bland? Rather, I am arguing against the position that confrontational politics is the only valid form of activism and that all others are intrinsically a compromise. ACT-UP-style activism is only one style among many. I believe all styles are valid, and the choice should be based on which is strategically advantageous.

12. The comparison by lesbians and gays of their struggle for civil rights to that waged by blacks is not limited to just the classic southern black civil rights period of 1954 to 1965. (My dates are borrowed from the PBS documentary series *Eyes on the Prize: America's Civil Rights Years, 1954 to 1965*.) For example, in the gay porn video *Body Search* (Chi Chi LaRue, 1993), during the prologue set in 1967, a character states, "You know, one of these days somebody out there is going to come down on a faggot once too often, and we are all going to riot just like the blacks are doing right now." During the early 1990s the lesbian and gay grapevine was abuzz with whispers about whether or not arms should be taken up (inviting comparisons to the Black Panthers and the riots of the late 1960s) because of the lack of progress made on lesbian, gay, and AIDS issues, especially considering the attacks by the radical right/fundamentalist Christians through such initiatives as the antigay video *The Gay Agenda* and the electorial actions in Colorado (Amendment 2) and Oregon (Ballot Measure 9) to strip lesbians and gays of equal protection under the law. Though many, if not most, of the fundamentalist Christian groups involved in these initiatives are not southern based, because of fundamentalist Christianity's strong association with the South through televangelists such as Jerry Falwell, Jim and Tammy Bakker, and Jimmy Swaggart, there is an unspoken assumption associating them with southern "backwardness."

13. One section of the 1997 documentary film *Out at Work* by Tami Gold and Kelly Anderson focuses on Cheryl Summerville, who was fired from the Douglasville, Georgia, Cracker Barrel in 1991 for being a lesbian. The documentary includes coverage of a Queer Nation Atlanta demonstration and sit-in at Cracker Barrel in protest of Cheryl's firing. I think it significant that although a Queer Nation chapter, the Atlanta group used strategies of the black civil rights movement (lunch counter sit-ins) rather than those of the 1960s New Left and 1970s Gay Liberation Front favored by such groups as ACT-UP New York and Queer Nation New York (an offshoot of ACT-UP New York).

14. The title of the 1993 March on Washington for Lesbian, Gay and Bi Equal Rights was based on the title of the 1963 March on Washington at which Martin Luther King, Jr., made his famous "I Have a Dream" speech. See for example, Charles Linebarger, "1963–1993: A Story of Two Marches," *Christopher Street*, August 1993, 24, 26–27. As I find typical of much popular writing on the matter by white nonsoutherners, Linebarger displaces all of the country's racism onto the South. Why else would he make a statement such as "If there are lessons to be learned for gays and lesbians in all this, it is that for us, the entire country is our South" (26)?

15. See, for example, Eric Washington, "Freedom Rings! The Alliance Between Blacks and Gays Is Threatened by Mutual Inscrutability," *Village Voice*, 29 June 1993, 25, 31–33; "*NY Times* Sees Black Backlash Against Gay Rights Movement; Survey Finds Otherwise," *Stonewall News*,

19 July 1993, 8–9; *Gay Rights/Special Rights* (Traditional Values Coalition, 1993, video). At its 1993 annual meeting, the Southern Baptist Convention simultaneously approved a resolution denouncing racial and ethnic discrimination and hatred (forty years too late) and one condemning all homosexuality as sinful. The takeover of the formerly moderate-led Southern Baptist Convention by right-wing religious fundamentalists was solidified when the denomination adopted in 1993 its first-ever doctrinal restriction on convention membership. That restriction, predictably enough based on the congregational oustings of the prior year, condemns all member churches that "affirm, approve, or endorse homosexual behavior" as "not in cooperation with the Convention." A denomination that forty years ago fought against the integration of the races has finally acquiesced on that position and now fights instead a new form of integration, that of lesbians and gays into the Christian faith. The Southern Baptists exchanged one hated group for another and now seek coalition building with that formerly hated group against their new one. After the success, though limited, of the southern black civil rights movement, these "ex-bigoted" right-wing fundamentalist Christians know well the effects progressive social change, if won, can have on a community. See *Record: Newsletter of Evangelicals Concerned*, Summer 1993, 1. The experience of University Baptist Church in Austin, Texas, succinctly highlights the historical connection between these two struggles. Recently the Baptist General Convention of Texas (BGCT) "disassociated" itself from the church because of its lesbian and gay ministry. In 1948 the church was "disavowed" by the BGCT because it allowed blacks to sit in the same pews as whites.

16. This fear by many heterosexuals about the articulation of homosexuality derives from, as Suzanne Pharr expressed it in Heather MacDonald's 1994 film *Ballot Measure 9*, the belief that "if you talk about homosexuality, then people will become homosexual." And even if such people allowed a discussion of homosexuality for the purpose of warning about its "evil," they certainly would not permit its visualization, its imaging. One has to wonder if this objection is because such images would be too horrific (and therefore traumatize the weak) or too tempting (and therefore convert the weak). Although homophobia and racism may operate differently on a cultural level, an expression of racist sentiments is emerging that embeds itself within a hatred of lesbians and gays. This allows racists to avoid being directly labeled racist in a time when such labeling can possibly prove a social hindrance.

17. Though lesbians and gays in the South, unlike blacks in the South, operate as a public secret, the presence of the Ku Klux Klan in the South has historically positioned lesbians and gays similar to its positioning of blacks. For example, when Carson McCullers returned to Georgia in 1941 to convalesce at her parents' home, an alleged member of the Klan threatened to attack her because in her first novel, *The Heart Is a Lonely Hunter*, she showed herself to be a "nigger lover" and in her second novel, *Reflections in a Golden Eye*, "a queer." See Virginia Spencer Carr, *The Lonely Hunter: A Biography of Carson McCullers* (New York: Doubleday, 1975), 136–137.

18. Though Ku Klux Klan members and lesbians and gays are positioned differently within the public secret, they are still structurally a part of the same knowledge system. So, even if their positions change, only an inversion in the system will have occurred. The system itself will not have been disrupted.

19. The southern culture's rule of polite behavior or, if one prefers, "nice manners," has significant ramifications for gender roles in the South because it necessitates the use of "yes ma'am" and "yes sir" in responses, whether personal or business. As a result, one is constantly reminded of the gender role one is presumed to occupy and continually experiences an explicit

verbal assignment of that position during interpersonal communication, one which for lesbians and gays can sometimes be incorrect. A common jostling point among many southern lesbians in their early twenties is being mistaken for an adolescent boy and called "sonny." And now with drive-through windows proliferating across the South, if you are a man with the wrong voice tone or inflections you can be told by the speaker box: "Thank you, ma'am. Please drive around to the window."

20. Joan Riviere, in her classic 1929 psychoanalytic study "Womanliness as a Masquerade" (reprinted in *Formations of Fantasy,* ed. Victor Burgin, James Donald, and Cora Kaplan [New York: Routledge, 1986], 35–44), theorizes that "women who wish for masculinity may put on a mask of womanliness to avert anxiety and retribution feared from men" (35). In other words, womanliness is a mask worn by women to hide their possession of "the phallus." Feminist theorists, in their adoption of Riviere's article, typically overlook the fact that the professional woman in the primary clinical case study upon which Riviere bases her theory is a white southerner. Riviere only mentions the woman's southernness in passing to briefly explain a dream the woman had involving a black man (an even more telling moment about the South that I am unable to go into here). I believe the hyperfemininity worn by Riviere's patient is, in general, more typical of southern femininity than of women in traditionally male professions. And southern women have long used their femininity as a tool to partially counter the social, political, and economic power imbalance they experience with men. (There used to be a running line among many southern lesbians that you could always tell who the other lesbians were because they were the ones without make-up on.) Riviere equates the reaction by professional women who wear femininity as a masquerade to that of male homosexuals who "exaggerate their heterosexuality as a 'defense' against their homosexuality" (35). In other words, women and homosexuals (of both the male and female variety) masquerade in feminine and heterosexual guises, respectively, to avoid retribution from men and heterosexuals, respectively. What I take from this is that southern women and homosexuals (not two mutually exclusive categories, obviously), because of their social positioning, are acutely aware of the artificiality and plasticity of the gender system in America generally, and in the South specifically. And this awareness provides the necessary first ingredient for one to begin to interrogate the structures of that system and attempt to rearticulate its parameters.

Works Cited

Conroy, Pat. 1986. *The Prince of Tides.* New York: Houghton Mifflin.

Flagg, Fannie. 1987. *Fried Green Tomatoes at the Whistle Stop Cafe.* New York: Random House.

Foucault, Michel. 1991. "The Ethic of Care for the Self as a Practice of Freedom." Trans. Joseph Gauthier. In *The Final Foucault,* ed, James Bernauer and David Rasmussen. Cambridge: MIT Press, 1–20.

———. 1978. *The History of Sexuality.* Vol. 1, *An Introduction.* Trans. Robert Hurley. New York: Vintage Books.

———. 1988. "Technologies of the Self." In *Technologies of the Self: A Seminar with Michel Foucault,* ed. Luther H. Martin, Huck Gutman, and Patrick H. Hutton. Amherst: University of Massachusetts Press, 16–49.

Galst, Liz. 1992. "Southern Activists Rise Up: Lesbians and Gay Men Gain Ground by Speaking Out from below the Mason–Dixon Line." *Advocate,* 19 May, 54–56.

Godwin, Gail. 1987. *A Southern Family.* New York: William Morrow.

Miller, D. A. 1988. *The Novel and the Police.* Berkeley: University of California Press.

Simmons, Ron. 1991. "*Tongues Untied:* An Interview With Marlon Riggs." In *Brother to Brother: New Writings by Black Gay Men,* ed. Essex Hemphill. Boston: Alyson Publications, 189–199.

Taussig, Michael. 1992. "Secrecy" course syllabus, 10 April, Department of Performance Studies, New York University.

Taylor, Peter. 1986. *A Summons to Memphis.* New York: Ballantine.

Edward R. Gray

Looking for a City:
The Ritual and Politics
of Ethnography

Glenn Memorial Church sits on a hill at the edge of Emory University's green campus in Atlanta. Large, brick, with long white columns framing its portico, it strikes you with its importance. Going inside, I find a seat by myself in one of the first rows. I am early, but already there are familiar faces in the crowd. The audience grows steadily to perhaps just over one hundred. It is a large auditorium, so the assembly at first seems somewhat meager. But most, like me, take a seat near the front, creating a close-knit feeling. Tonight, Glenn Memorial is the venue for an Emory University–sponsored event. It is a familiar role for this mixed-use facility. Concert hall, lecture hall, town hall, it is also the sanctuary of a United Methodist congregation. Neither cross nor altar is visible on this night. I pick up the Methodist hymnal from the rack in front of me to pass the time. Except for such hymnals, there are no explicitly religious elements visible. The pews, of course, remain. They announce that the auditorium, despite its other uses, is most often a religious sanctuary. If the pews are not enough, the high steeple outside adds to the spiritual message a dramatic exclamation point.

Soon a recorded orchestral version of Handel's "Hallelujah chorus," familiar to many in the assembly, fills the vast space. It is a hot, late June night, pregnant with thunderheads. Handel's loud chords, however, cause in me no sense of contrariety with the seasonable weather. The familiarity of this version of the famous *Messiah* choral centerpiece as a prelude makes me comfortable as I sit in Glenn Memorial. In the pew behind me, everyone is singing the final, singular "Hal-Laaaay-Loooooo-YAAAAAH!" An amplified voice announces that "the Gospel Hour" is about to begin. Wearing a long sparkling gown and a bemused look, Morticia DeVille enters carrying a microphone and a handkerchief. Behind her come the Gospel Echoes, two men of early middle age. They look dapper in tuxedo shirts, red collars, and tight black vests. Standing on either side of Morticia's large frame—the corpulent drag performer I call Paul in this essay, when referring to his everyday persona—they begin to sing, "This is our joy. This is our survival. Let's have a revival!"

Morticia is a professional gospel singer who performs in drag. She has earned a living at it in Atlanta for some ten years. She is also an evangelist. One Sunday at the regular Gospel Hour held in a popular gay bar, Morticia read a card from a Metropolitan Community Church minister (a predominantly gay denomination). "You wear makeup and a wig," this regular participant wrote. "I wear a robe. But we both serve the same person."

As she read this, I remembered her unlikely drag origins. She and her manager, Gary Jeffers, met at mortuary school in Atlanta. "The first time I got in drag was in the basement of the funeral home using the makeup in the embalming room," she told me.[1] Before then they had made a practice of using the chapel to "hold services," as Morticia put it. They would sing the old songs. "I think we ought to try doing this at a bar," Jeffers suggested one day. The Gospel Hour was born.

When Morticia entered Glenn Memorial to enthusiastic applause, I remembered a conversation we had some months earlier.

> When I was very young I broke into my grandma's house and stole her lipstick. And I stole her sheets and I would wear the sheets. . . . Then I would pretend I was Billy Graham. I would have like a picnic table that was the organ. . . . And there was this huge gully behind our house—you know what a gully is? The wind would blow and that would be the people coming, and we would have mass turnouts of people coming.

The Gospel Hour is Atlanta's longest-running drag show, even as Gospel Girls such as Chocolate Thunder and Alicia Kelly have come and gone. The show, or "service" as many call it, has moved from one Midtown Atlanta bar to another. Recently Morticia DeVille has taken to performing almost exclusively with the Gospel Echoes during the Hour. Many times over five years in Atlanta, I attended these services. Besides enjoying the music, I was drawn to how well it demonstrated the reflexive, performative nature of modern religious identity.

This performance at Glenn Memorial was much like any other Gospel Hour in recent weeks. Tonight, however, the Gospel Girls and the Echoes were performing as part of the official program of the Emory University–sponsored "Queering the South" conference. Organizers invited me to talk about a study of the Gospel Hour I wrote with my former Emory colleague Scott Thumma (now a research associate at the Center for Religious Research at Hartford Seminary). Accepting their invitation, I suggested to them that they invite the members of the Gospel Girls to respond as part of a panel. The panel had convened earlier on the day of the performance. Thumma and I joined Morticia; the group's manager, Gary Jeffers; the straight black Gospel Girl, Ramona Dugger; and Mark Roberts (his stage name), one of the Echoes.[2]

I told the small group gathered for the session that the Gospel Hour merges gospel performance models with one from high drag. It artfully blends southern evangelical Christian sensibilities with urban gay ones. Most importantly, it makes the model it creates available to the audience for its appropriation. The southern gay men in attendance can therefore reconcile their newly achieved modern urban gay identity with their childhood and young adult evangelical Christian formation. They do so—as a performance, ritually—through the singing of still-cherished songs under the direction of drag performers and, importantly, despite tonight's exception, in the safety of an urban gay bar. For these men, not necessarily a majority on any given night but always the audience's center of gravity, participation is a rite of passage. It is a step in their coming out as *gay* Christians.

The blended model combines southern-style evangelical Christianity with a modern urban gay identity. Both gospel music and gay bars are institutions there for the taking. At the Gospel Hour, participants and principals use them to create a ritual that dramatizes their commitments to the way of life practiced in each institutional setting. The ritual of the Gospel Hour validates the coming-out experience of its gay audience and, as well, invites and endorses the decision to continue to identify—at least in some way—as Christian.

Drag is essential to this act of blending. It is the principal medium by which the blending occurs in the Gospel Hour. Drag is an ambiguous art.[3] The drag performer is a liminal figure, at the margins between and transgressing everyday social categories. She/he is a blending of cultural categories and an extension of them, often to the extreme. The drag performer embodies the male as the feminine. Many people, gay or straight, will have no truck with the presentation of the male, and particularly the gay man, as the feminine. Combining drag with religion is only adding to the contrariety and ambiguity.

Drag shows appear especially popular in the South and in Atlanta. This is an entirely impressionistic report. I wonder what, if anything, this has to do with southern evangelical performance models. One need only visualize Tammie Fae Baker in her television heyday or her current impersonators to think "drag act!" One is more likely to hear Christianity referred to during an Atlanta drag show—if only as part of the general cultural background—than during a drag performance in, say, New York or San Francisco. In most venues, drag shows are presented as pure, if bawdy, entertainment. That the Gospel Hour is a drag show is essential to, but not alone a guarantor of, its great appeal.

I wondered what drew this particular audience to the Gospel Hour tonight. I also began to reflect on what, after years of attending, continued to draw me. At its current regular venue at Burkhart's in Midtown Atlanta, people come and go constantly. Many are out with their friends to simply have a good time. The performance dominates, but it does not monopolize. I have seen reactions that range from taking offense at the seeming sacrilege being performed, to indifference, to inebriated attempts to join in what a few misconstrue as a mocking of religion. I have also seen people weeping, others just teary during the singing of "Amazing Grace." Some, from time to time, raise their hands in the air in the charismatic's sign of prayer and praise. The audience at Glenn, I was sure, comprised many who were curious. But the true believers, I knew from their familiarity to me, were there too.

One of them had told me the Gospel Hour is where he feels safe. It is where he knows that no one will condemn him—as either a gay man or a religious one. "The Gospel Hour has helped me find an outlet to develop my spirituality," he said. "This is [our] one touch with God." Others said: "Gay anger against God is dealt with here." "It showed me a void, a need in my life . . . [and] it created a hunger for [church] again." "The Gospel Hour made me aware of the longing I had for a relationship with God that I had turned away from." "I am able to be myself. . . .I can do both [be gay and Christian] and be happy!" The Gospel Hour is a place where condemnation is replaced by kindness.

All the principals of the Gospel Hour are evangelical Christians. They know that Jesus loves them, and they wish others to know that too. Most of the audience, judging from our formal interviews, informal conversations, and other clues, had Christian backgrounds, although Thumma and I had learned that many did not attend church. We discovered that many participants at the Gospel Hour are in complex ways still the choirboys, testifying congregants, clerical and lay leaders that they were in the evangelical churches of their youth and young adult lives. In such settings, many learned their identity as (white) Christian men in the South. In the more diverse and tolerant cultural spaces of Atlanta, they have learned to accept their sexual orientation and to live it out across a broad, if incomplete, spectrum of institutional settings. These participants are mastering new roles—ones of their choosing—as gay men in a leading center of the urban, corporate-dominated New South. Our interviews and participant observation drew Thumma and me to these conclusions. They also became the occasion for me to start to search for the intersection in my personal and professional life of religious and gay sensibilities.

It was Gay Pride week in Atlanta. The "Queering the South" conference, I was sure, had been planned for months. No one could have predicted that controversy over the place of gays in the full life of Emory University would be swirling, as the Gospel Girls performed at Glenn Memorial. The catalyst was again the intersection of religion and sexuality, specifically, the gay struggle for full social membership through same-sex marriage. Only a few weeks earlier, the dean of Emory's Oxford College campus in Conyers, Georgia, denied use of a chapel to a former staff member. This staff member, a gay man, wanted to use it for a commitment ceremony. Almost immediately after the denial became public, Emory's new president, William Chace, apologized. With no hesitation, he stated that the university's facilities were open equally to all members of the university. A subsequent meeting of the trustees resulted in the suspension of all marriages and commitment ceremonies in university chapels. In the interim, the question of the use of chapels for non–Methodist-sanctioned religious exercises of all kinds would be studied.

The United Methodist Church [UMC], to which Emory is historically, if ambiguously, affiliated, does not permit homosexual ceremonies of commitment in its churches or allow its clergy to officiate at them. Emory's trustees, a group that counts a number of UMC bishops in its ranks, later reported that they felt bound to honor the UMC policy. The United Methodists support, I am told, the civil rights of gays and lesbians. They oppose, however, same-sex marriage. Gay marriage, as Andrew Sullivan has pointed out, would be the single step signaling full social inclusion (1997, xxii). It was not surprising that the UMC would not allow same-sex commitment ceremonies to be performed unless they were fully sanctioned by a recognized religious body, unlikely to happen at Emory.

I wondered what the United Methodists would make of the Gospel Hour. Did they have a policy on drag gospel performers? The UMC bishops knew with certainty that they would not preside over or recognize a gay marriage. They could not, however, know beforehand where they stood on the question of gospel singing in drag at Glenn Memorial! How could they? I guessed that the UMC bishops might be just a little bit suspicious of some gospel music, given its Baptist and Pentecostal roots. But neither they nor the University were likely to have been able even to *conceive* of the Gospel Hour—let alone to confront permitting its facilities for such a use. Singing gospel music while dressed in drag is—until one thinks of it—inconceivable. It doesn't matter if the setting is a church or a bar.

This illustrates an important point about gays in most U.S. institutions: it is simply too difficult to exclude gays and lesbians from social participation of some kind, often at their invention. This is true because of practical considerations in a democracy and, as the Gospel Hour case illustrates, a cognitive one as well. Gays, like other marginal groups in America, have a genius for working at the margins of social institutions and of the wider culture. In addition, and unlike other minorities, gays are already present in every institution. This makes exclusion of gays from all American institutions—excepting an unthinkable program of outright elimination—simply an impossibility. Gays claim ownership of rituals and forms associated with mainstream culture as much as anyone. They are loathe to let them go. These include, as here, evangelical Christian ones like gospel music.

That night at Glenn Memorial I knew from the interviews Thumma and I conducted two years earlier that some in the audience had experienced firsthand the rejection of gays that is a hallmark of conservative biblical Christianity. Many had the experience of discovering themselves to be outsiders where once they thought they were at home. "If you are gay, you are going to hell!" was how one informant remembered the prevailing message of the church of his youth. Others grew up knowing that they "couldn't be both gay and Christian at the same time." "I realized that the God that the Baptists preached hated me," a former missionary said one Sunday between services. "I was told for so long that [as a gay man] I was hated by God." "I always thought that God completely hated me. I was told, 'You are gay and you are going to hell.'" By participating in a new religious ritual of their own making, these men began to undo this judgment. They made illegitimate the institutional authority of the religious groups that had made them illegitimate. They did so not so much by cognitively thinking it through as by participating in the model of blended identity created at the Gospel Hour and by listening to the authority of their own experience.

Interviewing, observing, and participating in the Gospel Hour over many weeks convinced Thumma and me that the Hour is a ritual or a dramatization of identity negotiation. The negotiation is not cognitive as much as it is performative. It challenges everyday categories of "gay" and "Christian" by absorbing and transforming them. At the Gospel Hour, Thumma and I discovered gay men creating this new model. We witnessed them choosing to combine their inherited Christianity with their acquired urban gay sensibilities. At the Gospel Hour, these men have found a public space, an urban precinct, that they did not know existed when they first came out, and they have made it their own. For the men in our study, the sexual and religious life cycles intersected here and to positive effect.

It was not long before Thumma and I concluded that the Gospel Hour is a fully religious ritual. We also think it is neither religious nor ritualistic alone. I presented our findings at a session of the Gay Men's Religion section of the American Academy of Religion. Afterward, the editors of a volume of religious ethnographies invited us to submit a longer version.[4] For that essay, we theorized as well about the ethnographic enterprise. The strength of ethnographic work is not that it uncovers *the* single answer to a research question. Instead, it addresses many questions as it explores the multiple levels of meaning in an event. Ethnography provides the "thick description" of a phenomenon that makes it available to others for their own interpretative frameworks and theorizing. Participants at the Gospel Hour certainly have different experiences and interpret them differently. That is part of what makes the event so compelling. Only now, years later, have I come to understand my own multiple experiences as its ethnographer. The desire to analyze how I negotiated, indeed ritualized, my identity as a gay man *and* a religion scholar fueled this revisiting of the original research and writing.

I first attended the Gospel Hour as a new graduate student in religion at Emory University. I had been in Atlanta only a few months and had spent almost no time at all in the South before then. I came by way of California, but with solid Yankee credentials earned by growing up in New York City. Only minutes into my first performance at Blake's, wall-to-wall with good-looking men, I wanted immediately to write about the Gospel Hour. However, I wondered about my career in the academy and more immediately in Emory's Department of Ethics and Society. All of its faculty was drawn from the Candler School of Theology, a United Methodist seminary. I was suspicious of what their reaction might be. I had never intended to study gay religion. Nonetheless, the Gospel Hour is an instance of what fascinates me most about religion. It shows gloriously the ability of groups to turn religion to some remarkable uses in some unexpected places. Despite a fear of being identified as a "gay scholar," I felt drawn to investigate this phenomenon. As I explored this new territory, I did not know how I would resolve this tension. Two years later, when Thumma and I began our work, I did not know I would create a model of my own, one blending scholarly and gay Christian sensibilities.

I *did* know that I wanted a research partner. My motives were personal and professional. Like every doctoral student, I already had enough to do and was reluctant to add more. Trying to do the study myself would mean it might never get done. I never considered the Gospel Hour for my dissertation topic, although I think it is rich enough for such a treatment. I realized how I feared inching closer to the inter-section of gay life and the study of religion. I am out, but I had never identified closely with research into gay culture. This I had perhaps unfairly judged as a hopelessly post-modern, "lit-crit" straight-jacketed enterprise. When it came to religion and gay life, the work that I knew was too theological and too desperately liberationist for my sen-sibilities. My training is in sociology and ethics. I wanted to be descriptive in my work, not normative. I did not want to become (to exactly what audience I was never clear) "that gay guy" who does sociology of gay religious groups.

To my mind, working with a straight male colleague was a shield over my own aca-demic identity. Therefore, Thumma was the perfect research partner. He had already published a study of southern evangelical gay men (see Thumma 1991). As we began our research, another set of issues loomed. I pondered what readers would make of us as a research team. Were we gay? Were we lovers? Did it matter? To whom? And in which ways? Scott and I became an ambiguous research couple during our sum-mer-long project. Teaming up also meant I could not be charged with being an unat-tached single gay man who claimed—with little to offer as corroboration—to be doing research in a popular gay bar.

Like my informants, I participate in a set of public activities and institutional prac-tices with their own logic, their own models of identity. Alongside my straight col-league, I *practiced* ethnography of a religious phenomenon *as* a gay man. This prac-tice was not a cognitive, proposition-driven working out of how gay or how out I wanted to be in the academy. Instead, I *acted* into a new kind of thinking through a set of practices that combined being a gay man and a religion scholar. My blended identity formed as I became practiced in it. I did not think it into existence. As I watched and theorized about others combining gay and Christian identities, I cre-ated a composite of my scholarly and gay sensibilities. And, as I would discover, of my Christian sensibilities as well.

I also did more. Like the subjects of our study, I had felt the sting of rejection from the Christian church. As a young graduate of Columbia College in the early 1980s, I was under care for entrance into a Lutheran seminary, which meant I had declared my intention to become a pastor. The assistant to the local ecclesiastical leader was my official mentor. The Lutheran Church in America however had just barred homo-sexuals from ordination. I told the clerical officer in charge of ordinations in New York that I was withdrawing my candidacy and I wanted him to know the reason was that I was gay. He was the second person to whom I had ever spoken those words. I told him that I knew the church did not want me. I had earlier resolved that I would not continue to live as a celibate and that I would not live closeted in any vocation. Lis-tening uncomfortably, he asked that I pray with him. We bowed our heads and he asked God to heal me. "Amen," we said. I remember thanking him for his time as I left, feeling like a burden, I suppose. I walked out onto a Madison Avenue bustling with strangers, an exile from the church, the most important institution in my life. I was sick. I had just participated in sentencing myself to this exile and asking God's blessings on it! After wandering alone along the busy streets of midtown Manhattan,

I got into the subway and returned to my parents' home in Queens, never to tell them of what had occurred.

I find it odd to write about this. It is not because I find it hurtful. Instead it seems irrelevant to my life today. It feels like the memory of a former lover after the magic has gone and that odd kind of indifference has set in. I have written about this incident before. I submitted detailed testimony during an ecclesiastical trial. The church to which I still belong had ordained a lesbian couple as assistant pastors. It was a clear, flagrant violation of church rules by St. Francis Lutheran Church in San Francisco. The congregation and supporters nationwide looked forward to the trial in part to testify to their experience as gay *and* Christian. I gave an account of this experience of official rejection and the homecoming I found years afterward at St. Francis. It did not, of course, do any good. The congregation was suspended, and the Evangelical Lutheran Church in America has since severed its ties to the congregation. But making the statement did do me a great deal of good. My statement was a no to my church's branding me illegitimate—coming ten years after that "Amen." Its writing and delivery in the context of a church trial gave it a ritualized elegance of which I am proud.

The Gospel Hour may not seem to be a liturgical event, but it has the regular rhythm and repetition of one. The performance at Glenn Memorial concluded in the same fashion as all services I have attended elsewhere. Perched on a row of stools, the Gospel Girls lip-sync a rousing version of "Looking for a City." Immediately before their performance, one of Morticia's regular cronies distributes cocktail napkins for the audience to wave as hankies, back and forth, to-and-fro, round and round, in time with the music. The Gospel Girls mirror the movements, as they always do, of the enthusiastic crowd.

"See You in the Rapture," a contemporary song, follows and is the grand finale. A dozen or more men take the floor without prompting to form a chorus line. Among them are some who join every week. New people also join, making the line several deep. The theology behind the lyrics of "See You in the Rapture" and "Looking for a City" is explicitly eschatological. The heavenly city sought is a place where residents will never die, where they "will be with Jesus and their loved ones too. Where the Holy Spirit all our hopes renew." Both songs promise an imminent new order marked by what Victor Turner called "communitas" (1969, 94–129). The eternal home "Looking for a City" envisions, like the bliss "See You in the Rapture" eagerly awaits, stands against all human works and ways. The hymns describe an eternal place of acceptance. Despite "all we have been through," sing the participants, they await the day they will see Jesus and each other—including those taken by age, accident, and disease—"in the air some sweet day." These hymns anticipate a place that, contrary to current social structure, is based on spontaneous relations among equal human beings.

Bronislaw Malinowsky (1965) believed that ritual made what was essentially biological change socially meaningful. It did so by making it public. He studied the Tobriand Islanders' rites of passage—puberty, marriage, childbirth, dying, and burial.

Gays and lesbians share these passages with heterosexuals. They also have another rite of passage, one of their own. This is coming out. Consider the close connections between rites of passage and sexual development. Participation at the Gospel Hour is not, of course, a sexual rite of passage. Participation in the Gospel Hour, nonetheless, enables participants who so choose to come out as *Christian and gay.*

Coming out is the equivalent of a biological rite of passage such as, say, puberty. Unlike puberty, of course, there is no biological clock ticking out an inevitable physical change. But at least for the most recent generations of gays and lesbians, sexual maturity and coming out are more closely connected. Coming out is, in many and remarkable ways, a social and personal rite of passagelike the born-again experience of evangelical Christians. Similarly, it is only rarely a single event. More often it is a series of steps, some large, some small.[5] For some gay men, participation in the Gospel Hour is one of those steps. It is an intersection of sexual and religious life cycles, like the intersection of the biological and the social in Malinowsky's interpretation of ritual.

Modern religious life, Robert Bellah has pointed out, operates without the formal direction of religious organizations. This cultural commodification of religion in the modern period means that religious symbolization, in which I include ritual, is available widely, and not only exclusively from or through religious institutions or organizations (Bellah 1970). There are many vendors of the religious today. In the urban gay milieu, one such vendor is a group of drag performers. Drag erases symbolically in a particular subcultural setting the gender lines created and maintained symbolically and socially in the dominant culture. Urban gay men must rehearse these categories daily in some segments of their lives. They are increasingly free in the U.S. urban milieu, however, to ignore dominant gender lines in other precincts of modernity. Although it is the creation of a small group of principals and their regular participants, the Gospel Hour is dependent upon both Christian gospel music and the bars of the gay ghetto. Its urban setting helps to account not only for its audience but for the institutions on which it relies. Atlanta, the self-styled premier city of the South, is a key player in the Gospel Hour.

The urban surround is critical. The Gospel Hour is an instance in which a city like Atlanta may come closest to the normative ideal of social life Iris Marion Young has advocated. This ideal is a form of social relations in which strangers come together. In this ideal vision of the city, "persons and groups interact within spaces and institutions they all experience themselves as belonging to, but without those interactions dissolving into unity or commonness" (Young 1990, 237). This is the danger of bland community. The city holds the promise of compatibility among strangers, of an eventual working out of respect among radically different parties. In this city, the difference between strangers is not fearful, but erotic.[6]

I know that many participants have found at the Gospel Hour their city. They have not dissolved entirely the distinctions, indeed the contradictions, between gay and Christian identities. Instead, they have learned to live with, accept, and embrace the contradiction, the inconsistency, the tentativeness of life in and outside the gay ghettos of the still-Christian South. To them, if not to most academics, multiple identities are not troublesome or hypocritical, but necessary. Some are even liberating. Their equanimity before such contrary and ambiguity allows them to move, sometimes fitfully, often with grace, from one social setting to another, from straight precinct to gay ghetto in the modern big city.

Lately, I have not attended the Gospel Hour. I did go for the tenth anniversary and once just before the "Queering the South" conference. I find it, sometimes, too much work. I am always observing, looking for clues to themes that Thumma and I might have missed, more often for confirmation of our analysis. When I go to the Gospel Hour, the scholar in me thinks about how it displays a narrative of the life cycle of many gay men in the South raised as Christians. When I have attended lately, I have wanted the scholar in me to be quiet. I want to participate as a gay man. It is during such moments that I see most clearly how the Gospel Hour can heal the wounds traditional Christianity has inflicted on many. I see this clearly as a religion scholar but want to see it simply as a human being moved by sweet singing. I enjoy participating as a cultural Christian and as a gay man who lives in the evangelical South. By "cultural Christian," I mean a person who recognizes and remains grateful for his religious formation but who does not otherwise believe.

The highlight of the Hour, the "High Church Sing-Along," especially moves me. It could not, if I did not share a Christian formation with the principals and participants. Morticia, Ramona, Tina, the Gospel Echoes, and the occasional guest singer sit on bar stools to lead the crowd in favorite hymns. Among these are "When the Roll Is Called up Yonder," "Because He Lives, I Can Face Tomorrow," and "There is Power in the Blood of the Lamb." None of these are high-church anthems like the ones I knew from the Lutheran Church, but good old gospel songs, at first hearing completely alien to me. But they also sing more mainstream Protestant hymns like "How Great Thou Art," and "Old Rugged Cross." During the "High Church Sing-Along," the Gospel Girls invite individual members of the audience to sing a verse of "Amazing Grace."

The performance reaches its climax for me now. There have been very young men singing, middle-aged women, trained and untrained voices. A crowd always gathers around, draws in, becomes intimate in a way I have seldom seen in a gay bar—or a church. Some sway, all sing the first and final verses of "Amazing Grace." Too often, when I am there alone, I fight back tears as I sing "Amazing Grace, how sweet the sound, that saved a wretch like me. I once was lost, but now am found, was blind but now I see."

I do not think my tears are a mere emotional response. I believe that it is a religious one. I find my emotion a troubling comfort. I no longer speak the language of the evangelical or the Christian. I do not search for spiritual direction, but I respect those who do and am drawn to them. I am a lover of things religious, of rites and ritual, of the ties that bind. I do not believe in the Christian God who loves me personally or guides the affairs of the universe. I do believe in something greater than the self, the family, sexual orientation, the market, and the nation. Through the practice of ethnography among gay men in the South, I have reconciled my identity as a sociologist of religion with one as a gay man. I have participated in—as I theorized about—the intersection of gay and religious life in the New South. Like my subjects at the Gospel Hour, I too, am looking for a city. I search for a place where often inconsistent, sometimes conflictual, social memberships, like being gay and Christian or queer and traditionally Southern, a scholar of American religion and a gay man, can be blended. A city in which everyone relies on the kindness of strangers.

Notes

1. All quotations, if not noted otherwise, are from interviews with Morticia, transcribed from either tapes or verbatim written notes. Scott L. Thumma and I conducted these interviews, usually as a pair, during the summer of 1995.

2. Stage names are accurate. Personal names are pseudonyms.

3. There is much scholarly work on drag. Esther Newton 1979 is the classic study; Roger Baker 1994 and David Bergman 1993 are more recent contributions.

4. Our AAR paper was published as "Amazing Grace! How Sweet the Sound! Southern Evangelical Religion & Gay Drag in Atlanta," in Clark and Goss 1996. Our fuller treatment is "The Gospel Hour: Liminality, Identity, and Religion in a Gay Bar," in Becker and Eiesland 1997.

5. See the chapter "American Religion, Gay Identity" in Browning 1996. Browning credits Randy Shilts in *The Mayor of Castro Street* (New York: St. Martin's, 1982) with making the claim for equivalency between coming out and being born again.

6. Strangers, to customers in a gay bar, of course, are candidates for cruising, potential sexual partners. To Christians, the stranger is not a stranger at all, but a neighbor, a brother. Participants at the Gospel Hour must negotiate this distinction too.

Works Cited

Baker, Roger. 1994. *Drag: A History of Female Impersonation in the Performing Arts.* New York: New York University Press.

Becker, Penny Edgell, and Nancy L. Eiesland, eds. 1997. *Contemporary American Religion: An Ethnographic Reader.* Walnut Creek, Calif.: Alta Mira.

Bellah, Robert. 1970. "Religious Evolution". In *Beyond Belief: Essays on Religion in a Post-Traditional World.* New York: Harper and Row.

Bergman, David. 1993. *Camp Grounds: Style and Homosexuality.* Amherst, Mass.: University of Massachusetts Press.

Browning, Frank. 1996. *A Queer Geography.* New York: Crown.

Clark, J. Michael, and Robert E. Goss, eds. 1996. *A Rainbow of Religious Studies, Gay Men's Issues in Religious Studies.* Vol. 7. Las Colinas, N.M.: Monument.

Malinowski, Bronislaw. 1965. "The Role of Magic and Religion." In *Reader in Comparative Religion: An Anthropological Approach,* ed. William A. Lessa Vogt and Z. Evon. New York: Harper and Row.

Newton, Esther. 1979. *Mother Camp: Female Impersonators in America.* Chicago: University of Chicago Press.

Sullivan, Andrew, ed. 1997. *Same-Sex Marriage: Pro and Con. A Reader.* New York: Vintage.

Thumma, Scott. 1991. "Negotiating a Religious Identity: The Case of the Gay Evangelical." *Sociological Analysis* 52, 4 (Winter): 333–347.

Turner, Victor. 1969. *The Ritual Process: Structure and Anti-Structure.* Ithaca, N.Y.: Cornell University Press.

Young, Iris Marion. 1990. *Justice and the Politics of Difference.* Princeton: Princeton University Press.

Laura Milner

From Southern Baptist Belle
to Butch (and Beyond)

There is no place for nonconformists in the Southern Baptist Church and no legitimate place for women, so it's no wonder that I and others like me have fallen away. Perhaps fled is more honest. No mere backsliders, we are fighting for survival and looking for salvation in a culture that says female is bad and lesbian is out of the question. Add to this the schizophrenic pride and shame of being southern and the expectations for southern girls to be belles—smiling, self-deprecating women dependent (or pretending to be) on the trinity of Daddy, Jesus, and Hubby—and there's no place to go but insane or incognito. Life and literature are replete with tales of "the opposition and triumphant destruction of women's love for each other by husbands and fathers" (Bernikow 1980, 160) and the destruction of women's self-esteem by patriarchal religions. Failing to find positive female images in the traditional institutions of church and family, many southern lesbians lose themselves in lying, drinking, or abusing drugs: anything to avoid the pain of being pushed to the margins, "no 'count," unworthy of grace. But running away is not the only option, and the Bible is not the only book; many women find redemption in feminist literature, where real stories of human experience affirm our existence through lesbian characters who are not dirty, not perverse, not worms. When history ignores us and religion shames us, we must create our own.

For at least a century, women writers such as Gertrude Stein have escaped "the oppressive world of fathers and brothers" (Bernikow 1980, 183) and the rigid rules of patriarchal religion and been liberated through language. Courageous southern lesbians such as Dorothy Allison and Blanche McCrary Boyd, both raised Baptist in belle country, write stories about what happens when we stop feigning weakness and start taking responsibility for our lives, pledging allegiance to ourselves and our sisters and female lovers in this culture that demands that we do no such thing. Allison acknowledges that she "gave up God and the church early on, choosing instead to place all [her] hopes in direct-action politics" and using "good writing as a way of giving meaning to some of the injustices" she has seen as a white, working-class, woman-oriented southern woman (1994, 166). Telling one's own version of the truth, Allison says, is "a moral act, a courageous act, an act of rebellion" that encourages other such acts; as a lesbian and a feminist writer, Allison wants "to remake the world into a place where the truth would be hallowed, not held in contempt, where silence would be impossible" (177). Allison and Boyd, along with Rita Mae Brown, Florence King, and other southern lesbians, write so that we might have life, and have it more abundantly. Otherwise, there's no room in the inn, unless it's the closet. Those of us who dare to step out and speak up receive the mixed blessing of the truth setting us free. Having waded in the waters of freedom and light, I can no longer remain silent about the misogyny inherent in southern culture, whether in churches or history or my own life, because covering up leads to complicity in perpetuating the abuses ingrained in these traditions.

As a young girl in Alabama, I wanted to believe in Jesus and did. I opened the door to my heart and was sure I felt, as the hymn says, "the Savior come in." In retrospect, I may have been better off doubting the deity and believing in my own inherent worth. The Baptists in my town did not discuss their history of being proslavery and antievolution. Like their counterparts across Dixie, they opposed anything that "threatened the ideal of southern Womanhood and White Supremacy" (Cash 1941, 346). Nor did they acknowledge that their gender-biased liturgy was (and still is) antithetical to the love they preached and therefore detrimental to the female psyche. Worshiping the God of Abraham, Isaac, and Jacob, many Protestant churches ignore half the population, the half that happens to be female. Singing to God "from whom all blessings flow," they praise the Father, Son, and Holy Ghost with no mention of anything feminine. Exalting Jesus as "the Lily of the Valley," believers are reduced to nothing without him: "in Him alone I see, all I need to cleanse and make me fully whole" (*Broadman* 1940, 363). Where are the women? Our conspicuous absence from hymns and our cardboard presence in the Bible leave us without a mirror in which to see ourselves whole. This can be fatal in a society in which "knowing the cultural mythology about your identity is vital to organizing your own survival," a knowing that "plays a part in developing an affirmative self-image" (Allison 1994, 199). It follows, then, that believing in the superiority of the male—"without Him I could do nothing, without Him I'd surely fail," as the hymn says—led me to conclude that I and my sisters were inferior. Exalting the power of the man on the cross and the men in the pulpit meant denigrating myself, a habit I still struggle to break.

Our parents and preachers and Sunday school teachers, no doubt in good faith, programmed us to "surrender all" (*Broadman* 1940, 82) and to "trust and obey for there's no other way" (390) in a system where the only one to be trusted was the all-powerful male, never the still, small voice within. We did not realize that the fundamentalist Christian experience had redefined masculinity and empowered men to do as they please. According to Shirley Abbott in *Womenfolks Growing Up Down South:*

Christ was divine but a man as well: bleeding and chaste but still a man. The metaphor of salvation—giving in to Christ, submitting to his will, accepting Him as Master—came naturally to women. Salvation was and is a poetic transformation of a relationship that women learn from early childhood. They trust and obey their fathers, look to their brothers for protection, and then become wives. Becoming the bride of Christ is not part of a man's training. (1983, 146)

For the young women in my church, surrendering to Christ came naturally. Like other adolescent girls looking for safe, sanctioned love, I gave myself completely and expected absolution. Any doubts or challenges I voiced were silenced immediately, and one of the strongest messages I heard was that doubting, lacking faith, would send me to hell. Dorothy Allison must have heard the same message, for in her novel *Bastard out of Carolina*, a Christian woman tells the ten-year-old narrator, Bone: "Questioning's a sin, it's pointless. He will show you your path in His own good time" (1992, 160). This same woman, the mother of Bone's best friend, laughs and pretends not to notice the heavy drinking and fondling—"hands reaching out to stroke our thighs and pinch the nipples we barely had"—that are common occurrences on the gospel circuit the family travels (163), and the young Bone marvels at the mother's blindness. I still wonder how many adults in my church suspected that children and vulnerable women were being manipulated in dim church chambers but did nothing to stop it. In their silence and fear, these adults allowed the abuse to continue, unaware that Jesus is not the only one who "paid it all" (*Broadman* 1940, 258).

Women and girls become easy targets for abuse when we have waning self-worth and have seen negative female images in the Bible and in Southern Baptist churches. Not surprisingly, many of us learn to deny our own voices and defer to any male authority; consequently, we accept the blame when we end up pregnant, abused, molested, or worse at the hands of men and in the face of a Savior we trusted to protect us. We were doing as we were told. We were remembering the evil temptress Eve, the stupid wife of Lot, the traitorous Delilah, and the worthless slut Jezebel, that is, the male-interpreted myths about them. In *To Love Delilah: Claiming the Women of the Bible,* South Carolinian Mary Cartledge-Hayes explores these myths and offers some alternative perspectives. She suggests that the Bible has "very little good to say about women," and in fact, biblical women tend to be adjuncts to the primary stories about men and therefore easy to stereotype (1990, 13). As a Christian, Cartledge-Hayes struggles with the dualism of God versus the Bible, with God saying "love thyself" and the Bible saying women are despicable. When women internalize the myth of Eve as the root of all evil, "it predisposes us to live our lives in shadows" with low self-esteem (23). Most importantly, she says, "faith tells us that God breathes goodness into each person. To believe in God and at the same time consider women lesser creations is an abomination" (24). Because we have been taught to think poorly of ourselves, breaking the cycle of self-criticism is difficult. When heterosexual women of faith have sex outside marriage, "God would (maybe) forgive you if you hated yourself sufficiently" (53), and "God loved best those who hated themselves most" (54). The Christian requirement for lesbians,

Cartledge-Hayes says, is "an exponentially increased amount of self-hatred" (53). Though many modern women flee Christianity in search of more female-friendly spirituality, Cartledge-Hayes refuses to be "shoved out" of her faith "by those who would be content with my alms and my body while ignoring my mind and my voice" (15). Many feminists choose to stay in their home religion and try to change it from within; for others, staying and fighting involve more self-denial and pain than we are willing to endure for what should be a welcoming spiritual environment.

For me, it is not enough to walk away, become a Buddhist, turn butch, and shed my hair shirt as many southern women have done to escape the suffocating sacraments. I must speak up! Contrary to what our churches, history, and southern culture have taught us, women—even lesbians—do have worth. In my grandmother's *Broadman Hymnal,* I find "Christ Receiveth Sinful Men," where not a thing is said in four verses about sinful women. Are we not worth mentioning, not worth receiving? Here our only hope is the "he," never the "she." Across the page, I see evidence of the source of Baptist self-loathing: "Alas and did my Savior bleed? And did my Sovereign die? Would He devote that sacred head / For such a worm as I?" (1940, 112). What is lower than a worm? No wonder I had no self-esteem, no sense of worth. I memorized every word, every stanza, and took them to heart. Memorization paved the way to winning the Sunday-night sword drills and a new white dress to be crowned Queen Regent—a coming-of-age ritual for smart Baptist girls who cannot hope to preach but can, if they grovel enough, become the brides of Christ. Unfortunately, being armed with Scriptures did not protect me from the Lord's messengers, some of whom proved unworthy of my trust.

Add a strong dose of Southern Baptist restrictions to the demands of becoming a belle and overlay these on a woman born loving women and the result is anathema. Self-loathing seems to be "the tie that binds" (*Broadman* 1940, 239) and oppresses southern women, whether Baptist, lesbian, butch, or belle. Whether high born or working class, "to grow up female in the South is to inherit a set of directives that warp one for life, if they do not actually induce psychosis" (Abbott 1983, 3). Florence King, the North Carolina journalist whose autobiographical *Confessions of a Failed Southern Lady* describes her bisexual experiences as a graduate student in Mississippi, says all southerners are insane, but especially the southern woman. The reason, King says, is that "'the cult of southern womanhood'" endows the woman with at least five different images "and asks her to be good enough to adopt all of them. She is required to be frigid, passionate, sweet, bitchy, and scatterbrained—all at the same time. Her problems spring from the fact that she succeeds" (1985, 3). Like charity, King writes, "schizophrenia begins at home" (5). In *Womenfolks,* Shirley Abbott recounts how she grew up in Arkansas believing that "a woman might pose as garrulous and talky and silly and dotty, but at heart she was a steely, silent creature, with secrets no man could ever know, and she was always—always—stronger than any man" (1983, 3). A true belle must never admit her strengths; "any form of intellectuality will have to be muted or even totally concealed, depending on the situation" (107). Indeed, "no matter how lowly your origins or how plain your person, you were expected to be a belle", Abbott writes (112).

As defined by the *Oxford English Dictionary*, the term "belle" is derived from the Latin *bella*, feminine of *bellus*, for beautiful or fair, used as early as 1668 in reference to kissing a maid who was "so mighty belle." Further, it is defined as "a handsome woman, one who dresses so as to set off her personal charms; the reigning 'beauty' of a place; a fair lady, a fair one." Beauty is not an absolute requirement, however; a belle could also be, as Somerset Maugham writes in *Magician*, 1908, a "plain woman whose plainness does not matter." *Oxford*'s only reference to southern belle is from Margaret Mitchell's *Gone with the Wind*, 1936, "a delicately nurtured southern belle with her Irish up." *Webster's New International Dictionary*, unabridged, describes a belle as "one whose personal charms make her attractive in society."

Succeeding as a southern belle requires the aspirant to finesse a multifaceted approach to life while pretending to live simply. Specifically, Shirley Abbott notes that the belle's

> first job in life was to attract boys. Second, although she was not stupid, neither was she excessively troubled by her own intelligence or cultural yearnings, which were nil, and she knew better than to display the slightest proficiency at anything. Third, she had the quality of being unattainable, of coming from that "pure, clean, sweet atmosphere" described by Mr. [Thomas Nelson] Page. Fourth, she . . . was pious, or appeared to be. That is the herbal bouquet for the sauce and an excellent mask for all the calculated moves that a belle has to make. (1983, 112)

The best belle Abbott knew as a teenager, Margaret Anne, "never missed a Sunday at the Baptist church" and sang in the choir as instructed by her mother (112). In so doing, she cultivated an "otherworldly image" while displaying herself, flirting with boys, and all the while keeping her eyes focused on the preacher and crying when the "stray lambs" walked down the aisle and gave themselves to the preacher as the choir sang "Just As I Am." Some women do not learn until years later that this game of deceit is one we cannot win. Believing that "we are weak but He is strong" (*Broadman* 1940, 307) does not equip a person for life in the real world. If we do not believe in ourselves, cannot rely on ourselves, we are lost. I came to this revelation slowly, in my thirties, after a long spell of spiritual deprivation. Returning to Emerson's essays on self-reliance, Thoreau's "lives of quiet desperation," and Whitman's "Song of Myself," which insists "it is as great to be a woman as to be a man," I cracked open the door and found myself there, waiting.

Recently, I have come to understand that religion and forced femininity are only symptoms of the chronic aches and pains in southern culture. Reading the history of how this intricate system evolved—this system of women lying and men placing them on the "lady" pedestal—increased my sense of shame as a native southerner and my determination to inspire change. Our cultural closet is crowded with skeletons! As early as 1897, Thomas Nelson Page received acclaim for his stories about plantation mistresses, "good darkies," and the white man's right to lynch anyone perceived as threatening a white lady (Abbott 1983, 83). Page defines the plantation mistress as a "queen" who was "delicate in frame and of a nervous organization so sensitive as to be a great sufferer" (quoted in Abbott 1983, 84). Many roles kept her at home: "She was mistress, manager, doctor, nurse, counselor, seamstress, teacher, housekeeper, slave, all at once. . . . Her life was one long act of devotion to God, devotion to her husband, devotion to children, devotion to her servants, to her friends, to the poor, to humanity"(84).

Page's description conjures not Scarlett, who is lusty and willful, but her mother, Ellen O'Hara, "the archetype of the southern lady" (Abbott 1983, 80). A fictional Savannah, Georgia, beauty, Mrs. O'Hara is "both practical and ethereal" as she "contrives to cover up her executive abilities so as not to embarrass her husband or startle the servants" (81). Her purity and long-suffering are ineffable as she supervises the poultry yard, visits the sick, and suppresses her true feelings. In fact, Abbott says, "her forte is management" (81).

Unlike her feisty, willful daughter, Ellen O'Hara sacrifices herself and has unlimited energy to give. She "pours water over Scarlett's rebelliousness, her boyishness, her lack of decorum," in an attempt to raise Scarlett as "a fading flower of Southern white womanhood" (Bernikow 1980, 243–244). Outwardly, this flower is passive and helpless, but a "lady" to the highest degree (244). What set the southern belle apart from ladies from other regions is that she "had to work," and "the richer the lady, the greater the job," because someone had to take care of all those servants (Abbott 1983, 82). English, French, and Yankee ladies may be "ethereal and reticent and loyal, but they were also supposed to be idle, delicate, slightly neurotic, and ill" (82), not a strong manager and self-effacing worker like Ellen O'Hara. My own mother modeled strength and self-effacement to the hilt, rising at 5:00 A.M. to hang clothes outside on the line, prepare breakfast and lunch for three children, sew curtains for the dining room windows, and study for a test—all before going to work as a secretary (and later a history teacher) at 8:00 A.M. She ended her long days with night classes at the local university and induction into Phi Kappa Phi and somehow managed to attend our never ending ball games, concerts, and scout meetings. When praised for her talent and skill in any of these areas, she smiled, shook her head, and insisted, "It was nothing!"

What many southern girls are never told is that the perfect Ellen O'Hara never existed and that perpetuating her myth only serves the southern patriarchy and oppresses southern girls. Far from the angelic stereotype promoted by Page and Mitchell, white plantation mistresses are depicted in slave journals as "demanding, harsh, impatient, capricious, and quick to call for the laying on of the lash" (Abbott 1983, 92). The mistresses' actions, while not justifiable, may be understandable. As Georgia novelist Lillian Smith writes in *Killers of the Dream:* "The more trails the white man made to back yard cabins, the higher he raised his white wife on her pedestal when he returned to the big house. The higher the pedestal, the less he enjoyed her whom he had put there, for statues after all are only nice things to look at" (1949, 121). Isolation and silence are essential to being a southern lady or belle, and this way of life is not acceptable to some of us. As Shirley Abbott would realize after many years of idolizing Margaret Mitchell's characters, "the southern lady is not so much a real person as a utilitarian device for covering up ugly reality." The reality was that this lady was only revered as long as she stayed put, as long as she kept to her plantation and remained "an uncomplaining, unquestioning collaborator" (1983, 84) in the system that used her as an excuse to keep black men from voting and to justify white men abusing, even killing, black men and women.

The submissive white southern woman's role in perpetuating racism, intentional or not, is unmistakable. In *The Mind of the South,* W. J. Cash recalls the "unusually intense affection and respect for the . . . wife and mother upon whose activities the comfort and well-being of everybody greatly depended" (1941, 88). The wife often knew but denied that the black maid in the kitchen was her own husband's lover or child; the wife "feigned blindness, as her convention demanded she should," while her guilty husband "must inexorably writhe in shame" and worship, even deify, his pure but distant wife (88). Cash quotes the words of aristocrat John Temple Graves, who blamed the great Atlanta race riot of 1907 on the white man's need "to protect southern womanhood by lynching any number of innocent Negroes" (309). Every theological, sexual, and economic argument was used to convince southern women that they must fulfill the roles and obey the rules promulgated by churches, schools, parents, and books, chiefly, "Be a lady and you will be loved and respected and supported" (Abbott 1983, 94). A lady should marry early, please her husband always, model Christian piety, and kindly oversee the slaves and the children, teaching them to play the roles that perpetuate the social system (94). The young belle learns that "being honest with men is a basic tactical error" (106). How many times was I reminded to "make him think it was his idea" and "You'll catch more flies with honey than vinegar"! How often was I instructed at home, "Don't tell Daddy," and at church, "tell it to Jesus, Jesus alone," unaware that secrets can lead to oozing sores and permanent scars.

Not all southern women, historically or in modern culture, have agreed to remain invisible, follow the rules, and abide slavery. The Southern Association of Women Against Lynching organized in the early 1900s in an effort to destroy the idea that lynching protects "Southern Womanhood" (Cash 1941, 311). Contrary to the Southern Baptists and the popular opinion of the time, these women knew that owning another human being is intolerable in a nation that calls itself Christian and democratic. They knew that slavery was "evil and un-Christian and it deprived white women of the very ease it was supposed to provide" (Abbott 1983, 97). Only in the 1990s has the Southern Baptist Convention apologized to African Americans for condoning racism and slavery and for failing to support civil rights initiatives in the 1950s and 1960s (Blumenfeld 1997). Shortly after the Baptists apologized to one oppressed group, they began openly discriminating against three others. Delegates at the 1996 Southern Baptist Convention in New Orleans "passed a resolution committing to put more energy and resources into converting Jews to Christianity," as if Jewish people do not have the sense to choose their own way of life and worship.

In 1997, the convention voted "to boycott Walt Disney theme parks, movies, and products over what they see as Disney's 'promotion of homosexuality' and retreat from 'traditional family values'" (Blumenfeld 1997). In the summer of 1998, the convention publicly reaffirmed its position that wives should submit and be subservient to their husbands. As long as such bigotry and prejudice continue among the Baptists, the denomination is going to lose members, and the members who are female are going to lose self-esteem. We former Baptists who happen to be gay are not taking the bit into our mouths anymore; we will not be denied dignity, regardless of whom we love.

Though feminist historians tend to blame the patriarchy for all of society's evils against women and children, the "good old-fashioned Southern lady" is a collaborator for believing what she was told and keeping silent when in her heart she disagreed (Abbott 1983, 102). This tendency to obey and play stupid did not die when the slaves were freed or when women won the right to vote or went to work. In the new millennium, belles continued to be formally trained and displayed in debutante balls, cotillions, sororities, and Sunday schools across the South. Like her predecessor, today's belle appears shy as she quietly checks her image in her mirror; she speaks softly and expresses nothing but admiring opinions about any subject, and most importantly, she smiles. As a naive young journalist at the *Birmingham News* in the early 1980s, I was writing a story to meet a deadline one day when the publisher walked by my desk and stopped. He stood there until I looked up, and then he said, "Smile!" I probably responded with a plastic smile, the kind modeled by my editor, aptly named Jo Ellen O'Hara, but inwardly I fumed. This man would not dare interrupt one of my male colleagues on deadline with an order to smile or be charming. Fiercely independent but well-coached by Mother to swallow my rage, I knew better than to waste a diatribe on my boss and risk losing my job. Surely he suspected, as Abbott cautions in *Womenfolks,* that "you cannot judge a southern belle by what you see," for she is "ostentatiously charming, polite, enthusiastic, sincere, and soft-headed ... [and] it takes a keen eye to know what the performance conceals" (106). What the belle wants, Abbott says, is power, glamour, and a man she can rule so that ultimately, and ironically, she becomes independent, calling the shots economically and otherwise. Inner conflicts are inevitable, considering that seeking power, glamour, and dominion is forbidden in many conservative Baptist churches.

Southern women who lack the drive or the stomach for catching and managing a man may find themselves floundering, at least initially, for if the old code does not work, what does? Feminist literature offers an alternative to the Baptist hymns, Bible verses, and antithetical messages from southern culture that remain part of our core, even as we try to drop the charade and live honest, deliberate lives without a man at the center. Florence King offers hope as she writes of her mother, a tomboy who smoked and boxed and "was not interested in creating illusions" despite Granny's attempts at "ladysmithing" (1985, 6). Granny hated female intellectuals because they "could never be ladies" (3) and encouraged Florence to practice Christian charity by comforting "the sick and afflicted" (66). Florence's father, a musician and self-taught scholar, called the southern belle "a state of mind, a product of the Deep South which is a product of the nineteenth century and the Age of Romanticism" (53).

When Florence attempts to join the military her senior year in college, her sorority sisters respond with horror at her desire to live and work with so many lesbians. Stereotypes abound as the sisters discuss their suspicions about female military life: "'I feel sorry for women like that.' 'They have to turn to each other because they're so unattractive that no man will look at them.' 'I'd die if a woman touched me. I'd feel robbed of my femininity'" (170–171). Finally, Florence fights back, telling them, "If ya'll are against lesbianism, it can't be too bad" (171). The sisters then excommunicate her, which she does not necessarily mind.

In graduate school in Oxford, Mississippi, Florence lives in a female residence hall where she meets "a classic southern belle" named Tulip Lee, "a cuddly barracuda; mad, bad, and dangerous to know, but she commanded respect" (211). Florence is surprised in the end to learn that Tulip Lee "took care of" the unfriendly talk about Florence and her female lover, Bres, whose affair "automatically made us 'niggah-lovin' Jew Communists'" (221). Apparently, Tulip Lee asked her rich daddy to call off the White Citizens Council so that night would no longer be "fear time" in Oxford (226). After Florence's lover is killed by a drunk driver, Florence seeks solace in sex with a soft-hearted bubba in a Memphis motel, but she ends up crying: "There is nothing sadder than being with one sex when you want to be with the other" (256). Upon returning to her parents' home in Virginia, Florence seeks but cannot find any lesbians. She finally meets two in the nursing home where her Granny is dying; "Look at those poor twisted women who love other women," Granny says, nodding toward Mrs. Kincaid's daughter and female friend across the hall (276). Granny speculates that Mrs. Kincaid's "heart is just broken right in two," then thanks the Lord that she has "been spared that" (276). Florence stays with her unknowing granny until death. Ultimately, Florence decides that her mother, her granny, and their black servant, Jensy, are "better than ladies," they are viragoes: "a woman of great stature, strength, and courage who is not feminine in the conventional ways" (218).

The virago could be sister to the butch, defined by the *Oxford English Dictionary* as "a tough youth or man; a lesbian of masculine appearance or behavior." The word "butch" is considered slang and of unknown origin; in the United States, the term also applies to a short haircut, a crew-cut. *Oxford* traces one of the earliest references on record to the *San Francisco News*, 10 September 1954: "Then some of the girls began wearing mannish clothing. They called themselves 'Butches.'" Later that month, the *Observer* noted that the "rejection of the female role is very common among the 'butch' type of lesbian." While many women, regardless of sexual orientation, have quietly resisted or attempted to reshape traditional female roles, the mannish lesbians have openly challenged and to some extent changed the patriarchal system by designing their lives without men at the center.

Contemporary lesbian novels offer myriad variations of butch (virago), femme (bellelike), and androgynous characters, some of them flat, others complex. Blanche McCrary Boyd draws characters who suffer marginalization because they are "different," though for the most part they survive. The women in Boyd's autobiographical *The Redneck Way of Knowledge,* a book given to me by a federal judge when I was a newspaper reporter in Nashville, portray a range of possibilities for living as nonbelles in the South of the 1970s and 1980s. Dixie, a nineteen-year-old Charleston aristocrat who speeds down the magnolia-lined highway under moss-draped trees with the sunroof open on her Porsche, smokes pot and tells stories as she and Blanche head for the culture-packed 1979 Spoleto festival (1982, 35), an event revered today in the South. Heir to "an old fortune and an even older name," Dixie is "charming, beautiful in an androgynous way, and wild," or so Blanche thinks (36). A scar runs across Dixie's face from a mishap at age twelve, when Dixie's cousin "swiped at her with his great-great-grandfather's Civil War sword" (36). Having been married, as Blanche says, "for a few weeks on an extended drug trip when she was seventeen" and now divorced, Dixie is not allowed to go with her family to the annual ball hosted by the St. Cecilia Society, "Charleston's most prestigious organization," which admits no women who are unmarried or divorced (39). Dixie's friend Shreve, however, has attended several times, wearing long white gloves and watching the debutantes in long white gowns dance in lines. Shreve drives an English Jaguar limousine, is "tall, angular, has a waist-length braid," and usually wears jeans and tennis shoes (40). No match for Dixie's beauty, Blanche says Shreve's eyes "have a quality of looking inward" (45). Rebelling against the role of belle, Dixie, Shreve, and Blanche take control of their own lives. They write their own scripts and, like many of my southern lesbian friends, sometimes bloody themselves and others by racing numbly through life on the razor's edge. Desperate and running from their own identity, they find temporary relief in addictions to alcohol, sex, or work, determined to define their own lives. Some, like Blanche McCrary Boyd, stop and wake up and live to tell their stories; others do not.

When Blanche asks Shreve why storytelling is so important to southerners and such a source of pride, Shreve suggests that it started with the Civil War: "The winners write history and the losers write poetry and all that" (46). Then Shreve adds that storytelling thrived in the South even before the Civil War because it is "spellbinding . . . wishful thinking. The love of illusion. This is one hell of a romantic place" (46). Blanche says she and her mother and sister tell stories over and over as "a way of expressing complicated feelings about each other. With our tales we entertain, comfort, make order, instruct, chastise, and preserve" (46). I remember sneaking into the kitchen when my mother and her sisters or women friends were sitting around the table, sipping coffee and swapping stories about work and men and what seemed like magic. Their laughter and talk pointed to a knowing I longed for, a safe place where I could curl up for life. What they left unsaid loomed larger than their actual words, somehow, and their stories seemed to be manifestations of something more powerful than they could name.

In painfully realistic fashion, Boyd's three characters drink and drug their way through Spoleto's parties, operas, and chamber music until Blanche, who acknowledges having grown up "medium-rich" but not aristocratic, cannot take anymore.

Years later, Dixie invites Blanche to go hunting with her, and Blanche declines; the same day, Blanche learns that Dixie has shot herself while "drunk and drugged," leaving Blanche to wonder "if [Dixie] would have shot me too" (159). At Dixie's house before the ambulance arrives, Blanche realizes she could have put her fists "into the hole Dixie blew through her gut out her back" (159).

Dixie survives this suicide attempt, and Blanche recalls surviving an attempt of her own after losing a lover. Blanche took 105 aspirins "to soothe [her] headache" after a painful breakup with a woman lover she thought she "couldn't live without" (81). Blanche's lover had returned to her husband after "the magic receded," and Blanche, for the third time in her life, lost love. She remembers that the word "'passion' originally meant suffering, agony, as of a martyr. The passion of Christ. No wonder being in love made [her] feel out of control" (82). Blanche concludes that "falling in love is the only religious experience my generation legitimizes. We cannot talk about magic or seeing God or believing in astrology without seeming silly. Even those of us who still read the *I Ching* or *Holy Bible* do so surreptitiously. But falling in love is as democratic as puberty: It happens to almost all of us" (83).

For many southern lesbians like Boyd who grow up Baptist and balk at the pressure to be a belle, falling in love with a woman can be both devastating and liberating. A voice inside says, "Yes, I'm home," while everything outside screams, "No, you know better than that."

Blanche McCrary Boyd, like many southern women, attempted to reconcile her life by leaving the South. I did this at twenty-two to attend graduate school in Connecticut, a move that revolutionized my life. One lesbian feminist professor—the first such creature I had knowingly encountered—walked us through Virginia Woolf and showed us the necessity of having a room of our own, a concept foreign to me until then but suddenly and completely familiar. Reading about the ways women reflect and aggrandize men at the breakfast table and in so doing lose themselves, I saw myself, my relatives and friends, and was horrified. Once enlightened, I ended a self-destructive relationship with an older man who had done most of the talking while I smiled and nodded for three years, and I began to accept myself as a woman-oriented woman. Boyd, too, recalls leaving the South at eighteen "with a pose of ferocious finality," determined not to let her family's "smothering abuse" seduce her, a family that was "ideologically up-front right wing" (1982, 7). After a "vulnerable relative was quickly institutionalized for being homosexual," Blanche knew that she, too, was at risk: "We all know where we stand, and we don't discuss our differences. I . . . admire their eccentricities, and love them with the same complexity with which I once despised them" (7). When Aunt Jenny visits Blanche in New York and says she would "like to get a vacuum cleaner and clean out [Blanche's] mind" (9), Blanche laughs. Her aunt then replies, with watery eyes, "I view your life as a tragedy, Blanche," to which Blanche responds, "How can it be a tragedy if I'm doing what I want?" Jenny finally acknowledges that "that's the problem" (9). I, too, have been pitied and admonished by relatives who said, "What a waste!" to which I wanted to reply, "A waste of what? My reproductive organs?"

Boyd writes that she has spent years sorting through "the good ways [her] family and being a Southerner" have affected her and trying to "separate out the destructive influences," but it is not easy (9). Sometimes she feels "as if the pieces of [her] psychic makeup have broken off from each other in chunks," and she is "mourning a personal loss," mourning her family's myth about her (10). As a lesbian writer, Boyd can never be the belle they wanted her to be, though she has tried. Those of us born lesbian in southern Protestant families have to mourn and move on; our survival demands it, and our families, for the most part, must adjust or lose touch with us. When I called off my engagement at age nineteen to a medical student my mother adored, it took months for everyone to recover, and I never came that close to marriage again.

When Blanche married at eighteen, she considered sex "holy" and agreed with an Episcopal bishop that "religious emotion and sexual feeling come from the same mysterious depths" (67). When she divorced seven years later, she still saw sex as holy, but marriage to her had become "part of the property system . . . an institution whose very nature ran counter to deep personal meaning. Like, say, organized religion. Or belonging to a sorority" (67). Later she lived with a woman for several years and began to see sex as "the inner world, an altered state; it was speaking in tongues" (67). As an adolescent, Blanche rebelled against her baptism by considering conversion to Catholicism and spending six months in that faith. In her thirties, Blanche returned to her hometown and developed two butch interests, skydiving and stock-car racing, "falling and noise . . . the only fears we're born with" (17). Though she did not return to South Carolina "to get religion," Blanche says she has found herself in a "total immersion. If I wash in the blood of the past, I tell myself, maybe I'll be free of it" (31). Her lovers, friends, and a stint in a commune "never replaced the special feeling" she had with her family, the same family that institutionalized a gay relative. Blanche acknowledges feeling "confused about God" (63) but says "in outliving Jesus, I haven't managed to outgrow him" (68). She recalls her love for Noreen, a woman whose eyes made Blanche "feel forgiven . . . and now I'm not sure what I needed forgiveness for . . . I want to hang it up about Western guilt" (80). Guilt holds many southerners in place, even when the stench of racism, misogyny, and homophobia tells us the place is rotten. Feeling locked in, we do not realize we have choices, even about our guilt.

In another autobiographical book by a South Carolina lesbian, Dorothy Allison's nationally acclaimed *Bastard out of Carolina,* the protagonist and narrator, Bone, grows up in a poor family in rural South Carolina—a family where the men drink heavily and the women work hard to keep the children fed and clothed. From age six, Bone is beaten and molested by her stepfather while her mother deludes herself about the abuse. Bone often wishes she were male so she could "run faster, stay away more, or even hit him back" (1992, 109). She learns quickly that "men could do anything, and everything they did, no matter how violent or mistaken, was viewed with humor and understanding," leaving her "wishing I had been a boy" (23). Instead, she stands scared and ashamed, "unmoving and desperate, while he rubbed against me and ground his face into my neck. I could not tell Mama" (109). Like other southern girls, Bone has been taught to conceal her pain and protect the man in charge, no matter what. Telling the truth means risking ostracism, and for some of us, hiding our shame is easier than disappointing and being rejected by the people we love.

Unable to burden her mother, Bone turns to religion and tries to cast her cares upon Jesus. At tent revivals and cinder-block churches, Bone dreams of becoming a gospel singer: "the music [is] a river trying to wash me clean" (136). Hearing the choir sing "Swing Low, Sweet Chariot" in church, Bone realizes that "all my nastiness, all my jealousy and hatred, swell in my heart. . . . The world was too big for me, the music too strong. I knew, I knew I was the most disgusting person on earth. I didn't deserve to live another day" (136). When her stepfather, Daddy Glen, repeatedly beats her with a belt, breaks her collarbone and coccyx, and molests her, Bone is convinced that she is "evil" (110). She "lived in a world of shame" and hid her bruises "as if they were evidence of crimes" she had committed (113). For Bone, gospel music could "make you hate and love yourself at the same time, make you ashamed and glorified. It worked on me" (136). Bone wants "to be washed in the blood of the lamb" but says, "I could not tell if what I truly hungered for was God or love or absolution. Salvation was complicated" (148). She comes close to being saved fourteen times in fourteen different Baptist churches (151), but each time Bone is asked to fill out the membership card and commit herself to the preacher, she hesitates:

> I wanted, I wanted, I wanted something—Jesus or God or orange-blossom scent or dark chocolate terror in my heart. Something hurt me, ached in me . . . everything . . . drew me down the aisle to the front pew. . . . I wanted the way I felt to mean something and for everything in my life to change because of it. (151–152)

Instead of feeling cleansed, Bone leaves each church feeling ashamed and empty because the magic never happens: "Jesus' blood was absent" (152). This self-hatred permeates and often debilitates the lives of girls like Bone who are abused sexually, physically, or emotionally in churches and homes across the South. Unlike Bone, not all of them find support in friends, lovers, or family members, and many kill themselves.

Ultimately, Bone's salvation lies not in religion but in her Aunt Raylene, a lesbian virago who lives alone by the river, beyond the city limits, and always arrives when her sisters or nieces need her most. Unlike Bone's mother, Anne, and other aunts who move frequently, Raylene has rented the same house for most of her adult life and enjoys fishing, cooking, gardening, and canning. When Anne loses a baby, Raylene "showed up in overalls and low boots to clean the house" (49). When Raylene's sister, Ruth, dies after a long bout with cancer, Raylene cleans the house and cooks a ham and two casseroles, then slaps Ruth's selfish daughter, DeeDee, and orders her to go to the funeral. Another sister is jealous of Raylene and insists that Raylene should "learn to use makeup and fix her hair, start working on getting herself a man" (89). Bone's mother, Anne, respects Raylene and entrusts Bone to her, even though Anne acknowledges that "Raylene had always been different from her sisters: she was quieter, more private, living alone with her dogs and fishing lines, and seemingly happy that way" (178). Raylene's stability and success in taking care of herself and her family provide a much-needed positive role model for Bone and for southern lesbians who want to be "good" but cannot fit the belle-shaped mold society has cut for us.

At *Bastard's* end, we learn the truth about Raylene's reasons for dropping out of school and joining the carnival at age seventeen; she left home to be with the woman she loved. Raylene "worked for the carnival like a man, cutting off her hair and dressing in overalls. She called herself Ray, and with her short, stocky build, big shoulders, and small breasts," Bone could imagine how no one questioned her (179). Raylene finally tells Bone about loving this woman "better than myself, a lover I would have spent my life with and should have" (300). But the lover had a husband and a child, and Raylene returned home alone. She tells Bone that "it should never have come to that. It never should. It just about killed her. It just about killed me" (300).

Though Raylene left the carnival and her lover behind, she brought her butch way of life back home with her. She worked at the mill for twenty years, keeping her gray hair cut short and wearing "trousers as often as skirts" (179). One sister admits that Raylene was "probably the only person any of us would ever meet who was completely satisfied with her own company" (179). Bone, too, notices that Raylene "always seemed completely comfortable with herself, elbows locked around her knees and one hand drawn up to smoke. Sometimes she'd hum softly, no music I'd ever heard" (182–183). Raylene praises Bone for helping find the "good trash" in the river and not being afraid of falling in or drowning. She advises Bone: "I am so tired of people whining about what might happen to them, never taking no chances or doing anything new. I'm glad you ain't gonna be like that, Bone. I'm counting on you to get out there and do things, girl. Make people nervous and make your old aunt glad" (182). Unlike Bone's mother and the other aunts, Raylene cautions Bone against keeping secrets and challenges her to be authentic.

Raylene nurtures her niece in ways that would win a star in any belle's crown. Being a virago does not preclude a woman from being a nurturer. In fact, a true belle and a butch share common traits: a strong will and fierce determination to do what they consider "the right thing," without whining or complaining. Both know what they want, and both work hard and wear a facade in order to have their way. In Raylene we find an authentic blend of the butch and belle, a courageous woman and family manager who is more concerned with the well-being of her family than with what other people think of her. She listens to her inner voice and encourages her niece to do the same. When Bone is beaten the first time, she cries "until Aunt Raylene took me out in her truck and rocked me to sleep with a damp washcloth on my eyes" (49). When Bone is beaten severely again, it is Raylene who sees the bruises and tells her brothers to kill Daddy Glenn. When Bone is hospitalized after the final brutal rape, it is not Mama but Raylene who wrestles the nurse and finally "shoved the woman away and came forward like a tree falling, massive, inevitable, and reassuringly familiar" (297) because "there was no stopping Raylene" (299). It is Raylene who assures Bone that her mama loves her and encourages Bone to give her mama time to forgive herself for allowing the abuse to happen (250). Raylene tells Bone to "think hard . . . about what you want and who you're mad at" as Bone decides how to live her life (263). Raylene confides that she ran off to the carnival, "but not for no man. For myself. And I ain't never wanted to marry nobody. I like my life the way it is, little girl. I made my life, the same way it looks like you're gonna make yours—out of pride and stubbornness and too much anger" (263). Motivating from anger may be less than ideal, but for many of us, rage catapults us toward survival. Anger is not pretty, but it can push us to create what eventually becomes a more peaceful, productive life.

Finding peace can be almost impossible after a violent rape such as the one Bone endures at the hands of her stepfather. After the rape, which her mother witnessed before disappearing for several days, Bone sits on Raylene's porch and whispers, through torn lips, that she hates Mama for abandoning her. Raylene quietly says, "You'll forgive her" (302). Bone then leans against Raylene, "trusting her arm and her love. I was who I was going to be, someone like her, like Mama, a Boatwright woman. I wrapped my fingers in Raylene's and watched the night close in around us" (309). Without Raylene, the butch lesbian, Bone would have been alone, betrayed and battered, with little hope for recovery.

Allison's and Boyd's narratives feature working-class and upper-class white lesbians, respectively, but white southern lesbians are not alone in being oppressed by church and family for their sexual orientation. In her short story "Be Still and Know," black lesbian author Brigitte M. Roberts presents a narrator who "comes out" to her mother and is sent to a church deacon for counseling. Roberts's narrator quotes John 3:16 about God sending his son to save the world, not just to save a righteous, heterosexual few: "Whosoever, Momma, not just the straight, childbearing, churchgoing folks. Whosoever. The pussy loving . . . bulldaggers . . . who believe in Jesus will walk beside you and rest at His feet in heaven" (38). The mother eavesdrops on a telephone conversation between the narrator and her butch girlfriend, Linda, as they are breaking up and suddenly intrudes: "Don't you be trying to teach my child your funny ways, them unholy things . . . call here one more time and I will call the law on you, you child molester" (38). Ironically, the child molester is not Linda but the revered deacon. Roberts writes:

> I allowed Deacon Carter to counsel me. I studied [verses in Leviticus, Deuteronomy, I and II Kings, Romans]. . . . But I refused to allow him to lay hand on my breasts, my ass, slip his tongue in my ear or mouth. When he threatened to reveal "my sin" to the church I promised to cry rape and named four less determined victims of his godless counsel.(39)

The narrator concludes with this message to her mother: "You taught me to see God in all things, in everyone. How could he be absent in the faces of the women I've held in my arms? You taught me that God will never forsake me. . . . I will be still and know that it is God who put the love for women in my heart" (40). Regardless of color, many lesbians reared in Christian families suffer when the parents and preachers who promised to love them end up denouncing and degrading them. Black southern women do not have the same pressures to become belles because they can never achieve such "status"; since slavery, black women have been dehumanized as sexual objects, "warm and earthy, while white women are disembodied, desexualized, and distant" (Bernikow 1980, 244). Whether lesbian or not, black and white southern women are expected to seduce and keep a man, or at least defer to Jesus, without whom they are deemed nothing.

This essay is an attempt to explore the options for southern women like me, women who love women, women who want to be good but rail against submission to and submersion under male domination, holy or otherwise. We want to be heard. We do not want to drown in the baptismal pool. We may blaze and inflame, but we know that the path of lies and secrecy leads to more shame and oppression and that truth telling is redemptive, so we proceed, in literature and in life. Allison challenges us to tell our stories, especially when they are mean, hard, or offensive (1983, 219); she encourages us to "give some child, some 13-year-old, the hope of the remade life. Tell the truth. Write the story that you were always afraid to tell . . . there is magic in it" (219–220). This kind of candor does not come easy for Allison or any southern woman whose mothers and aunts cautioned: "Don't tell nobody nothing . . . telling the truth is too dangerous, too expensive," because it gives people weapons to use against us (240). In disclosing her truth, Allison discovers that the primary use of writing is to "reject hatred, simple categories, shame," a process that requires her to love the people she writes about, "and loving my mama, loving myself, was not simple in any sense. We had not been raised to love ourselves, only to refuse to admit how much we might hate ourselves" (237).

Allison's conflicting feelings for her mama remind me of my own. Shortly after coming out at age twenty-nine to my mother, a complicated woman who dropped out of high school to marry a musician, then divorced and married my father and earned three college degrees, I sent her a copy of Adrienne Rich's *On Lies, Secrets, and Silence*. Nothing could have prepared me for Mother's negative response. She scribbled across the book's margins and returned it, along with a two-volume set of "real history" by a credible authority, William Manchester. As a history professor who forfeited her doctoral dissertation for a life at home with her new husband, she must have seen herself in Rich's prose about the dangers of pretending and deferring. As Mother always said, "The truth hurts," and "Be careful what you wish for, you might get it."

Oh, yes, "we've a story to tell to the nations" (*Broadman* 1940, 379) that could turn their hearts inside out. The good news is not that I *was* blind, but that *now I see*! So this is my story, this is my song of grace, an ongoing ballad of moving toward salvation through loving women and loving myself, and yes, loving men, but not in the biblical sense. My brother, three years older, has come a long way. This summer he taped a movie for me, "When Night Is Falling," because, as he put it, "it's about a lady professor who gets turned into a lesbian." I had to laugh. It was the first time I'd heard him say the *L* word, although at Christmas last year he surprised me with the latest compact discs by k.d. lang and Melissa Etheridge—out-of-the-closet mainstream lesbians, an oxymoron until recently. Not bad for a boy raised Baptist, son of a tool-and-dye maker and a hard-working, eyelash-batting belle. My sister has not rejected me, and my mother, not known for encouraging the truth to come out, shocked me by applauding my decision to write this essay, to set the record as straight as possible, to tell those Disney-boycotting Baptists that I, too, have a right to sit at the communion table.

Like Dorothy Allison, I began to see the light—or had it snuffed out—at thirteen, when the a music minister in our church offered to give me voice lessons and then molested me behind locked doors. A few years later on a school trip to Montgomery to meet Governor George Wallace, I confessed my sin to a trusted teacher, who understood that a child had been violated and decided to help. Help came in the form of a prayer session with a respected preacher who knew the music minister and had moved to another church in a bigger city, the preacher who had baptized me at nine and to this day claims me as his other daughter. His response to my ruination by molestation was to pat my knee and insist that God would forgive me. Thinking this preacher would take care of me, I chose a Baptist college close to his church and joined. By twenty-one, I was sure there was no God and no such thing as a "good Baptist," after this preacher decided that he, too, had rights to my body and crossed the line one day in his office. One minute we were reading the Bible together—"Let not your heart be troubled," he read—and the next he was gripping my shoulders and pushing his tongue down my throat. Shocked and shaking, I tripped down the dark steps and did not look back. What followed were years of rage, alcoholism, and refusal to associate with anything or anyone religious. Being grabbed by other male authority figures was painless compared to this betrayal by the preacher who had cupped my first-grade face in his hands and called me his "Sunshine."

At age twenty-six I found a real woman to love and therein a path to integrity and authenticity. I found a liberal religious community whose members strive to honor the inherent worth and dignity of every person, ordain hundreds of female ministers, and celebrate the interdependent web of life—even gay and lesbian!—in its hymnal. I found relatives—some of them Southern Baptists—willing to embrace and encourage me, and for this I am grateful. I found Rita Mae Brown's classic coming-of-age novel, *Rubyfruit Jungle,* about a tomboyish lesbian growing up with a sense of passion and humor, and without apology, in the South. When first published in 1977, *Rubyfruit* provided a long-overdue positive role model for southern women like me, as its "freedom takes the form of refusing self hate, moving outside and laughing" (Bernikow 1980, 183). Brown paved the way for other southern lesbian writers to come on out and be proud.

I found Dorothy Allison, and I found a job teaching writing and literature that stops my heart. Like Allison, "I am the woman who lost herself but now is found, the lesbian, outside the law of church and man, the one who has to love herself or die" (1995, 67). Like Allison, I have hope in "the remade life, the possibilities inherent in our lesbian and gay chosen families, our families of friends and lovers, the healing that can take place among the most wounded of us" (1994, 215). Before the women's movement, Allison recalls, "too many of us hated ourselves and feared our desire. But when we found each other, we made miracles—miracles of hope and defiance and love" (157). I, too, found strength in the women's movement. Working as a community educator and volunteer coordinator for a Tennessee women's clinic that offered a range of services, including abortion, I discovered the value of joining with others and putting our values into action. When an antichoice protester appeared outside the clinic one Saturday with a "Repent, Laura Milner!" sign, my coworkers and I laughed and fetched the camera. Several weeks earlier, I had physically blocked two Bible-toting men from sneaking in the side door of our clinic, and they were not amused when I filed trespassing charges against them and stopped their marching for six months. Between working with those volunteers to protect our patients' rights and writing news stories for years about activists and families working to ease the pain of poverty, sexism, racism, and homophobia, I began to regain faith. Now, as an assistant professor of writing in a university setting, I am inspired and empowered by my students' stories as their truths often touch my own.

One steamy summer day in Savannah, I came upon a sidewalk sale where a white cotton dress hung on a headless mannequin. Seeing the sheer fabric rippling in the breeze, I inhaled sharply, then stepped closer to touch the hem of this, the uniform of the virgin, the femme, the belle. I checked the price tag, then checked myself for considering such a feminine purchase. Perhaps the white dress brought back bittersweet days as a trusting Baptist G.A., member of Girls in Action, aiming for the only available title, Queen. Or maybe it piqued long-buried memories of the white robes my brother and sister and I were baptized in, or of the white sheets worn by hate-filled Klansmen when I was a reporter covering a Ku Klux Klan march in Birmingham in the early 1980s. No longer ladies in waiting, perhaps my partner and I will wear white dresses—or white tuxedos!—to our wedding, which will be holy, blessed by God.

Works Cited

Abbott, Shirley. 1983. *Womenfolks Growing Up down South.* New York: Ticknor and Fields.

Allison, Dorothy. 1992. *Bastard out of Carolina.* New York: Plume.

———. 1994. *Skin: Talking about Sex, Class, and Literature.* Ithaca, N.Y.: Firebrand.

———. 1995. *Two or Three Things I Know for Sure.* New York: Plume.

Bernikow, Louise. 1980. *Among Women.* New York: Harper and Row.

Blumenfeld, Warren J. 1997. "Southern Baptists Will Have to Apologize Again." *Boston Globe,* 23 June.

Boyd, Blanche McCrary. 1982. *The Redneck Way of Knowledge.* New York: Knopf.

The Broadman Hymnal. 1940. Nashville, Tenn.: Broadman Press.

Cartledge-Hayes, Mary. 1990. *To Love Delilah: Claiming the Women of the Bible.* San Diego, Calif.: LuraMedia.

Cash, W. J. 1941. *The Mind of the South.* New York: Vintage.

Faderman, Lillian. 1981. *Surpassing the Love of Men: Romantic Friendship and Love Between Women from the Renaissance to the Present.* London: Women's Press.

King, Florence. 1985. *Confessions of a Failed Southern Lady.* New York: St. Martin's.

Roberts, Brigitte M. 1997. "Be Still and Know." In *Does Your Mama Know? An Anthology of Black Lesbian Coming Out Stories,* ed. Lisa C. Moore. Decatur, Ga.: Red Bone.

Smith, Lillian. (1949) 1961. *Killers of the Dream.* New York: Norton.

Vicinus, Martha. 1993. "'They Wonder to Which Sex I Belong': The Historical Roots of the Modern Lesbian Identity." In *The Lesbian and Gay Studies Reader,* ed. Henry Abelove, Michele Aina Barale, and David M. Halperin. New York: Routledge.

Mab Segrest

"Lines I Dare": Southern Lesbian Writing

for Dorothy Allison

I did not know the word "homosexual" until I was twelve and read an article on the subject in *Life* magazine. It worked on me like a silent bombshell, this revelation that a whole group of people—enough for there to be a word for it—were powerfully drawn to members of their own sex. As I looked at *Life*'s sinister pictures of sad, scared men walking down dark and deserted streets, I saw that those feelings reverberating in me meant a life of loneliness and alienation. This knowledge so overwhelmed me that I pushed it to the back edge of my brain, where I developed a secret homesickness—maybe I had always had it—for these people I could love, a conviction that someday I would find them. Even though I loved my family and felt that love returned, I told myself in private conversations that I had to get away from home to be myself. I figured it meant somewhere far away and very exotic—like London, or an island in the Caribbean. I resolved to travel. I got as far as Durham, North Carolina.

When I fell unmistakably in love with another woman, in Durham, in 1973 (at the age of twenty-four), I was not sure that I had come far enough for this. But my brain was in open rebellion, not to mention the rest of my body and spirit. I sneaked over to the Intimate Bookstore in Chapel Hill to see what books they had on the subject (I had developed a habit of approaching books first, then proceeding sometimes to life). So I bought the only book that had "lesbian" in the title and went to sit beneath the trees by the stone wall on Franklin Street. I read with a sinking heart as a clinical voice explained how lesbian lovemaking, and love, was basically hollow because there was no penis to insert into the lesbian vagina. That turned out to be the biggest lie I ever got told, but I sure didn't know it then.

A previous version of this essay appeared in Mab Segrest's *My Mama's Dead Squirrel: Lesbian Essays on Southern Culture* (Ithaca, N.Y.: Firebrand Books, 1985). Copyright © 1985 by Mab Segrest. Reprinted with permission of the author and Firebrand Books.

So when I went to my first Southeastern Gay and Lesbian Conference in Chapel Hill in 1977, I headed directly for the session on lesbian literature. There sat a whole roomful of lesbians, including two novelists (Bertha Harris and June Arnold, flown in from New York), and Catherine Nicholson and Harriet Desmoines, the editors of a lesbian magazine in, of all places, Charlotte, North Carolina. It was like coming home.

Now, this literature I stumbled into was very different, you had better believe it, from what I had been reading while struggling to acquire a Ph.D. in English. In graduate school, other miserable graduate students and I spent long hours of research on literary history, theory, symbolism, and all, wondering over lunch in the cafeteria, day after day, why we put up with the bullying tactics of professors, why we and they were doing what we did. In my courses on twentieth-century literature, I learned about how Ezra Pound claimed to have invented modernism in the early part of the century and then forced it on everybody else because, as he explained, there was nothing new to say, only new ways to say it. His buddy T. S. Eliot went on to define poetry as the "escape from emotion." With these two men, literature took a great leap into academic obscurity, from which only scholars called New Critics could hope to rescue it.

The modern writer became a suicide. As A. Alvarez's book *The Savage God* documents, writers jumped off boats and bridges, blew their heads off with shotguns or stuck them in ovens, or slowly and loudly drank themselves to death.[1] Most of the "great works" of this century traced the dissolution of Western white male culture, in works by male writers who could identify only with its demise. Listen to the titles: *The Waste Land,* "The Second Coming," *For Whom the Bell Tolls, Love among the Ruins.* As graduate students, we sat around in despair trying to explain all this and lamenting that our own students, whom we as teaching assistants taught, didn't lap it all up as we did—a failing we explained as the decline of literacy.

With lesbian literature I remembered how it's supposed to be. No lesbian in the universe, I do believe, will tell you there's nothing left to say. We have our whole lives to say, lives that have been censored, repressed, suppressed, and depressed for millennia from official versions of literature, history, and culture. And I doubt that many lesbians will tell you that poetry, or anything else, should be an escape from emotion. We have spent too much of our lives escaping our emotions. Our sanity has come when we have turned to face them. The lesbian's knowledge that we all have stories to tell and that each of our cultures produces its own artists lessens the suicidal alienation between modern writer and audience.

Lesbian literature, like all the best women's writing today, is fueled by the knowledge that what we have to say is essential to our own survival and to the survival of the larger culture that has tried so hard to destroy us. The lesbian's definition of herself is part of the larger movement by all oppressed people to define ourselves. For some time I taught a survey of British literature using the Norton Anthology of British Literature, and for its first thousand years not a single woman's voice can be heard—though it is filled with plenty of usually hostile male definitions of what women are. There are no writings included in the book by people of color or Jews during the centuries when Europeans were burning women and conquering darker peoples for gold, glory, and the gospel. When excluded people begin to define ourselves, much of conventional literature (not to mention the rest of society) must be redefined, rejudged. Nothing left to say? My god.

So what does all this have to do with southern literature? Potentially, a lot. There was a spate of essays after Faulkner fell off his horse, drunk, and died, asking "Is the southern novel dead?" and "Is there writing after Faulkner?" Obviously, there is. But it is not a literature that like Faulkner's establishes a mythic country unto itself, a "postage stamp of native soil." It is rather in the tradition of liberation, as black poet June Jordan explains it: "the movement into self-love, self-respect, and self-determination is the movement now galvanizing the true, the unarguable majority of human beings everywhere."[2]

Within this broader tradition, the origins of southern lesbian literature can be traced to the beginning of the twentieth century. It emerges full blown in the 1960s wave of liberations: black civil rights, women's, and homosexual. It extends into the 1980s, when lesbian writers with southern roots take their places openly in the "movement now galvanizing the true, the unarguable majority of human beings everywhere."

Phase One: "Lines I Do Not Dare"

Angeline Weld Grimké, Carson McCullers, and Lillian Smith are the earliest southern and lesbian writers I can locate. Among them, they raise themes that later lesbians either develop or redefine, and they help set the terms with which we can understand lesbian literature.

Angeline Weld Grimké was the daughter of Archibald Weld Grimké, who was the nephew of the abolitionist Grimké sisters from South Carolina. She grew up in Boston (where the Grimkés brought her father from the South Carolina plantation on which he was a slave) as a "light-skinned, mixed blood black girl," according to Gloria T. Hull.[3] She lived in Washington, D.C., from 1902 until 1926.

Grimké's love poetry establishes her lesbianism and shows the self-silencing that accompanied it—like this from "Rosabel":

> Leaves that whisper whisper ever
>   Listen, listen, pray!
> Birds that twitter twitter softly
>   Do not say me nay
> Winds that breathe about, upon her
>   (Lines I do not dare)
> Whisper, turtle, breathe upon her
>   That I find her fair.

"Lines I do not dare"—when a lesbian denies her self and denies her sexual energy, she denies her creative energy as well. Gloria Hull finds these lessons in Grimké's life:

The question—to repeat it—is: What did it mean to be a black Lesbian/poet in America at the beginning of the twentieth century? First, it meant that you wrote (or half wrote)—in isolation—a lot which you did not show and knew you could not publish. It meant when you did write to be printed, you did so in shackles—chained between the real experience you wanted to say and the conventions that would not give you voice. It meant that you fashioned a few race and nature poems, transliterated lyrics, and double-tongued verse which—sometimes (racism being what it is)—got published. It meant, finally, that you stopped writing altogether, dying, no doubt, with your real gifts stifled within—and leaving behind (in a precious few cases) the little that manages to survive of your true self in fugitive pieces.

Grimké, who felt herself "crushed" and "smothered . . . under the days," has received little critical attention, no doubt because of her triple jeopardy—she was black, female, and lesbian. Yet my tracking of southern lesbian literature leads back to her—a woman born in Boston who never lived in the Deep South, yet whose slave father and abolitionist great-aunts give her undeniable southern roots. Her "fugitive pieces"[4] bring up the painful question of home—who owns it, who must flee it, who wants to claim and how do we reclaim regional culture soaked in the heritage of human slavery.

The next two women I locate are Lillian Smith and Carson McCullers. Writing in the southern renaissance, these two white, middle-class women also voice themes that help shape later southern lesbian literature. Like Grimké's, their lives and work show the effects of lines they "dare not write." They also illustrate further the kinds of problems that lesbians encounter in trying to reconstruct their culture. With them we meet not so much the question, What is southern? as What is lesbian?

For instance, neither woman ever publicly defined herself as a lesbian, and both might be upset that I am now proceeding to do so. A recent biography of McCullers, *The Lonely Hunter* by Virginia Spencer Carr, establishes McCullers's emotional ties with women, although in a disgusting heterosexist way:

> Reeves (Carson's husband, probably bisexual himself) was incapable of coping with his or his wife's sexual inclinations or of helping her to become more heterosexually oriented. Carson was completely open to their friends about her tremendous enjoyment in being physically close to attractive women. She was as frank and open about this aspect of her nature *as a child would be in choosing which toy he most wanted to play with*."[5] (Emphasis added)

Identifying Lillian Smith as lesbian presents more complex problems. As yet there is no definitive biography, though there is the fact that she never married and that she lived and worked with a woman companion for decades. There is no way to prove a sexual relationship between them, nor is there a need to do so. This puritanical culture defines homosexuality as sexual activity only: in this way it can then self-righteously condemn it, rather than seeing homosexuality as a question of emotional identity. (It's harder to be self-righteous about telling people they can't be who they are or love whom they need to.) I am sadly certain that many lesbians have lived out their entire lives fearing and repressing their sexuality. Smith's commitment to women, her analysis of oppression, and the nature of her criticism of the surrounding culture are enough to show me her lesbianism. But my best argument comes from my gut—a sixth-sense way by which lesbians have always known each other, a way of knowing not given much credence by most literary scholars. And in treating only two women from this period, I am being fairly discreet. For example, if Flannery O'Connor, of whose self-life there is no public record, cannot be put clearly into a lesbian column, it makes no more sense, and maybe less, to consider her heterosexual. Her letters show that her closest emotional relationships are with women.

The lives and work of McCullers and Smith present complementary studies in white lesbian response to a repressive culture. For most of her adult life, McCullers acted out internalized homophobia without overt political insights into the world she wrote about, insights important in Smith's writing. Living in a culture that pretended only men can love women, Carson once wrote to a friend: "Newton, I was born a man." She thought of her attraction to a female friend as "the devil at work" in her.[6]

McCullers entered into a horrible marriage with a bisexual man and spent most of her adult life in self-destructive confusion. It is little wonder that loneliness and displacement suffuse her writing. I am not saying that all kinds of people are not lonely or that a certain kind of loneliness is not the inevitable result of being the only person inside one's own skin, but, as a lesbian, I know that we are lonelier than we have to be. This unnecessary loneliness is rooted in the various forms of self-hatred so virulently promoted by our culture. And when characters and writers swallow that self-hatred uncritically, they become what literary critics call grotesque.

The Heart Is a Lonely Hunter,[7] McCullers's first novel, spirals toward a hollow center: Mick, the teenage protagonist, loves the deaf mute Mr. Singer, as do many other lonely people in the town who come to tell the perplexed man their troubles, interpreting his silence as understanding. Mr. Singer loves his retarded mute friend. His friend loves only food. In McCullers, human love is seldom returned. As the narrator explains in "Ballad of the Sad Cafe," the lover and the beloved are "from a different country."[8]

A Member of the Wedding shows McCullers investigating the complexities of belonging.[9] The novel opens in the summer with twelve-year-old baby-dyke Frankie Addams entering the terrors of adolescence, "not a member . . . [but] an unjoined person" (12). Two of the adjectives that resonate throughout the story are "afraid" and "queer." "The spring of that year had been a long queer season," blooming wisteria and the wild bright green of trees stirring sexual feelings in Frankie that she did not understand, leading to a summer of glaring sun and sidewalks too hot for Frankie's feet (20). To keep out of "secret trouble," she stays at home with her black maid, Berenice Sadie Brown, and her six-year-old cousin, John Henry West, who exhibits traits as queer as Frankie's. The drawings he hangs on the kitchen wall are "crazy" and make the kitchen look to Frankie like a crazy house (4). The three of them sit at the kitchen table playing cards and fantasizing about how they would improve the world if they were God. (Berenice's vision: "No killed Jews and no hurt colored people. . . . Free food for every human mouth.") Fearing she will grow into a nine-foot freak, Frankie hates herself and longs to be anyone else: "I wish I was somebody else except me" (91).

Her brother Jarvis's wedding offers her the fantasy of escape—from the heat of the summer and her feelings to the coolness of Winter Hill, where the wedding will be held when her brother returns from Alaska. When she first sees her brother and his fiancée together, she thinks: "They are the we of me. . . . The three of them would go into the world and they would always be together" (92). Although in her fantasies they have no faces, she imagines them as "the prettiest people" who have a "good time every minute of the day" (6). Berenice tries to explain Frankie's growing sense of anxiety: "We are all of us somehow caught. We burn this way or that and we don't know why. . . . And maybe we wants to widen and bust free. But no matter what we do we still caught." Berenice understands this especially because "they done drawn completely extra bands around colored people" (43).

Frankie's attempt to bust free ends in humiliation, as her father drags her scream-ing out of the bride and groom's car as they are about to drive away for their hon-eymoon. The Addamses move to a new house, and Berenice no longer works for them. Frankie spurns her black friend for the "lumpy and marshmallow white" Mary Littlejohn, whom she loves and latches onto as her entry into the club of adolescent girls (114). John Henry dies of meningitis, suffering terribly, during the week that the fair arrives with its freak show again. The book ends with Frankie thrilling at the ring-ing of the doorbell, announcing the arrival of Mary and what Frankie hopes is her own arrival into the heterosexual world in which she will someday have her own wedding.

In McCullers there is love and heartbreak—as well, sometimes, as self-hatred—in her examination of her hunters—her characters hunting for belonging amid a great loneliness. She examines people who are viewed by the world, or who view them-selves, as grotesque, who feel the danger—as Grimké would say—of being flattened under their days.

McCullers had Frankie and John Henry and Berenice sitting around the kitchen table remaking the world. Lillian Smith's writing searches in more explicit ways for "how to make into a related whole the split pieces of the human experience."[10] This vision gave her hope for change. It made her into not only a writer but a radical and brought her into conflict with her white culture. For twenty years, she and Paula Snelling published *South Today,* one of the outspoken southern voices to oppose seg-regation in the 1940s and 1950s. Her *Killers of the Dream* is the most profound analy-sis I know of the causes and effects of racism on the whites who practice it. Smith's life and writing embody what later became the feminist manifesto, "The personal is political." She delved into her own life as a white southern female and came up with a radical analysis of southern and Western culture, an understanding of the power-ful links between race, sex, Christianity, economics, and politics. When she wrote, she put her life on the line. Her house was burned three times. But she proceeded to develop not only an antiracist but a feminist analysis, seeing and establishing con-nections among the culture's virulent forms of oppression.

Smith's analysis proceeds out of a southern lesbian sensibility. Her main theme is repression. Influenced by Freud, she discusses the "hidden terror in the unconscious," and she traces the ways white culture built itself on lies: "A system of avoidance rites that destroyed not bodies but spirits."[11] Her fiction gets its energy from exploring sexual taboos: "One Hour" tells the story of a doctor accused of molesting a child. *Strange Fruit* chronicles a tragic relationship between a black woman and a white man. In *Killers of the Dream* she analyzes "ghost relationships" between the races: white man/black woman, white father/unacknowledged child, white children/black "mammy." I can't help thinking she was sensitive to these because of the ghost relationships in her own life, between woman and woman, that she used *Strange Fruit* to explore obliquely.

Among them, Grimké, Smith, and McCullers introduce themes and concerns that figure in later southern lesbian writing and life: repression, the triple jeopardy of the black lesbian, the concern in both black and white work with the grotesque, the need for a political understanding to preserve life and sanity, the awareness of the interrelatedness of oppressions, the figure of the fugitive, and the need to bust free.

Angelina Grimké died in 1958, "flattened" and "crushed"—to borrow Hull's description. Lillian Smith died in 1964 of a cancer she saw as symbolic (Smith's family would not allow Paula Snelling into the hospital during Lillian's final days). She died in the midst of a thirst for justice that was sweeping the South and that later would bring change to the rest of the country. It is from this burst of liberating energy, unleashed by black southerners who said *no* to write racist ways, that the second generation of southern lesbian writing emerges.

Southern Gentlemen and Disciplinary Power

To understand these three women and the lesbian writers who follow them, we must understand the two traditions that produced them, the one they followed and the one they resisted. Before moving on to the second stage of southern lesbian writing, I want to look at the white southern male upper-class literary tradition that held sway during the lifetime of Grimké, McCullers, and Smith. It was a tradition with roots in European aristocracy and southern slaveholder attitudes and practices, and it helped define modern poetry and criticism in the United States. This examination shows that to understand southern lesbian writing, I must construct a new understanding of southern literature.

Vanderbilt University in the 1920s, 1930s, and 1940s was the center of a movement known variously as the Fugitives, the Agrarians, and the New Criticism. Its advocates were a group of southern white male poets and critics, many of them academics: Allen Tate, John Crowe Ransom, Donald Davidson, Robert Penn Warren, Stark Young, and John Peale Bishop, to name the most well-known. Tate, Ransom, and later Cleanth Brooks were its most prominent spokesmen and propagators. These southern men of letters were in positions of tremendous privilege, as artists and academics go (which is to say, they weren't generals or senators). They were "honored with an array of awards not to be matched by any other collection of writers grouped in a common cause."[12] Among them they won six Guggenheim grants, two Library of Congress poetry chairs, three Yale Bollinger Prizes in Poetry, two Pulitzer Prizes, two National Book Awards, various special lectureships—the list goes on and on. They also controlled at least three journals during those years: The *Sewanee Review,* the *Kenyon Review,* and the *Georgia Review.* They gathered this harvest of reputation, respect, money, and the financial freedom to continue their work while in the 1950s black southern female writer Zora Neale Hurston—the most published black woman in America at that time—spent the last ten years of her life in poverty, working as a maid, and finally was buried in an unmarked grave.

These gentlemen critics imported Eliot's patriarchal modernism to the United States. Ransom gave it its name—the New Criticism—in a book by that name in 1941. This New Criticism defined the poem as an object on a page, to be analyzed in terms of its form—its ambiguities, ironies, texture, and structure—separate from its connections to the reader, the author, or the age. The poem is thus autotelic, having no other purpose than itself. The folks who think otherwise are guilty of various heresies and mistakes: the "affective fallacy" that a poem has to do with feeling: the "fallacy of communication" that a poem conveys ideas and feelings to an audience: the "heresy of critical relativism" that believes that aesthetic values are not absolute but are influenced by historical contexts. As Tate explains in "Three Kinds of Poetry": "[Poetry] proves nothing: it creates the totality of experience in its quality, and it has no useful relation to ordinary forms of action." He finds poetry a medium of "perfect inutility, a focus of repose for the well-driven intellect that constantly shakes the equilibrium of persons and societies with its unremitting imposition of partial formulas." He concludes that "when we are put back into an explicit relationship with the whole of experience, we get the true knowledge which is poetry."[13]

By defining the poem as just an object on a page, the New Critics do not have to account for which poems get to the page and which don't, and then which pages get printed and by whom, whose books are burned, what writers or would-be writers were killed, whose spirits were denied and destroyed by the dominant culture. In denying the feeling element of poetry, New Criticism denies the base of a literature that must tell truths previously repressed, with the love, anger, and pain necessary to make itself felt. Ransom exhibits an amazing arrogance: "The economic system provides sufficiently for art, on the whole, in its haphazard way. Art remains in continual production, or very nearly, and the artist secures his livelihood and is a free man. On the other hand, the public is furnished with the art it requires."[14]

The other arrogance in this New Critical approach is the assumption that white class-privileged European men have produced a complete tradition: in Tate's words, "the whole of experience . . . the true knowledge which is poetry," as opposed to society's "unremitting imposition of partial formulas." What these men have produced is in itself a terribly partial formula, a projection of their values, an imperialist pretense to wholeness that, acted out in history, has sought to destroy the nonwhite, the nonmale, the poor, the earth itself.

Southern New Critics got this assumption of wholeness from T. S. Eliot. Eliot called his white-male-European-Christian privilege tradition and anything that deviated from it eccentric. It was to this tradition that the male poet sacrificed his emotions. "One error, in fact, of eccentricity," Eliot explains in "Tradition and the Individual Talent," is to "seek for new human emotions to express; and in this search for novelty in the wrong place it discovers the perverse." He explains, "This business of poetry is not to find new emotions, but to use the ordinary ones." Any great new work of literature expands this tradition. "The existing order is complete before the new work arrives." The poet's absorption into this impersonal tradition allows him to escape his personality, his emotions, his eccentricity.[15] The poetry that Eliot himself produced was, consequently, tremendously obscure. Perhaps New Criticism was necessary to explicate the obscurities. In any case, poetry and criticism moved into the academy.

If the New Critics got their objectivity from Eliot, they also shared his lament for a past order. Eliot is clear about the relationship between his art and his politics. He declares himself "a classicist in literature, a royalist in politics, and an Anglo-Catholic in religion." In "Notes Toward a Definition of Culture," he argues with the notion that it is "in the nature of things for a progressive society eventually to overcome [class] divisions," arguing that they are a necessary breeding ground for the elite who produce art. Recognizing that many in the upper class are "conspicuously deficient in culture," and many from lower classes have natural abilities, he nonetheless figures that without a class structure the elite would have "no social cohesion . . . no social continuity" and therefore would meet "like committees." The transmission of culture therefore requires that there are "groups of families persisting, from generation to generation, each in the same way of life." Eliot concludes, "If it seems monstrous to him that anyone should have advantages of birth I do not ask him to change his faith, I merely ask him to stop paying lip service to culture."[16] Both Eliot and Ezra Pound, the other male founder of poetic modernism, supported fascist regimes in Europe.

The southern critics likewise lamented the passing of the traditional social order of the South in their guise not as New Critics (who should, after all, not care about historical contexts) but as Agrarians. The group got together in *I'll Take My Stand*, a collection of essays that advocated a southern agrarian and humanistic way of life opposed to the onslaught of Yankee industrialism. The Agrarians claimed that what gave the South its superior tradition (the most European of U.S. cultures) was its "humane relationship to the land," rather than the worship of the Yankee idols of Progress and Service. The southerner, wrote Ransom, is not

> addicted to work and to gross material prosperity. . . . His business seemed to be rather to envelop both his work and his play with a leisure which permitted the activity of intelligence. On this assumption, the South pioneered her way to a sufficiently comfortable and rural sort of establishment, considered that an establishment was something stable, and proceeded to enjoy the fruits thereof.[17]

Need we ask, comfortable for whom? Ransom's agrarian analysis, based on the South's "humane" relationship with the land, must completely deny the reality of slavery, which Ransom manages to do in a few sentences: "Slavery was a feature monstrous enough in theory, but, more often than not humane in practice; and it is impossible to believe that its abolition alone could have effected any great revolution in society."[18]

As New Critics, these southern gentlemen divorced the poem from its cultural context; as Agrarians, they clearly advocated the racist, classist southern tradition that gave them their leisure and status as poets. They had their cakes and ate them, too, plus their Guggenheims and their Pulitzers. Their objectivity was the subjectivity of the powerful, who can force their own definitions by denying what doesn't fit them. They clearly illustrate what gay French philosopher Michel Foucault calls "disciplinary power"[19]—in this case the use of the discipline of literary criticism to turn their power base into truth and right.

Lillian Smith, who took them on directly and whom they helped isolate from the literary mainstream, sums them up:

> Instead of confronting these new realities the Fugitives turned away, after some eloquent denunciations, and sought the ancient simplicities. In their search most of them ended up on northern university campuses. They were so nearly right to be so wrong. And because their tones were cultured, even though their minds were not wholly so, they had great influence on the youngsters, sensitive, bright, who were their students: persuading many of them to refuse commitment to a future that was bound to be difficult, tangled, ambiguous but which must be created and should be created by the best minds and most sensitive spirits of our time. Instead, the Fugitives urged their students to busy themselves with literary dialectics, to support the "New Criticism" instead of a new life.... The quickest way for a writer to be banned as an Outsider who did not belong to this little clique was for him to seek new words, new ways of interpreting the earth-shaking hour we live in.[20]

Lillian Smith rephrases Foucault: "The winner names the age."

If the Agrarians have roots in European modernism, their other ancestors are southern slave masters. Comparing *I'll Take My Stand* (from the line of the Confederate anthem that continues, "to live and die in Dixie") with *The Ideology of Slavery* (a collection of antebellum essays defending slavery) shows parallels. Both celebrated the "humane" southern labor system over the avaricious materialism of the industrial North, with slavery as a relatively harmless (if not beneficial) part of the system. Both drew on theories of social organicism that advocated stability, slow change—basically maintaining the status quo—over any more rapid correction of social injustices. Both promoted a dichotomy between art and life, preferring discussions of aesthetics and form to a more uncomfortable personal examination of the moral underpinnings of the society reflected in their art.[21]

The Agrarians, in fact, were the direct descendants of the slave advocates who invented southern literature. In 1847, South Carolina senator John C. Calhoun told the white defenders of southern slavery: "We want, above all other things, a southern literature, from school books to works of the highest order."[22] By 1856, slavery apologist George Frederick Holmes could write: "Out of this slavery agitation has sprung not merely essays on slavery, valuable and suggestive as these have been, but also the literary activity, and the literary movement, which have lately characterized the intellect of the South."[23]

It is not this literature of masters but the literature of slaves that is the ancestor of southern lesbian literature. Afro-American slave narratives, like lesbian literature, could not be autotelic but must be understood in the context of history. They are rooted not in class stasis but in social change. They urgently seek to communicate with an audience (slave narratives were usually first worked out orally as escaped slaves repeated their stories to abolitionist audiences). Thus they are action, part of a movement that resulted in the emancipation of slaves in the southern United States. And they root the Afro-American literary tradition in autobiography. As critic James Olney explains, "Black history was preserved in autobiographies rather than in standard histories and . . . black writers entered the house of literature through the door of autobiography."[24]

When we consider that slave narratives as a genre and the proslavery white southern literature came into their own near the same time—1820–1860—then we can begin to view southern literature as arising from two poles, human enslavement and human liberation.[25] This differently mapped terrain gives a place to the literature of all who are not slave masters and opens up new associations and suggestions. To refuse to be a slave is to refuse the grotesque, as *The Life of Frederick Douglass, An American Slave* illustrates.[26] Before Douglass can escape North, he must rid himself of the slave mentality. His narrative reflects what a century later Frantz Fanon would identify as the "decolonization of the self."[27] It is the kind of decolonization that Carson McCullers and Tennessee Williams could not manage, but it defines the second generation of southern lesbian writers.

We are moving toward a southern lesbian literature that explores the connections between seeing the world differently and making it different. Several years ago, a friend quoted to me a South American poet: "Justice now, art later." If art is not to wait for justice, it must help bring justice into being. The literature of human liberation will never be autotelic, or art for art's sake, but art for the sake of life.

Phase Two: The 1960s and 1970s

The 1960s brought what Grimké, Smith, and McCullers had needed desperately: a feminist analysis of a sexist society, a liberative understanding that gave lesbians support and a basis for self-respect. As Sara Evans shows in her book *Personal Politics*, feminism first burst forth in the urban centers—New York, Chicago, San Francisco, Washington—but its roots were in the southern civil rights movement.[28] There, white women gained skills and self-respect (especially from examples set by southern black women) but were denied roles commensurate with those skills by male leadership as the New Left exited the South and took on Vietnam. In 1967, New Left women in Chicago formed the first autonomous women's group working solely on women's issues. By the next year this feminist movement had spread to New York and other major cities.[29]

In 1969, with riots by gay queens against police in Greenwich Village, the gay movement entered a militant phase. As John D'Emilio's *Sexual Politics, Sexual Communities* shows, the homophile movement from the end of World War II to Stonewall was shaped by other radical movements. The Mattachine Society, the first openly homosexual organization, was founded by former Communist Party member Henry Hay, who saw the country moving toward McCarthyism and anticipated that homosexuals would be the target of scapegoating, as we turned out to be: more homosexuals than Communists were fired from government jobs in the 1950s. The purpose of Mattachine was to "unify isolated homosexuals . . . to educate homosexuals and heterosexuals . . . and to assist our people who are victimized daily as a result of our oppression." In the 1960s the example of the civil rights movement gave new militancy to homophile demands—as the self-analysis shifted from understanding homosexuality as a disease to understanding it as an oppression.[30]

Lesbians gradually emerged in, and many moved out of, women's and gay liberation. An autonomous lesbian feminist movement and analysis developed as lesbians began to define themselves, working not only on broad-based feminist issues but also on rediscovering, extending, and preserving a culture nearly obliterated by centuries of misogyny and homophobia.

Little of this took place in the South, but southern emigrants to northern and western cities helped create this emerging lesbian feminist analysis and culture. Fugitive lesbians and gay men left the South in large numbers, looking for increased freedom and safety, as openly homosexual cultures developed in northern and western cities.

And these queer fugitives, what did they flee? In 1903 a Texas doctor advocates castration and removal of ovaries of homosexuals to "bring to bear in breeding of people the principles utilized by intelligent stock raisers in improving cattle." A doctor in Atlanta reports in 1937 that "all homosexual desires disappeared after the 19th shock [treatment] . . . said to have been a lesbian since puberty . . . grand mal seizures induced." In the 1960s parents commit a son to a mental hospital in a southern state; he later reports that "for the first eight years after shock treatment I never knew if I would be able to connect my thoughts. Amnesia happened 1000 times." A Miami vice squad officer asks: "How do you love a homosexual? You put him in prison. I would rather see my children dead than homosexual."[31]

Rita Mae Brown's *Rubyfruit Jungle,* a much loved lesbian novel of the early 1970s, traces the archetypal journey from the Deep South to New York.[32] The departure is precipitated by the "apple-cheeked, ex-marine sergeant" dean of women at Florida State, who accuses the first-year woman of seducing "numerous innocents in the dorms," various black women and men, and the president of Tri Delta sorority. When Brown pointed out indignantly that the dean was a dyke also, Brown was put under house arrest.[33]

In the cities to which they migrated—especially New York and San Francisco—southern lesbians such as Ti-Grace Atkinson, Rita Mae Brown, and Pat Parker benefited from and helped give birth to the emerging movement. In New York, Atkinson and Brown both bolted from the local National Organization for Women. Atkinson left protesting NOW's hierarchical organization and soon helped form a group called the Feminists. Influenced by socialism, the Feminists worked to develop egalitarian process within their collective. This dual focus—on men's oppression of women and on women's "lateral oppression" of one another—became characteristic of much lesbian feminist analysis.[34]

Meanwhile, in the South in 1976, two lesbians in Charlotte—Catherine Nicholson and Harriet Desmoines—founded *Sinister Wisdom,* a magazine begun after the demise of *Amazon Quarterly* that was to become one of the main vehicles for lesbian writing in the 1970s. (The New York–based *Conditions* began at about the same time.) The writing that emerged in *Sinister Wisdom* was a response to Catherine and Harriet's call for a vision "of the lesbian or lunatic who embraces her boundary/criminal status, with the aim of creating a new species in a new time/space."[35]

Much of the work of the seventies is also highly autobiographical. It reflects Harris's perception about the lesbian's work on her "sense of reality"—her need to re-understand a world that had denied her very existence. It shows the need for testimony: this happened to me and my people; believe me and change it.

Again I find comparisons with slave narratives instructive. James Olney in his paper "I Was Born: Slave Narratives, Their Status as Autobiography and Literature" lists characteristics of slave narratives that have their counterparts in coming-out stories.[36] Slave narratives invariably begin "I was born"—asserting the fugitive's need to establish human existence in a world bent on his or her destruction. "Coming out" is a metaphor of birthing—out of the closet's door, out of the womb into a new life. Escaped slaves, like lesbians, often took new last names to reflect their transformation. Slave narratives, like coming-out stories, contain accounts of both victimization and resistance. Language and literacy are important in both sets of narratives. Learning the forbidden skill of writing allowed Douglass to write his own pass to freedom; lesbian literature has emphasized themes of silence and the power of naming. Both slave narratives and coming-out stories are told from the vantage point of freedom/the present—the plots move from worse to better, as the narrative starts in a place where the writer can finally afford to begin to remember.

If much of it is rooted in autobiography, much of this decade of lesbian feminist writing has undertaken the work of decolonizing the self. The 1970s women-identified woman proclaims that a lesbian is not, as McCullers feared, a woman who "should have been a man," but the essence of womanness—anger and "primacy of [all] women relating to [all] women," as *The Woman-Identified Woman* had defined the lesbian.[37] Judy Grahn takes the charge of perversion, formerly internalized, and directs it outward; the act of one woman kissing another is not grotesque; the culture that would destroy both is—and in this context, the kiss comes as a blessing and an act of resistance.[38] The lesbian in these contexts is not alone: she moves, as Pat Parker shows, in her love and anger with other woman.[39] And, as Nicholson and Desmoines proclaim, the marginal status of lesbians is really the new center from which we can create a transformed society.

In addition to the parallels between lesbian coming-out stories and slave narratives in terms of the decolonized self, there is another similarity. As Olney points out about slave narratives, these stories of liberation easily become constrained by new conventions. The assertion of the decolonized self—the master is enslaved by his domination, the society is perverse in its hatred of otherness—can trap the fugitive into a need to be too pure, too free, which leads back into a new repression, into another death-dealing denial of our complex selves. And if the decolonized self slips into the born-again self, we are really in trouble! We are liable ourselves to stone those among us who speak too loudly of their impurities, of their heartbreak and grief, and thus endanger our hard-won salvation. As Bertha Harris (here a daughter to Carson McCullers) warns: "Monsters are, and always have been invented to express what ordinary people cannot: feeling."[40]

It is a radical loyalty to feeling and to the complexity of our identities that characterizes the best of the most recent southern lesbian literature.

Contemporary Southern Lesbian Literature

Contemporary southern lesbian literature begins, as the tradition itself did, in Boston, where Angelina Weld Grimké was born and where in 1977 a group of black feminists produced the Combahee River Collective Statement. The women named themselves after a river in South Carolina along which Harriet Tubman led a guerilla action that freed 750 slaves. The statement clarifies concepts that would prove central to the lesbian writing that followed.

The first concept was identity politics. The group wrote: "We believe the most profound and potentially radical politics come directly out of our own identity, as opposed to working to end somebody else's oppression." This concept of identity was inherently complex for women of color and led to the corollary concept of simultaneity of oppressions. "We also find it difficult to separate race from class from sex oppression because in our lives they occur simultaneously."[41]

Barbara Smith, a member of the Combahee River Collective, went on to become one of the shapers of the black feminist movement and a reshaper of lesbian politics and literature. "Nothing is more important to me than home," she begins *Home Girls: A Black Feminist Anthology.* Although she grew up in Cleveland, an important part of this concept of home for Smith is the South. She writes of her grandmother: "To her and her sisters, home meant Georgia. . . . Their loyalty to their origins . . . provided us with an essentially southern upbringing, rooting us solidly in the past, and at the same time preparing us to face an unknown future." Smith retraces her family's fugitive journey, visiting Dublin, Georgia, in 1982. "I thoroughly understood their longing for it, a longing they had implanted sight unseen in me," she recalls, "for its beautiful, mysterious landscapes." But she also understood their need to leave—because of "race lines [still] . . . unequivocally drawn." She takes a handful of red clay from the side of the road "to remind me of where my family had walked and what they had suffered."[42] This handful of Georgia clay is the soil in which much of the work of Barbara Smith grows.

Dorothy Allison's writing shows the fierce refusal to deny any of her selves, a temptation at least as difficult within the feminist movement as beyond it. "A River of Names" sets out her dilemma. It is a story about stories, about storytelling—a narrative containing almost thirty separate tales. Its frame is a conversation between the narrator and Jesse, her middle-class lesbian lover, whose oblivion to class differences leads the narrator to lie in various ways about her own family, delivered by poverty into levels of violence and vulnerability unimaginable to the lover, whose grandmother smelled like dill bread and vanilla. "Somehow it was always made to seem they killed themselves," the narrator writes of her cousins. "Somehow, car wrecks, shotguns, dusty ropes, screaming, falling out of windows, things inside them."[43]

She mercilessly chronicles the fate of these cousins for the reader, while at times refusing to do so for the lover. Again, the theme is narration itself, and the ways it can be blocked or distorted because of the narrator's fears or the listener's insensitivity. Here the lover's bed, with all its cuddling and conventions of support, is not safe for the narrator. At times, she lies outright—inventing a grandmother who smelled like lavender instead of sour sweat and snuff, a character stolen from a novel. She also distorts through tone—drinking bourbon to tell stories that "come out funny." There is distortion that acts out the listener's misinterpretations—Jesse's attributing her stories to a "fascination with violence" rather than to heartbreak and grief and a need to make peace with a violent past. Then there is silence, the absence of narration—"all the things I just could not tell her, the shame, the self-hatred, the fear" (177).

"A River of Names" also shows the reasons for telling stories true, in spite of the obstacles. There is the need to establish a genuine relationship with the listener ("by not speaking I am condemning us"). There is an even greater need to be loyal to those she has survived, the need to address the self-hatred of the survivor, the "why me, and not her, not him?" by "saying something" about their lives. True narration carries a psychic risk for the woman who feels herself the "point of a pyramid, sliding back" under the weight of characters who are also kin, a woman whose voice can mingle dangerously with the voices of "all those children screaming out their lives in my memory," making her "someone else, someone I have tried so hard not to be" (182).

We can assume that such trying has led her into her middle-class lover's bed, which is both an escape and a torture, because she carries with her loyalty to the names floating in the "dust river" in her head.

If "A River of Names" contains the impediments to narration, it also contains in its final sentence the moment when true narration starts—the moment of honesty in spite of risk, when Jesse says, again, "You tell the funniest stories," and the narrator replies, "But I lie" (178). We can assume that it was such a moment that led to the narrator's ability to reveal to the reader the real stories—told without making them terribly funny, told for the narrator's own motives with herself as her necessary first audience—that become the story "A River of Names."

This loyalty to "a river of names" leads Dorothy Allison to challenge basic assumptions of feminism, both as poet and organizer. In her book of poems *The Women Who Hate Me,* she is not willing to go along with a sisterhood that denies her blood sisters, who lived in "the country where we knew / ourselves / despised."[44] This hatred of southern poor people was articulated in neighbors' voices: "no-count, low down, disgusting." She will not deny the grief between them, "our stepfather running after us / caught me more often than you / ran blood down my body," or the hate and love and desire for the sister who turned "quick to fuck" men. She can no longer deny that, in spite of her feminist "woman-identification," her relationships with women have often been like theirs with men: "sucking cunt, stroking ego, provoking / manipulating"; and violent, "her fist swinging up to make a wind / a wind blowing back to my mama's cheek / past my stepfather's arm." It is her mama and her blood sisters, one of whom is numbered among the women who hate her, that Dorothy claims as home: "the hatred we have resisted / the love we pretend / never made any difference."

The poet refuses a "sisterly" standard set by middle-class women who never had "got over by playing tough":

> God on their right shoulder,
> righteousness on their left
> the women who hate me never use words
> like hate, speak instead of nature
> of the spirit not housed in the flesh
> as if my body, a temple of sin,
> didn't mirror their own.

She hears in their derision earlier, less sanctified slurs—"White trash / no count / bastard."

Allison's essay "Public Silence, Private Terror" addresses again the issues that the women who hate her would have her deny. She speaks from her experience at the 1982 Barnard Scholar and the Feminist Conference in "Towards a Politics of Sexuality"; there, she and other members of the Lesbian Sex Mafia (LSM) sponsored a speak-out on politically incorrect sex to coincide with the conference. In its consciousness-raising sessions, the LSM had addressed the central question of the conference: "What would it be like to organize for our sexual desire as strongly as we have tried to organize for our sexual defense?" The reaction indicated the level of repression and denial around sex. "Even for those of us with backgrounds as political activists who had thought we had some handle on sex and its variations in this society, the revelation of shame, fear and guilt that we produced was overwhelming," Dorothy wrote of the sessions.[45] The conference produced another surprise: "critics who were horrified at our behavior as lesbians, never mind 'queer' queers."

Allison addresses the terror beneath the shock she encountered: "If we get into this, what might we lose? If we expose this, what might our enemies do with it? And what might it mean? Will we have to throw out all that theory we have built with such pain and struggle? Will we have to start over? How are we going to make each other safe, while we work through all it means?" Not to address these questions "reinforces the rage and fear we all hide, while supporting the status quo of sexual oppression."

Not to address these questions also means that we will never have a place where we are safe, we will always be fugitive. "Home is what I want, what I have always wanted—the trust that my life, my love does not betray those I need most, that they will not betray me." In spite of her rage and her sense of betrayal—more because of it—Dorothy Allison holds out, for herself and for us, for a more genuine sisterhood:

> I am saying that the world is wider
> than anyone thought, the women
> far more important, their true voices,
> the real events of their lives
> not cleaned up, not lied about
> stark, dirty, and hard.[46]

The moment of truth at the end of "A River of Names" is the fountainhead of lesbian writing. To reach it is to begin to conquer the survivor's self-hatred. It requires faith. This faith is the subject of Adrienne Rich's work from this period, a search for sources that leads her South to the home of her Jewish father and gentile mother. In Rich as well as Allison, loyalty to loved family members makes the poet shred the temptation of ideological self-righteousness in order to find more complex truths.

In the essay *Nice Jewish Girls: A Lesbian Anthology,* Rich ends up almost obsessively factoring her identities—"white, Jewish, anti-Semite, racist, anti-racist, once-married, lesbian, middle-class, feminist, exmatriate southerner"—a process that leaves her "split at the root," feeling she has "seen too long from too many disconnected angles." Her essay ends not with the resolution she had hoped for but with increased tensions: "if you really look at the one reality, the other will waver and disperse." She can only resolve the contradictions temporarily, in a "moving into accountability" of all her contradictory selves."[47] There is irony here that the feminist search for wholeness has led instead to a sense of fragmentation; female power must come from a centered self, but what happens when the center doesn't hold?

Rich again tackles the contradictions in her poem "Sources" and wins a resolution. The poem is framed by a trip to a former home in Vermont that makes her think back to her family home in the South. White male Christian voices confront her with the questions all her poems have sought to answer:

> From where does your strength come, you
> southern Jew? . . .
> With whom do you believe your lot is cast?[48]

She travels back to the beginning where "we grasp whatever we can to survive." For Rich, this was her Jewish father's "rootless ideology / his private castle in air"; "the floating world of the assimilated who know and deny they will always be aliens."

She speaks to her father directly and in doing so reenters "the kingdom of the fathers" too closed off by lesbian theory and by her own earlier work: "For years I struggled with you . . . as the face of patriarchy . . . there was an ideology at last which lets me dispose of you, identify the suffering you caused, hate you righteously as part of a system, the kingdom of the fathers." Now, as the poet/daughter struggles with the complexities of her own identity, she can allow more for her father's, can see beneath the male arrogance "the suffering of the Jew" that he had carefully hidden. With a "powerful, womanly lens" she can "decipher your suffering and deny no part of my own."

As a child, Rich had attributed to "some special destiny" her safety from the Holocaust. Now she sees that belief in one's destiny is "a thought often peculiar to those who possess privilege." "But there is something else," she affirms—

> the faith
> of those despised and endangered
> that they are not merely the sum
> of damages done to them:
> have kept beyond violence the knowledge . . .
> of being a connective link
> in a long, continuous way
> of ordering hunger, weather, death, desire
> and nearness of chaos.

This faith leads her to its sources: "The Jews I've felt rooted among are those who were turned to smoke." This smoky air is the answer to her father's "rootless castles of air." Her search for the origin of her power leads to "the place where all tracks end"—the death camps of the Holocaust—where the pattern of faith (that we are more than damages done to us, a faith kept beyond violence) "was meant to give way at last" in the face of genocide, "but only becomes a different pattern / terrible, threadbare / strained familiar on-going."

Finding these roots, she can speak finally to her husband, "the other Jew . . . who drove to Vermont in a rented car at dawn and shot himself." She talks at first *of* him, but *to* her father—men she had seen for years as opposites, in whom she now sees the likeness of brothers—"The one who, like you, ended isolate, who had tried to move in the floating world of the assimilated who know and deny they will always be aliens."

Then she has to speak to this other Jew, to decipher his suffering in order to find the way to an "end to suffering."

> You knew there was more left than food and humor. . . . it was a formula you had found, to stand between you and pain. . . . That's why I want to speak to you now. To say: no person, trying to take responsibility for her or his identity, should have to be so alone. There must be those among whom we can sit down and weep, and still be counted as warriors. (I make up this strange, angry packet for you, threaded with love.) I think you thought there was no such place for you, and perhaps there was none then, and perhaps there is none now; but we will have to make it.

By the end of "Sources," Rich can view her complexity of identity without feeling split—"dragged by the roots of her own will / into another series of choices"— a refusal of destiny but an assertion of faith: to make an end to suffering, to change the laws of history.

Like Adrienne Rich, Minnie Bruce Pratt works the poetic ground of identity politics—sifting through contradictory identities, detecting a series of choices that confront a will determined to change the inherited pattern of her life.

"Reading Maps," a series of three poems written from 1981 to 1985, shows Pratt exploring the metaphor of territory as the ground on which these choices emerge. These are also fugitive poems by a poet both driving (a VW) and driven to find an end to suffering.

"I never had any need to read / a map, every place I go it's already charted," a voice in the office begins "Reading Maps: One."[49] The poet sets out to "imagine a place not yet marked on any map." But she cannot escape charting the territory in which she and other women live: a territory littered with the corpses of women's bodies. "WOMAN'S CHARRED / BODY SHOVED INSIDE INCINERATOR," read the headlines of the daily paper, or "WOMAN KILLED." It is a landscape that fills her with despair and rage: "If I had an M-16 / I could go shoot them down." Her marriage is very much on this map, with a husband who did the driving, leaving her with "no belief that I could get myself from here to there."

She determines to "drive right off the map." She locates women friends and, "gathering the bones of memory"—the stories they tell each other—begins to construct a different reality. At first her husband asks, "smiling, about the revolution," until she insists: "I did not want the place he gave me in the world as it was." He shoves her "against the stove, / out the door." She lies on the porch cement:

> I could smell the back yard, the dusty smell
> of sasanquas, the rotting leaves gone to earth,
> smell of the memory: all living things
> change themselves. He could be different,
> but he wasn't. I would be.

For Pratt, the natural landscape holds out this possibility of change to humans who stumble through it. It is the link to wildness, to the uncharted terrain. With a new job and growing self-sufficiency, the poet ends the first poem in a roomful of women tracing angers to the point of origin to locate forbidden places—"the kind marked *dangerous / swamp, unknown territory* on the old charts."

"Reading Maps: Two" takes the poet back into the territory of the past, a "place, once familiar as my own body / where now the ground heaves around me with secrets." If the women in her consciousness-raising group had begun her escape, she hopes a more primal circle of women, the women in her family, will provide answers and company. "I want to know / if sometimes she veered from the road she was told to take," the poet says about her mother, but it's a wish not to be granted in this second reading of maps.

To get home, she follows a familiar road that leads to a front porch where she sat within the circle of family women, but now the poet has a new vision of its paths and turnoffs:

> During the day we didn't mention
> how the road from Mobile and Jackson, from
>   Montgomery,
> Birmingham, connected to our road, or how
> that road became the path that went behind
>   the house,
> wore down the grass to the backyard where a
>   black woman
> did our wash in an iron pot over a slow fire.

The women on the porch remain silent and complicit, and she sees her identity in them in ways that make her uncomfortable. She has the look, for instance, "of Mary when she sat her horse over fields / rowed green with corn, black with fifteen slaves." She wants to "follow this road, the unwinding grey thread" to their graves to tell them "I want / to alter the pattern we were born into, to ask them / to help me."

Instead, she meets greater silence when she breaks her own silence to tell her mother she is a lesbian. "I would burn like the woods / on fire in September." She has found little consolation.

"Reading Maps: Three" begins on the day of the invasion of Grenada. "The foot, boot, kicks down a fragile door," leading the poet to commune with "betrayed mothers" who have given her the company and guidance she longed for. One of these is Laura, the black woman hired to raise her. "I can no longer deny / I am a child of hers." Others are the black women in the delivery room who helped her through the birth of a child.

She travels to visit Barbara Deming—"to the very end of land"—to ask for the secret: "how to find a place without sorrow." Barbara replies with a parable that warns: Don't let your heart shrivel. The other poems in the collection show that for the heart not to shrivel, the cunt shouldn't either. Pratt writes to a lover: "with your hand in my cunt. Your fingers explain / the future by scrawling lines of exquisite pleasure / on the walls of my vagina, urgent graffiti." "Reading Maps: One" wondered about a "charred and smoking heart." Part of finding a new territory for Minnie Bruce Pratt is the need "to admit the need: to lie beside you in common struggle."

Barbara Deming tells the poet the secret she already knows: "Of the way there, she replied: *Tell me your piece of the truth.*"

"Reading Maps" ends as it began, in a terrain of male violence, but it also ends with hope. The place-of-no-sorrow is still mythic terrain, imagined as a swamp where once slaves escaped, now women do; as the poet herself does to "lay myself down there, light-hearted, naked," with her lover. But Minnie Bruce Pratt has traveled much territory in the space between the poems. She ends them with images of hope— laundry flapping from behind a battered women's shelter; people she loves (mother, sons, lover) with her in natural terrain, in the *wichity-wichity* of frogs' songs; and a visit with a girlfriend from home—both grown lesbians now admitting each had thought the other lost.

"No one knows where the end to suffering will begin," Nadine Gordimer wrote from South Africa, stirring Adrienne Rich. For Pratt it began in a polka with her girlfriend twenty years ago, "galloping, staggering . . . our thighs clearing / a wider and wider space on the cold slippery floor."

Allen Tate wrote of poetry's power to resist "the unremitting imposition of partial formulas." It is such a resistance—though different perhaps than Tate imagined—that marks the best of contemporary southern lesbian writing. "It would not be about betrayal," writes Barbara Smith. "Loving doesn't terrify me. Loss does."[50] It is the work of survivors, and it does not deny the burden of the "river of names" of the people who did not survive—the white-trash cousins, the Jews in the smoky air. It clings to the faith that we and they are more than the sum of damages done to us; that we can create a deserved place to sit down and weep, a place where love does not betray, a world that lets all the caught souls widen and bust free.

It is a literature of life taken back from fear. As Joy Harjo, whose Creek ancestors lived in southern territory before their betrayal, writes:

> Oh, you have choked me, but I gave you the
>   leash.
> You have gutted me, but I gave you the knife.
> You have devoured me, but I laid myself
>   Across the fire.
> You held my mother down and raped her
>   but I gave the heated thing.
>   I take myself back, fear.[51]

Conclusions

Black critic Louis Gates Jr. explains the black Afro-American tradition in terms of "signifying." Signifying includes all the forms of black rhetoric, such as testifying, rapping, and playing the dozens. It is a method of speech "full of punning and ambiguity . . . ever embodying the ambiguities of language" and as such becoming "a vehicle for narration itself."[52] Signifying is embodied in the trickster figure of the Signifying Monkey, who from his tree fools the far stronger lion and elephant into attacking each other and leaving him alone. Signifying is a survivor's form of language, and it happens in the air "above the heads" of the powerful. "The speaker attempts to transmit his message indirectly, and it is only by virtue of the hearers' defining the utterance as signifying that the speaker's intent (to convey a particular message) is realized."[53]

Queer literature has its analogy in works of encoding and in the parody of camp. For Gates, "signifying" also becomes the term for the Afro-American literary tradition, each writer signifying off of two or three others in a process of "tertiary revision": "It is clear that black writers read and critique other black texts as an act of rhetorical self-definition. Our literary tradition exists because of the precisely chartable formal literary relationships, relationships of signifying."[54] Afro-American writers signify off of a tradition that goes back to the first slave narratives and beyond that into art forms from Africa.

The walls of the closet—cultural invisibility and erasure—have tended to dull the resonances between works of lesbian literature, to obscure the tradition. As Eliot remarked, "No poet, no artist of any art, has [her] complete meaning alone." Any literary tradition grows in subtlety and complexity as text answers and elaborates on text, author on author, generation after generation, over time. By this process, writers give their people back a deepened sense of reality, a survival tool if there ever was one. In a tradition, the individual author feels less desperate and responsible for saying it all, getting it right. As Gates quotes Ralph Ellison on the work of Richard Wright, "I had no need to attack what I considered the limitations of Wright's vision, because I was quite impressed by what he had achieved. . . . Still, I would write my own books."

"Who will find me buried under the days?" Angelina Weld Grimké had asked. A tradition unburies people, provides content, so no author or work ends up lonesome with the lonesomeness of McCullers's Frankie Addams sitting in her kitchen miserable all summer, longing to be straight and so denying the importance of the company she already had—her little faggot cousin and her black woman friend, both of whom gave her love and support—"that we of her and John Henry and Berenice . . . the last we in the world she wanted." Here at the end, I have to believe in the irony of McCullers's words, in their signifying to me over the years that there is company for people who grow up and decide to be themselves, there is a tradition that does not escape from eccentricity. An eccentricity of traditions—of freaks and queers and survivors, of black people and white trash and Jews—fugitives making themselves a home, their traditions as their *we* of *me*.

Notes

1. A. Alvarez, *The Savage God: A Study in Suicide* (New York: Random House, 1972).

2. June Jordan, "Where Is the Love?" In *Civil Wars* (Boston: Beacon, 1981), 142.

3. Gloria T. Hull, "'Under the Days': The Buried Life and Poetry of Angelina Weld Grimké." *Conditions Five: The Black Women's Issue* (1979): 17–25. The information on Grimké and the quotations that follow in the text may be found in this article.

4. Thanks to Dorothy Allison for showing me the importance of this phrase and the theme of the fugitive in this essay.

5. Virginia Spencer Carr, *The Lonely Hunter: A Biography of Carson McCullers* (Garden City, N.Y.: Doubleday, 1976), 295.

6. Ibid., pp. 159, 226. Carr's biography offers a titillating glimpse of a possible network of lesbian writers: it was while visiting at Lillian Smith's house that Carson learned of her husband's suicide.

7. Carson McCullers, *The Heart Is a Lonely Hunter* (New York: Bantam, 1978).

8. Carson McCullers, *The Ballad of the Sad Cafe and Other Stories* (New York: Bantam, 1976), 26.

9. Carson McCullers, *A Member of the Wedding* (New York: Bantam, 1979); the page numbers in the text that follows are from this work.

10. Lillian Smith, *Killers of the Dream* (New York: Norton, 1949), 21.

11. Ibid.

12. Virginia Rode, "The Twelve Southerners: Biographical Essays," in *I'll Take My Stand: The South and the Agrarian Tradition* (Baton Rouge: Louisiana State University Press, 1977), 367.

13. Allen Tate, *Essays of Four Decades* (Chicago: Swallow, 1960), 196.

14. John Crowe Ransom, "The Community of Letters," in *Poems and Essays* (New York: Vintage, 1955), iii.

15. T. S. Eliot, "Tradition and the Individual Talent," in *The Sacred Wood: Essays on Poetry and Criticism* (London: Metheun, 1957), 15–21.

16. T. S. Eliot, *Notes Toward a Definition of Culture* (New York: Harcourt Brace, 1949), 35–48.

17. John Crowe Ransom, "Reconstructed but Unregenerate," in *I'll Take My Stand*, 12.

18. Ibid., 14.

19. Michel Foucault. *Power/Knowledge: Selected Interviews and Other Writings; 1972–1977* (New York: Pantheon, 1980).

20. Smith, *Killers of the Dream*, 224.

21. Drew Gilpin Faust, ed., *The Ideology of Slavery* (Baton Rouge: Louisiana State University Press, 1981).

22. Louis Rubin, *The Literary South* (New York: Wiley, 1979), 69. Rubin shows his Agrarian biases in *A Gallery of Southerners: Essays* (Baton Rouge: Louisiana State University Press, 1982), venerating Allen Tate more than any other writer in the century. In his essay "Thomas Wolfe and the Place He Came From," Rubin lauds "the traditional southern literary virtues of formal excellence and moral relevance" over "ideological gimmicks." In *The Literary South* he shows remarkable nonchalance about black southern struggles: "Then almost overnight the whole complex structure of racial segregation collapsed." Nor does he include Alice Walker in the authors he anthologizes in this text, when she had already produced a significant body of work and within five years would win a Pulitzer Prize. Rubin was not on a critical trajectory to be able to appreciate or predict the work of a black woman writer like Walker.

23. George Frederick Holmes, "Bledsoe on Liberty and Slavery," *De Bow's Review 21* (1856), quoted in Faust, *The Ideology of Slavery*, 5.

24. James Olney, "Autobiography and the Cultural Moment," in *Autobiography: Essays Theoretical and Critical* (Princeton: Princeton University Press, 1980), 15.

25. William Andrews, "The First Fifty Years of the Slave Narrative, 1760–1810," in John Sekora and Darwin Turner, eds., *The Art of the Slave Narrative* (Macomb: Western Illinois University Press, 1982) discusses the shift in early slave narratives from the "slavery of sin" to the "sin of slavery" (12).

26. Houston Baker, ed., *The Life of Frederick Douglass, An American Slave* (New York: Penguin, 1982).

27. Frantz Fanon (*Black Skin, White Mask* [New York: Grove, 1967], 18) defines a "colonized people . . . in whose soul an inferiority complex has been created by the death and burial of its local cultural originality."

28. Sara Evans, Personal Politics: The Roots of Women's Liberation in the Civil Rights Movement and the New Left (New York: Random House, 1980).

29. Leah Fritz, *Dreamers and Dealers: An Intimate Appraisal of the Women's Movement* (Boston: Beacon, 1980), 25–26.

30. John D'Emilio, *Sexual Politics, Sexual Communities: The Making of a Homosexual Minority in the United States, 1940–1970* (Chicago: University of Chicago Press, 1983).

31. Jonathan Katz, ed., *Gay American History: Lesbians and Gay Men in the U.S.A.* (New York: Avon, 1978), 208–209, 188–189, 252–255, 306–315.

32. Rita Mae Brown, *Rubyfruit Jungle* (Plainfield, Vt.: Daughters, 1973).

33. Rita Mae Brown, "Take a Lesbian to Lunch," in *Plain Brown Rapper* (Baltimore: Diana, 1975), 76–87.

34. Fritz, *Dreamers and Dealers*, chapter 3.

35. Harriet Desmoines, "Notes for a Magazine," *Sinister Wisdom* 1 (1976): 3.

36. James Olney, "I Was Born: Slave Narratives, Their Status as Autobiography and as Literature," in *The Slave Narrative*, ed. Charles T. Darwin and Henry Louis Gates (New York: Oxford University Press, 1984).

37. Sidney Abbott, Rita Mae Brown, March Hoffman, and Barbara Love, "The Woman-Identified Woman," in *Plain Brown Rapper* (Baltimore: Diana, 1975), 2.

38. Judy Grahn, "A Woman Talking to Death," in *The Work of a Common Woman: The Collected Poems of Judy Grahn* (Oakland: Diana, 1978), 73.

39. Pat Parker, *Movement in Black* (Oakland: Diana, 1978).

40. Bertha Harris, "What We Mean to Say: Notes Toward Defining the Nature of Lesbian Literature," *Heresies* 3 (1977).

41. "The Combahee River Collective Statement," in *Home Girls: A Black Feminist Anthology*, ed. Barbara Smith (New York: Kitchen Table, Women of Color Press, 1983), 275. Two white women who point out the importance of these concepts to lesbian writing are Elly Bulkin, "Hard Ground: Jewish Identity, Racism, and Anti-Semitism," in *Yours in Struggle: Feminist Perspectives on Racism and Anti-Semitism* (New York: Long Haul, 1984), and Jan Clausen, *A Movement of Poets: Thoughts on Poetry and Feminism* (New York: Long Haul, 1982).

42. Barbara Smith, ed., *Home Girls: A Black Feminist Anthology*, (New York: Kitchen Table, Women of Color Press, 1983), xxi–xxii.

43. Dorothy Allison, "A River of Names," in *Lesbian Fiction*, ed. Elly Bulkin (Watertown, Mass.: Persephone, 1981), 176; the page numbers in the text that follows are from this work.

44. Dorothy Allison, *The Women Who Hate Me* (New York: Long Haul Press, 1983), 9.

45. Dorothy Allison, "Public Silence, Private Terror," in *Pleasure and Danger: Exploring Female Sexuality*, ed. Carol Vance (Boston: Routledge and Kegan Paul, 1984), 112.

46. Allison, *The Women Who Hate Me*, 37.

47. Adrienne Rich, "Split at the Root," in *Nice Jewish Girls: A Lesbian Anthology* (Watertown, Mass.: Persephone, 1982), 83–84.

48. Adrienne Rich, *Sources* (Woodside, Calif.: Heyeck, 1983), 11.

49. Minnie Bruce Pratt, *We Say We Love Each Other* (San Francisco: Spinsters Ink, 1985), 7.

50. Smith, *Home Girls*, 69.

51. Joy Harjo, "I Give You Back," in *She Had Some Horses* (New York: Thunder's Mouth, 1983), 74.

52. Henry Louis Gates Jr., "The 'Blackness of Blackness': A Critique of the Sign and the Signifying Monkey," *Critical Inquiry* 9 (1983): 636.

53. Claudia Mitchell-Kernan, "Signifying," in *Language Behavior in a Black Urban Community*, Monographs of the Language-Behavior Laboratory, No. 2 (Berkeley, Calif: Language-Behavior Laboratory, University of California, 1971), 87–129.

54. Gates, "The 'Blackness of Blackness,'" 693.

Jim Grimsley

Myth and Reality: The Story of Gay People in the South

Part One: We Come From the Country

We live in the South, that strangest of regions, where pigs once ranged free over the land. We descend from people who settled in wild country, who carved farms out of forests, who hated fences and yet built them anyway. We descend from people who were stolen from their land and imported for their labor. Some of us are the people from whom this land was stolen, whose lives were forever shattered by the arrival of the others. We have all lived in the same neck of the woods, on the same hills and strewn across the same sandy plains, for generations. All that time we have been caught up talking about ourselves, about what happened to us, about what some of us did to the others, often while eating and drinking; if not talking about ourselves directly then about our friends and relations, our neighbors down the road, or those people who live away over yonder in the next county, the next state. We have been telling each other the story of the South, not as something precious with melancholy or cheap sentiment, but as something real, an actual place that has happened to all of us. We have lived here, gay and lesbian, silenced by the others, the heterosexuals, unable to tell our own stories or live our own lives, until lately.

In Atlanta we can sometimes numb ourselves to the weight of the southern hand, because we are in a city and the countryside seems far away. We have moved to Atlanta from other places, most of us; we never pictured ourselves living in a city like this, because we are sons and daughters of the backwoods, of country roads, of shadowy

Earlier versions of this essay appeared in the March 1998 issue of *Brightleaf: New Writing of the South* and the 18 and 25 July 1996 issues of *Southern Voice*, Atlanta's Gay and Lesbian Newspaper. Reprinted with permission of *Brightleaf* and *Southern Voice*.

riversides and mossy coasts. Some of us, queer ones often enough, moved to the city to escape the trees and the shadows of trees, to escape our families, but we come here to this city only to learn that the country, the southern landscape, our own past, has etched its imprint on us in ways that will never change. We live in Atlanta with shade trees in our yards to block out the sight of the big buildings downtown, on streets that wind and twist like the country roads they used to be, us hardly knowing our neighbors but talking about them anyway. We attend symphony or theatre or museum shows as if they are great novelties. We live as if we are miles from town. We live with the memory of our families, the place we grew up, the feeling that maybe we belong somewhere else; even when we are happy living here in Atlanta, there sometimes comes on us the feeling that there was a better place for us once, outside the city.

One can speak of the gay South, the gay southerner, the queer in the South, only after one allows oneself to consider the South as a separate idea. Apart from the myths, the storytelling, the hard-drinking, the good old boy, the steel magnolia; apart from the harder stories, the bondage of one people to another, the burning cross replacing the slave cabin, what is there in the South that can be described as belonging to us all?

The place itself is one answer. We have the heat, the wet hot summer followed by the mildness of the winter. Kudzu grows in all places everywhere, thick as women's arms, green and sculptural when consuming glades of trees. We have the roads winding through a countryside that, in places, has barely yielded to the asphalt, a landscape with a look of bleakness, old farmhouses rotting beside old tobacco barns, trailers parked under trees, brick ranch houses strewn like tiny boxes across fields of grass, between fields of cotton and tobacco and soy beans. We share the fields themselves, changing with the seasons, fallow in winter, humming with tractors in spring, yielding to green shoots that thrive in spring rain and summer thunder, then ripening toward the harvest and dying again. We have the front yard full of rusted cars, the minuscule cemeteries in the middle of the fields under a cluster of trees, the tiny white-shingled churches with hardly even a window. We have the past rotting beside the present, in town and out of town.

Here we find it hard to live without a goodly dose of the past, though our history has been hard and bloody, deeply scarred by the cruelty of one people to another. We remember our private pasts, our childhoods, our grandparents, our first day of school. We remember the first chicken we ever saw get its neck wrung and its feathers plucked, the smell of the wet feathers and the flash of Grandma's fingers. The first fish we saw jerked out of a dark river remains with us, beheaded, slitted, and gutted in our sight. We remember the larger past, the old cotton-gin houses with their brick walls falling down, the mill at the edge of the mill pond, the places where plantations used to be and sometimes the places where the old plantation house still stands, half-seen down a lane of oaks. The slave cabins have mostly been torn down or fallen down but they have left their own shadow where they stood. White southerners speak in awed tones of places where slaves were traded, or where they once lived; and black southerners set their mouths in bitterness at any such reference. When we sit, black and white together, we remember that white people held black people in chattel bondage, that white people broke apart black families and sold loved one away from loved one like a bale of cotton or a sack of rice. We remember separate schools, separate bathrooms, separate water fountains, separate worlds. We have that in our past together to bind us with bonds of bitterness and hatred, strong as love any day, as binding as any feeling can be. That history belongs to all of us, spreads itself over all of us, whether we like it or not. The food we eat drips with the flavors of grease, bacon fat, chicken fried to a perfect turn, cornmeal dumplings floating in a pot of greens. Biscuits light and fluffy rise in our ovens, some from mix and some from scratch. Children learn to boil grits that never stick. Black pepper is the spice of choice, Texas Pete the hot sauce, at least where I come from, and when traveling before the days of fast food we stopped at a Piggly Wiggly for white bread and cold wienies.

We argue over how barbecue ought to taste, what kind of sauce to use on it, whether it ought to be beef or pig, whether you ought to cook the pig in a pit or an oven, we taste each others' barbecue, we critique our neighbor's potato salad and deviled eggs and slaw, we fry our hush puppies in tubs of fat.

No one would claim that any of this is universal, even in the midst of the South, where we like a person to conform quietly to our expectations. Even here in the land of greasy meat we have southern vegetarians; even here in the land where the Civil War was fought we have people who don't give a damn about that war, or cotton, or history, or storytelling. We have southerners who could not spell Piggly Wiggly, who loathe black pepper and never sprinkle it on fried eggs. We have black people living here whose ancestors never were held as slaves. Yet when we talk about ourselves, we reach for this common material, the grotesque South, the soul-food South, the South that never forgot the Civil War, that never forgave slavery. We reach for a South that has simmered in its own traditions, that has a past. We remember a South that made us suffer in one way or another, and we hold onto that.

We gay ones have a similar ambivalence about the region as a whole. Do we have a southern gay identity? Do we buy all that talk about the past, about our supposedly common heritage? Is there any truth in it at all?

We wonder about these things; we tell each other stories. Now that we have moved to the city—to Atlanta, or Birmingham, or Charlotte, or Columbia, or New Orleans, or Nashville, to one of those places—we can find each other, we can sit down and chat, and we do sometimes. Most of the time we find the ones who are most like us; we white queers sit down with white queers, we black queers sit down with black queers, latinos talk to latinos y latinas con latinas. We rich sit down with the rich and we poor sit down with the poor. We men talk to the men and we women talk to the women. In this we are like the rest of the South, where the colors have rarely mingled, even under court order. In the South, the social hierarchy has remained strong, and distinctions of every kind have kept one category of person from dealing with another.

We tell stories about our families, what it was like to be different, to be homosexual, among our particular kin. The stories have a common thread: we all have strange families, strange parents, odd aunts and uncles, dozens of crazy cousins, all of them warped by the life they have lived, isolated on farms, living in shacks in the swamp or in the backwoods, suffocating in small towns. Crazy relatives are the great common denominator of the South, and they come in all shapes, sizes, genders, and colors. Every family, at least of a certain class, has its story of Aunt Edna who lived forty years with that woman Miss Jane, because they were real good friends, in a little house in some town that had once seemed large, the women growing old together raising tomatoes and collards, one of them working as a schoolteacher, maybe, or in the library, or taking in washing, or cleaning somebody's house. Everybody had a bachelor Uncle Homer, known for his neat-as-a-pin house where he lived alone; everyone tells stories of his frequent trips to New York to see Broadway plays, how sophisticated he is, if only he had ever found a good woman, he must be terribly lonely.

Cousin Mike got a reputation for giving a pretty good blow job, what you did was you would take him for a walk down by the creek, and you would just lean against a tree, easy as you please, and Mike would take care of you. Or that Elizabeth, Becky's oldest girl, she's a hard one all right, plays ball better than her brothers and runs like a little locomotive; she broke her cousin's nose when he called her a girl. She'll learn though, when she gets older and develops. She'll learn that boys don't like it when a woman is tough like that.

For some the stories are dark and hard and never can be told, like the daughter of the poorest family in town where the daddy sometimes visited his daughters at night; like the sissy son whose brothers beat him up so often he got crazy in the head. The rich man's son tells the story of how his daddy found out about him and had him put away, sedated with pills, believing himself crazy, and withering every day. The rich man's daughter was offered up like a prize to the son of a family who owned barbecue restaurants all over the eastern part of the state; she had to run away to find out she never wanted to marry any man of any stripe.

We have this much in common with gay people everywhere, that for us our families are our first battleground. We must survive our families in order to become ourselves, to realize that we are gay, even though our families never want us to be gay. But for us in the South, the family is a field where craziness grows like weeds.

We have the church in common too, all of us, even the ones who never attended any service or sang any hymn. The church has reached its hand into every corner of the South, into every black place and white place, and has set about its task of telling people how to live, of telling women to be subject to their husbands, of telling husbands how to rule over their wives and men how to rule over women. Most of all we have the church that tells us sex is nasty, never to be discussed except in its nastiness. For gay people, this is the hardest part of all: because we can only identify ourselves as ourselves through what we desire, and we learn, from the first moment of life in the South, that desire is a deadly evil thing.

So we have the country inside, and the church inside us, and the memory of a harsh childhood where everybody was watching us and talking about us. Then we grew up and moved to the city.

Part Two: We Live in the City

We came to the city for shelter, for a place where we could escape our families, many of us; if we did not move from the country to the city, then we moved from one city to another, or from one part of one city to another part of it; we left home in order to find some space for ourselves. We moved to places where gay people were said to have congregated, to Atlanta, to New Orleans, to Charlotte, to Miami, to other places. Many of us chose Atlanta because it seemed the largest, closest place, central in the region.

I moved here in 1980, after living for a while in New Orleans, and I settled in Little Five Points, which was already then a famous lesbian neighborhood, with a woman's bookstore, Charis, and a food co-op, Sevananda, a vegetarian restaurant, and several used-clothing stores. I had never lived near such innovations as these before. I had only ever lived in the tiny farm village of 400 people where I grew up, and Chapel Hill, North Carolina, a large small town, and New Orleans, an even larger small town.

In New Orleans I had lived near many gay men in the French Quarter and had pursued a life much like that pursued by those around me: I cruised the bars as often as I could, seeking companionship in the era when companionship meant sex, and cruising meant looking for sex, and going to the bars meant wishing for sex, or at least placing yourself somewhat closer to the possibility of sex. I visited lesbian bars at times, with friends, to see if the women's bars seemed any different from the men's, and I found that, as far as I could tell, there were differences of style but not of substance. The women leaned on the bar in butch or femme poses, drank thin-tasting North American beer, bathed themselves in ear-splitting disco, ate dry peanuts, and ogled each other from the deepest throes of lust and longing.

That world of French Quarter bars was so consumed with sex that I found myself terrified most of the time, awaiting the wrath of God. I had taken the lies about Jesus too far into my bones and smelled sin everywhere. I had no notion of what being a gay man meant, I had no idea of sexual freedom. Perhaps I might have explored those ideas in New Orleans, as many people had and continued to do. But I moved to Atlanta instead.

In New Orleans I had known mostly gay men, but in Atlanta, almost immediately, I found myself drawn to lesbians and to free women, women who had ideas about themselves independent of men. Through this mixing, the women's wild need to talk and my need to listen, began my long education in what it means to be homosexual.

The same discussion had been going on in Atlanta for a long time before I fell into it, but in the early 1980s we gay people were at the beginning of a cycle of years that would lead us to a greater visibility, if, alas, not a greater unity, than we had ever before enjoyed. Gay organizations existed then, but mostly along segregated lines; the Atlanta Gay Center existed, mostly staffed by men, and published a newspaper, mostly written by men. The Atlanta Lesbian Feminist Alliance (ALFA) had already been around for many years. Rumors of this group fascinated me. I knew of ALFA through my friends, through the rumors of dances the organization held at which lesbians gathered, and other events they sponsored, which seemed to me better places for gathering than the gay bars that gay men habituated.

Through a twist of fate I even attended one of these dances, which were mostly closed to men, and I felt, at this extraordinary gathering where women held women and loved each other and chased each other to mate with each other, the raw power of free women in a way that I had never felt it before. I felt, for the first time, the certainty that women exist outside of my male definitions of who they are and what they do. I felt their strength and fire filling the room, and even though it frightened me, I knew it was a real path to the future.

The plague swept in and killed many of us in those following years, and changed our lives forever, and changed the shape of our organizations and the tenor of our politics. Men came together, as women already had, for a purpose other than to find sex; men watched each other die and moved to help each other and, miraculously, women moved to help because they understood it was their own who were dying. The plague changed our bars, closed our sex rooms, made us learn how to put on condoms, changed our mating habits, infested our art.

One woman, Rebecca Ranson, wrote a play called *Warren*, the first play about the AIDS epidemic in the country, and men and women got together to do the play and got together to make the audience for the play and got together to build organizations to fight the disease and take care of the sick.

Because we felt ourselves so embattled by disease and by years of a government that hardly cared for us at all, that hardly wanted to face our sickness or our deaths in any real way, we joined together in dozens of organizations, and these organizations, as often happens in our world, soon divided themselves into more organizations through disagreements over this and that or changes in direction or simple need for change. A group of artists came together to make Southeastern Arts, Media & Education Project (SAME), with the idea of fomenting a southern-based movement in gay arts. SAME produced plays and involved the community in making plays, SAME began to publish a literary magazine, *Amethyst,* and through all the energy that the group was able to create simply by bringing people together a gay theater was born and a gay magazine was created and, later, in those same offices, Chris Cash started a gay newspaper, *Southern Voice.*

AID Atlanta got birthed in those years, and Project Open Hand, and national organizations began to notice that southern queers were stirring up a little energy, with a chapter of People With AIDS forming here, and a group called Black and White Men Together, and later ACT UP and Queer Nation, and probably a dozen others I never heard of.

The March on Washington in 1987 stirred thousands of us. We stood together in the gathering place near the Mall, all of us from Georgia, some of us running over to check the size of the delegations from other southern states to see how we compared. We had slept ten and twenty in a room to be there; we had waked just after dawn to walk to the Mall in time to see the Names Quilt unfolded, slowly, under a perfect lightening autumn sky.

Flying back to Atlanta that night I sat with two men who had been committed lovers in Virginia-Highland for nearly thirty years, who told me stories about the former world of gay people here, the hidden life they had led, the essential "Don't ask, don't tell" policy that we all face every day. They told me things had gotten better, and I believed them, though we all agreed it wasn't enough. They held hands on the plane, free to do so, and proud of themselves, and seeing so much more in the moment than I understood, while the flight attendants offered beverages and a group of lesbians at the back of the plane chanted, "What do we want? Gay rights! When do we want it? Now!" Softly, voices mellowed by joy.

In Atlanta, Gay Pride weekend drew hundreds, then thousands, then tens of thousands, then hundreds of thousands, over the course of the years that I have watched. Even in the days when the march was small, some image of our life here etched itself in memory indelibly: the truck bearing the sign "Truck Load of Fat Dykes" with lots and lots of burly women packed in the back: a carnival in Piedmont Park where men and women were parading themselves in every direction, holding hands by the tens of thousands; the Digging Dykes of Decatur appearing in their stylish chapeaux with attractive gardening accessories; a straight friend flushed with a sense of righteousness because he had come to visit me fresh from the march one year I didn't go. Feeling, it seemed to me, as though he had won more freedom for himself by standing up for mine.

What was southern in any of this, beyond the fact of our location here? Maybe a sense of wonder at our freedom, at the fact that we had finally found our voices, or, at least, the beginning of a voice. We have lived, after all, in one of the last places in the world where one people legally held another in slavery. We are aware, from our own history, that freedom can vanish, never to return. We grew up steeped in the notion that one kind of people always tries to dominate another; we grew up surrounded by a complicated class system driven by wealth and privilege; we lived in a world where women were always subjected to men's ideas, men's power, men's definitions.

Our own first steps toward finding our gay and lesbian freedom have led us to understand that we must work not only for ourselves but for each other, even if we lose sight of that fact at times. We have given it a try, we southerners, even though we were skeptical and never really believed our freedom would amount to much. We stuck our noses out of the closet and took a look around at one another. Liking what we saw, what we still see, we set about the business of making a place for ourselves out in the open, in sunshine, in our city.

Carlos L. Dews

Afterword

> *Discriminating and broad-minded criticism is what the South needs.*
> *W.E.B. Du Bois,* The Souls of Black Folk

I remember the exact moment when the idea for this collection of essays came to me. I was at home in Pensacola, Florida, reading Mab Segrest's essay, "Southern Women Writing: Toward a Literature of Wholeness," in which she develops a groundbreaking reading of southern women writers, and indeed of all of southern literary history, from her position as a southern lesbian. As I read Segrest's essay I kept thinking that we southern queers have a unique perspective of the South. It seemed clear to me that despite our myriad differences across gender, geography, race, and class, our queerness gives us a distinct point of view from which to critique the South, a point of view that until very recently has been totally absent in print and is still greatly underrepresented. My idea was to compile a book of examples of this queer southern perspective, and in so doing, I hoped to stimulate some degree of change.

The queer southerner's position relative to the South is split—insider/outsider—thus creating a double or triple vision of the world, a position from which one may both participate in southern culture and yet remain apart from it. Like the double consciousness of African Americans that Du Bois described, the double vision of southern queers, inside/outside members of southern families and southern communities, becomes a survival strategy in a world simultaneously nurturing and hostile toward its queer children. Many southern queers, myself included, simultaneously hate, and love, the South. We feel split between a desperate need to flee yet an equally urgent desire, once we are away, to return to it as well. In my case, I love the South abstractly but find it difficult to tolerate in reality.

I grew up in East Texas, a part of Texas that takes great pride in its southernness, and as I grew, Nacogdoches County became increasingly unbearable for me as a gay teenager. Two examples from my adolescence might make clear the unbearable nature of my hometown. I clearly remember when my father pulled me aside, for what I thought was the inevitable discussion of sex, to declare that he would rather see me dead than "queer, on drugs, or dating a nigger girl" and that if he ever heard I was any of these things he would kill me. And I also remember, after one too many fire and brimstone Southern Baptist sermons, driving home from church one Sunday praying for God to strike me impotent and thereby cure me of my homosexual desire.

As I looked around East Texas trying to imagine a future for myself there, I simply could not see it. I could not imagine myself surviving, literally and metaphorically, as a gay man in East Texas. It had been made very clear to me that queers were not welcomed in our neck of the Piney Woods of East Texas. I knew I had to leave. So at age nineteen I went to Austin to the University of Texas. I had seen bumper stickers that proclaimed "Steers and queers, no place but Austin," and I longed to go there to live in internal exile in what I thought at the time was the one safe haven for gays in the South. Austin is still the least Texas-like of Texas cities—politically liberal and socially progressive. I helped organize the first two annual gay and lesbian awareness weeks on campus. Even there, though, I felt conspicuous, too close to danger, not far enough from home. I moved with my partner briefly to Spain, then to Minnesota, becoming increasingly conscious that these moves were attempts to break entirely away from the oppressive atmosphere of the South and my family and to find a community accepting and supportive of gay men and lesbians.

While living in Minnesota, I got great mileage out of my southern heritage. To my surprise, I met many gay men and lesbians from the South in my doctoral program at the University of Minnesota. There were so many of us, in fact, that we formed a kind of little expatriate community. And we were romantic the way all expatriates are romantic. The South is quaint when viewed from afar, but the South is frightening as hell experienced up close. We often talked about whatever region of the South we knew best as we might talk about a narrow escape from a near-fatal car accident. We were all thankful to have survived the South, glad that we were no longer there, but also proud of our common roots in a peculiar kind of way.

On the faculty there was a lesbian feminist from Alabama who had escaped the South to progressive Minnesota yet retained her southern accent and identity. She offered a model to me, a confirmation that I could be queer and southern. I had self-consciously worked to erase my southern accent as best I could, thinking that complete dissociation was the only means to success, to finding an accepting place, to constructing an accepted self. I thought that being queer and southern was an impossibility, an oxymoron. What I had not fully realized until I heard my professor's beautiful southern accent was that I had thrown out my southern baby with the homophobic, racist, xenophobic bath water. Wider life experience and the emotional and geographical distance I found in Minnesota helped me to reconsider my relationship with the South. I found that in addition to running me off, the South had also shaped me and my perception of the world in positive ways as well. I know my deep seated desire for social equality and my love for storytelling and the oral tradition are both deeply indebted to my southern heritage.

In the end, I earned my doctorate in southern literature and with it, ironically, virtually guaranteed my return to the South, where I was reminded almost immediately that there is always suffering behind the South's quaint cover. I study and teach primarily queer southern writers and their own attempts to write their way out of the South, either through a queer point of view on the South or their own distancing of themselves from their native region. But those of us who specialize in southern studies and profess to interrogate the South intellectually are not exempt from perpetuating the South as an idea. Every day I meet or read the work of folks who study the South and its institutions who use their pursuit of the unique characteristics of the South only to mask their reluctance to challenge the South to change. I am tired of the noncritical worship of the South's quaint aspects passing as genuine scholarly study of the South. The South needs to be taken to task for its past and its hateful desire to remain in it. Southern studies must be southern critique.

I offer a challenge for scholars of the South to examine an attribute of the South thought of as characteristically southern, truly examine its cultural genealogy, without finding beneath it either misogyny, homophobia, racism, or classism. Perhaps at its core the South cannot be defined without these terms. If this is the case, then we must ask, is it perhaps necessary to sacrifice "The South" to help rid the region of its homophobia, racism, classism, and misogyny? The South I envision free of hatred ends up lacking all the attributes for which the South is known.

It took my return to the South, specifically to Pensacola, Florida, with its strange mix of a large gay community and a frighteningly active fundamentalist Christian population, for me to remember why I had felt such urgency to leave the South in the first place, why I both love and hate the South. I love it as an idea and find it endlessly fascinating, but I hate it in reality. The South in my head is peaceful and welcoming, the one I live in can kill me. Had I not lived in Minnesota for seven years during graduate school, I might not have the perspective I do about the nature of the South vis a vis its queer sons and daughters. Today the South seems to me nearly uninhabitable. But take me out of it for three months altogether and I am inexplicably drawn back. When I am back in the thick of things, I resent the South for making me feel unwanted again.

Now that I am living in Florida, I meet queer southerners who have returned to the South after living in other regions of the country who tell me they came back for the warm weather, for family obligations, but ultimately they all confess that they missed "something" about the South, though not one of them can really name it. I can easily state the reasons I hate the South—religious conservatism, blatant racism, homophobia, classism, anti-intellectualism—yet I find it almost impossible to name the reasons I feel drawn back here.

In some ways, I respond to the South as I respond to my family. I like some members of my family, I do not like others; I am loved by some and hated by others. At times I am proud to be a member of my family and want to champion its ideals, its history, and the things that I am thankful for having learned from it; at other times I am embarrassed by what it considers important. My family articulates the same strategies in dealing with a queer son that the South uses to deal with its queers sons and daughters. Like my family, the South created me and gave me the conflicting desires to be its harshest critic and its most loyal son. Being queer and southern, I am simultaneously my own worst enemy and my own most vehement defender.

I recently drove through Florida, Alabama, and Georgia on a motorcycle, and as I rode past fields of cotton, soy beans, and kudzu-covered red clay hills, I felt acutely the ambivalent emotions I have toward the South. I am drawn to the familiar landscape that I recall so fondly from childhood. Yet I cannot dwell too long on these familiar, comforting recollections of my East Texas upbringing in the piney woods without quickly sensing a vague fear of this place. I am frightened by the reactions I imagine I would receive should I return to live in my home town as the openly gay man I am or should I decide to settle in any other small southern town. And although I know there are queer southerners in every town I drove through on my motorcycle, my cowardice, complicit in a conspiracy of silence, prevents me from knowing them or feeling at home in their place.

I had often thought that I would live in a small southern town, perhaps in the country outside a small southern town, if I were straight. I sometimes think about what my life would have been like if I had been the boy my father wanted. For starters, I would not be concerned with political activism; my life would not depend on social change. In fact, my life would depend desperately on things staying the same. I would not have been propelled outward and awayward because, had I accepted my birthright in the patriarchal, heterosexist, racist South, I would have been welcomed and the object of much privilege and attention. My abdication of that position is simply unfathomable to my father. Should I be thankful to the South for hating me for who I am because the hatred and violence actually saved me by pushing me out? If I answer yes, that would amount to complicity—I made my way through it, so can others. If I answer no, it means I must work to change it for others.

The South is in need of change and ripe for critique, but another book will not change the South. In many ways the South finds books, except for the Bible, all too easy to ignore. Like the necessary stories gay men and lesbians tell each other, recounting their individual experiences of the coming out process, this book is perhaps best described as a necessary place to begin, especially for other queer southerners to turn to for support and encouragement, to hear that they are not alone. But books alone cannot change the South, only activism can. I know I am willing to take on the South in print, but I am not sure I am courageous enough to take on the South in the streets, in the fields, or in the woods.

It would be very easy for me to turn my back on the South, to escape northward, but I know this flight would only lead to guilt—survivor's guilt, defector's guilt. I understand now that I escaped into the academy and away from my family and the South and that my return to the South is in response to my need to walk out of the academy and into activism. I know that I live and work in a privileged corner of the South. In many ways by associating myself with a university, even in the South, I avoid the harshest realities of life for queers who work in mills, haul logs, or serve in the military in the South. It is easy for me to sit in my university office and take pot shots at the South. I am protected by something called academic freedom and a union contract from the fallout from my queer activism in the South.

I know the South the contributors to this book and I describe, the South I respond to so viscerally, is not what it once was. The fact that this book can exist is proof of that. The fact that I can keep my job as a university professor at a state university in a southern state despite being out of the closet and doing my work on this book is proof that the South has changed and is continuing to change. It is less rural than when I was growing up here, and in some respects it is less racist and perhaps less homophobic. Yet, that South of my childhood still exists in my psyche. So I continue to respond to the South out of the anger, ambivalence, frustration, and maybe just a bit of the hope of my childhood.

Du Bois writes, "Discriminating and broad-minded criticism is what the South needs—needs it for the sake of her own white sons and daughters, and for the insurance of robust, healthy mental and moral development." I believe the South's queer sons and daughters can provide the South with the discriminating and broad-minded criticism called for by Du Bois. The lessons and development brought about by this criticism, though based in a queer understanding, will ultimately benefit all southerners. The South is not hopeless thanks to its own queer children. We undertake the difficult work of queering the South not just for our own queer selves but for all the South's sons and daughters. I hope this collection can participate in the much-needed process of transforming the South into a more livable place for all people. If this transformation means the end of the South as we know it, it is a sacrifice I am willing to make.

About the Contributors

JOSEPH BEAM, writer, founding board member of the National Coalition of Black Lesbians and Gays, edited the groundbreaking 1986 *In the Life*, a collection of writing by black gay writers. He died shortly before his thirty-fourth birthday in December 1988.

KATE BLACK was born and raised in a big Catholic family that lived in a sea of Protestants in northeast Arkansas. She is a librarian and teaches in the Appalachian Studies and Women's Studies Programs at the University of Kentucky.

R. BRUCE BRASELL is a Ph.D. candidate in Cinema Studies at New York University; he is completing a dissertation titled *Imag(in)ing the American South in Documentary Film and Video*. He has published articles in *Wide Angle, Jump Cut, Cineaste, Southern Quarterly*, and *Cinema Journal*.

CARLOS L. DEWS is an associate professor of English at the University of West Florida. He is the coeditor, along with Carolyn Leste Law, of *This Fine Place So Far from Home: Voices of Academics from the Working Class* (Temple University Press, 1995) and is the editor of Carson McCullers's unfinished autobiography *Illumination and Night Glare*.

PATTI DUNCAN is currently a visiting assistant professor of women's studies at Emory University in Atlanta. Her work focuses on Asian Pacific American feminist writings, especially in relation to notions of speech, language, and silence. She is also a founding member of Asian Pacific Islander Lesbian Bisexual Transgender Network (APLBTN) of Atlanta.

EDWARD R. GRAY is the director of academic relations for the American Academy of Religion and visiting assistant professor of religion at Emory University. He has written about gay religious life and the religious and moral dimensions of natural disasters and their aftermaths.

JIM GRIMSLEY is the author of two novels, *Winter Birds* and, most recently, the award-winning *Dream Boy;* a forthcoming novel, *My Drowning;* and a book of plays. Among his work for the stage is "Math and Aftermath," which was produced in New York; he has for ten years been affiliated with Atlanta's Seven Stages theater company, which recently mounted a Jim Grimsley Festival.

JAMES R. KELLER is associate professor of English and director of the Honors College at Mississippi University for Women. He has a doctorate in sixteenth- and seventeenth-century British literature and has written two books and more than thirty articles on subjects including African American literature, film, and cultural studies.

CAROLYN LESTE LAW is dissertation advisor in the Graduate School at Northern Illinois University and an independent scholar interested in activist scholarship and social justice. She is coeditor (with Carlos Dews) of *This Fine Place So Far from Home: Voices of Academics from the Working Class* (Temple University Press, 1995).

LAURA MILNER teaches writing at Georgia Southern University in Statesboro. A native of north Alabama, she wrote for daily newspapers in Birmingham, Nashville, and Savannah for more than twelve years before taking her concerns for social justice into the classrooom.

BONNIE J. MORRIS is a women's studies professor and lesbian author who has worked and performed at the Gulf Coast Women's Festival for almost ten years. Her two most recent books are *Eden Built by Eves: The Culture of Women's Music Festivals* and *Girl Reel: A Lesbian Grows Up at the Movies.*

CHARLES I. NERO is an associate professor of African American studies, American cultural studies, and rhetoric at Bates College. His research interests include African American oratory, literature and drama, and black gay cultural expression. He is the author of an essay in *Brother to Brother: New Writings by Black Gay Men,* edited by Essex Hemphill (1991).

MARC A. RHORER is originally from Burgin, Kentucky. He is currently the director of undergraduate studies for the College of Business and an instructor of sociology at Florida Atlantic University.

MAB SEGREST was born in Alabama and now lives in North Carolina, where she worked for North Carolinians Against Racist and Religious Violence. She is also the author of *My Mama's Dead Squirrel: Lesbian Essays on Southern Culture* and *Memoir of a Race Traitor.*

DONNA SMITH is currently a Ph.D. candidate in the Institute of Liberal Arts at Emory University, focusing on southern studies and lesbian and gay studies. Her dissertation uses oral histories to examine the process of lesbian identity construction in women over fifty in the South.

BONNIE R. STRICKLAND was raised in Alabama and the river swamps of northwest Florida. On the psychology faculty of the University of Massachusetts, she is a teacher, researcher, and clinician. She is a past president of the American Psychological Association.

DAVID KNAPP WHITTIER is a sociologist who was born and raised in the South, although he now lives in San Francisco. His scholarly interests are mainly in the areas of sexuality, gender, and qualitative methods.